VIBRANT PROSE

BY
CHRISTOPHER CLOUSER

Also by Christopher Clouser

MARCO FLYNN MYSTERIES
As the City Burns
The Young & the Wicked
The Gold in Their Eyes
Legends in Addington

OTHER WORKS
The Unspoken Truths of Casemiro
Argent's Menagerie
Curator of the Gods
The Forsaken Protector
The Midwest Associate: The Life and Work of Perry Duke Maxwell
Trophies and Traditions
A Month of Saturdays
Craft the Draft

VIBRANT PROSE

Copyright © 2025 by Christopher Clouser

All rights reserved. This book or any portion thereof may not be reproduced or used in any manner whatsoever without the express written permission of the publisher except for the use of brief quotations in a book review or use allowed for "fair use" under section 107 of the Copyright Act of 1976.

For more information, or to book an event, contact:
Christopherclouser1970@gmail.com
https://clouserwritesbooks.wordpress.com

Cover art and design by Christopher Clouser

ISBN: 979-8-3481-4058-8

For all those people that ask me those questions

TABLE OF CONTENTS

Introduction · 1

The Vibrant Idea
1 - Beginning the Journey · 3
2 - Concept Development · 17
3 - Genre and Story Types · 31
4 - The Reader · 43

The Vibrant Story
5 - Developing Characters · 53
6 - Character Roles · 67
7 - Perspective & Interiority · 79
8 - Theme, the Narrative Fulcrum · 95
9 - Plot · 109
10 - Dramatic Structure · 127
11 - Scene Construction · 141
12 - Setting · 157
13 - World-building · 173
14 - Conflict · 185
15 - Dramatic Tension · 199

The Vibrant Narrative
16 - Voice & Prose · 217
17 - Showing & Telling · 235
18 - Dialogue · 249
19 - Descriptive Language · 263
20 - The Action/Reaction Cycle · 275
21 - Revisions, the Necessary Evil · 291

Afterword · 303
Glossary · 305
Bibliography · 313
Index · 321

INTRODUCTION

Are you wondering what differentiates this writing craft book from the others on the market? The same question arose multiple times in preparing the book. After contemplation, three priorities directed the drafting of this book and the associated curriculum.

First, *Vibrant Prose* is a practical guide intended to present tools and techniques for writing your story. This book walks through topics such as viewpoint, dialogue, and description, while addressing issues that trip up every writer. This book presents various tools and techniques to enhance your writing and turn the story in your head into vibrant prose on the page. The author designed *Vibrant Prose* to create an impression in your writing that leads to better stories.

Writers lament over the loose rules espoused by experts for writing, such as showing and telling, dialogue assignations, or plot construction, that make it difficult to write the way you want. The experts then contradict themselves, urging you to break the rules they mentioned. The "rules" exist for a reason: they work. However, these "rules" are not the sole method of storytelling. This book doesn't do that. Instead, it proposes ideas for you to implement as you wish.

The second priority addresses developing narrative prose; something lacking in most craft books. Some broach the subject, but none approach the level necessary to teach a new writer the principles to enhance their writing. This book's goal is to merge the theoretical, technical, and practical aspects by identifying tools and techniques any writer may use during the planning, drafting, or editing phase of developing a story.

Three well-known tomes approach the topic from various angles. *Writing Fiction: A Guide to Narrative Craft* by Janet Burroway covers the theoretical aspects of writing prose and approaches the topic from the angle of literary fiction. Mike Klaassan's *Fiction-Writing Modes: Eleven Essential Tools for Bringing Your Story to Life* teaches the technical rules for writing the various narrative modes. *Techniques of the Selling Writer* by Dwight V. Swain presents practical application while using the same academic tone geared toward genre fiction. *Vibrant Prose*'s format encapsulates those approaches while creating a fuller view of the discipline.

This book's third priority focuses on a logical presentation for readers. Each chapter presents that topic from a theoretical perspective, with recommended books for further study. This book combines the theory with technical information on what to do and what not to do with that writing element. Practical examples from the author's writing and well-known fiction demonstrate the techniques and use of the tools. The book also provides exercises for you to practice the techniques on your own.

The goal is to give each writer advice, and they decide whether to embrace it. This book encourages new writers by providing a path to creating a story without expecting them to know the rules or achieve instant success. The journey is challenging and presents a steep learning curve. Can you catch lightning in a bottle? Sure, but that seldom occurs.

The reader should find this experience enjoyable. This book's style presents a light-hearted and fresh tone to keep you reading to the end. The goal is for this guide, along with the accompanying author toolbox, to help you become a stronger writer and to write your story with vibrant prose.

There's more to this package than the book you hold. This book purchase entitles you to a set of tools. Also included with the purchase of this are a set of customizable presentation files, lesson plans, and quizzes that any teacher can use in implementing this as a curriculum to supplement their regular classroom plans. All these elements comprise a comprehensive toolset for teaching and students learning, along with application of text lessons.

https://clouserwritesbooks.wordpress.com/vibrant-prose-download-page/

1 – BEGINNING THE JOURNEY

The aspiring writer often asks, "What does it take to be a writer?" The candid answer is a gluttony for punishment. People often relish the idea of becoming a writer. They carry a romanticized view of a writer's life because of non-sense articles about Hemingway or poor Hollywood dramatizations. They view a writing career as little work, in the traditional sense, consisting of collecting royalties and acquisition payouts, along with financial freedom and fame. Writers shake their collective heads and laugh at the naivete.

Then, someone wishes to continue the conversation, and we return to the original question. What does becoming a writer involve? Not to squash their ambitions, but becoming a writer involves putting in the time, effort, and commitment. The occupation requires discipline, routine, ambition, study, and professionalism. The same as any other. Why expect less? That is the journey you now begin.

FINDING INSPIRATION

Perhaps the most important aspect of being a writer is finding inspiration. One of the primary ways to draw inspiration is through consuming media; either reading, watching, or listening to other people's work in the form of novels, poetry, music, television, or movies. The multitude of works features various qualities to provide inspiration and instruction. You must examine these works through the lens of a writer. Note the things you admire about the stories presented. What draws the audience in? Are there interesting characters? Is the dialogue witty? Do great plots keep the audience on the edge of their seats? Start absorbing these characteristics of the work and stew over what consumers appreciate. Conceptualize how to write the story differently. Document the ideas or techniques you enjoy in a notebook.

Most writers agree reading helps. If you read what other authors write, and study their works, you'll be able to find new ideas and illuminate the use of certain techniques. Allowing the media you ingest to trigger ideas of your own is suggested. Maybe you switch an idea around and change one factor to create a new novel. Perhaps you tell a story with similarities but from a different perspective. Two well-known novels, *Paper Towns* by John Green and *The Cartographers* by Peng Shepherd, center on a fictional town known as Agloe and around how this town serves a mysterious purpose on road maps of New York. The writers noticed this unique phenomenon and spun two different stories. Reading other writer's stories will open new doors to you.

Many things in your surroundings, often overlooked, can give rise to complex ideas. Imagine if some insignificant event never occurred, and the lack of action created the destruction of bees. The result leads to a huge world impact and creates a prompt for a dystopian story. Taking inspiration from the world is an inexhaustible source for your writing.

Draw inspiration for a story from the commute to your job. The author of *Curator of the Gods* passed a cemetery divided by a dirt road on his daily drive. He developed the idea of a farm housing the pantheon of Greek gods who were cursed to live in central Indiana for eternity.

Many writers keep a notebook handy to jot ideas as they arise. When you mill around the town or when you wake up from a dead sleep (which will happen), capturing random thoughts that coalesce into a story becomes paramount. Famous author Brandon Sanderson mentions mining his notebooks for ideas during his lecture series on YouTube. Maybe an image comes to mind, perhaps keep a sketch pad handy in case you wish to put together a rough drawing.

- Keep a notebook handy.
- Use a sketch pad.
- Use Post-it notes.
- Use notecards
- Dictate Ideas into your phone.

Figure 1-1 - A summary of items to capture ideas.

Notecards are a popular item for authors to use. Anne Lamott, of *Bird by Bird* fame, uses them to capture her thoughts. Other options include putting notes into your smartphone, or dictation into a recording device. The key is to find a method to collect and store inspirational moments for later use. The next chapter will cover the creation and cultivation of ideas in more detail.

CONTINUING EDUCATION

You might think being a writer means freedom from the daily monotony of life. Newsflash, if you want to be an excellent writer, you must continue your education. But this learning is much more pleasurable than sitting through high school English. Accountants, electricians, and plumbers continue to study their profession to stay current with the industry throughout their career. Every profession of any worth does this. Why should writing be any different?

This education begins with the words you use, your vocabulary. There are many ways to build your vocabulary. Word-of-the-day services enhance your vocabulary over time by presenting you rare words you don't use in everyday conversation. When you discover an unfamiliar word, look the term up in the dictionary. Note the synonyms and ponder how to use that word in a short story or sentence. Find words that rhyme or feature a similar cadence and build rhythms in your writing. Some authors compile word banks, or word journals, where they collect words until they master their usage and incorporate them into their writing.

Numerous disciplines and industries possess their own specialized terms, or jargon. Doing research on a topic for your story will help you learn this jargon and build your vocabulary. Accountants have their own language that makes many people's eyes roll back into their heads from boredom. But if you are writing a story about forensic accounting and trying to solve a murder, like Cory Doctorow's *Red Team Blues*, learning this jargon assists your writing to become more interesting, engrossing, and authentic. Let's say your character is a florist. Develop a list of words and phrases to create a specific botanical diction for your character to use in describing people and things with floral imagery. It will give the character a unique voice and add to your arsenal.

A focused vocabulary for a particular character is one way to build up your word vault. Use the exercises from the previous paragraphs to master unfamiliar words. The more words you possess, the more arrows in your quiver.

The next step is studying the craft of writing. To mature as a writer, understanding the various concepts and elements of writing is necessary. While this book is valuable, there are other sources dedicated to specific aspects of the craft. There are a litany of online classes and conferences to attend. There are lectures and discussions on YouTube; the Brandon Sanderson 318R lectures are an excellent place to start. Select a few of the overwhelming number of writing blogs or podcasts like *Writing Excuses*. Numerous writing books are available, but it's a costly habit. Become a patron of the greatest friend to any writer: your local library. Search out new techniques, tools, and generally accepted guidance and advice (GAGA).

Many believe a Master of Fine Arts (MFA) degree might be necessary to becoming a skilled writer. Hogwash! There are many wonderful writers out there that learned their trade without getting an advanced degree. It is a noble pursuit if you wish to go that route, but you are not lesser if you don't pursue that path. The best education arises from reading, gathering information, and practical application. This includes reading the craft books mentioned at the end of each chapter. Any skill, whether it be hitting a baseball, painting a landscape, or building a shed, requires study and practice.

WRITING ADVICE

The most important thing to do, for anyone wishing to be a writer, is to write. Initially, writers ponder where to begin. View this new pursuit as initiating a workout regimen. You begin with the basics. Writing the great American novel requires adequate preparation, like running a marathon.

Consider if starting with the age-old advice of "write what you know" is the right approach. Many writers consider the adage garbage. What we absorb from our real life will seldom make for an exciting book. We must use our imagination. As mentioned previously, imagination is one of the two limiting factors for a writer. Don't stifle your imagination with a quote from an old white dude (Mark Twain, in this case). Instead, the adage should have been, "write what you care about" and use verisimilitude to convey your emotions. Use your life as a reference to produce events and emotions readers relate to.

Perhaps an example would prove helpful. How many of us relate to flying through space, getting stuck on a giant space station, and trying to escape a million guys in white armor? Absolutely zero. How do we relate to the scenario? Most of us understand the pain of losing a hero, brother, or mentor. We see what Luke experiences in *Star Wars* when Ben dies at the hands of Vader. That loss and sorrow hits home, and we sympathize. We understand being chased, like Han and Leia in the Death Star's corridors. Everyone understands the trying to find an answer to a problem. The movie evoked the same feelings and emotions for George Lucas and his writers. That is how we write what we know.

Try to avoid "writing to the market." Understanding industry trends is beneficial, but your story may not mesh with this trend. Write your story the best you can and only concern yourself with the market once you get the ear of an agent, editor, or publisher. But if paranormal romance with blue aliens is your jam and is the current number one book on the market, then write away. If you are writing a story bearing no comparison to the books sold at the checkout of your big box store, don't fret. The publishing world is full of different stories.

Having said that, never let the market compromise your story. While editing *The Unspoken Truths of Casemiro*, an editor provided feedback without understanding the story. The editor advised adopting a closer point of view, amplifying tension, and prioritizing the romantic aspects of the story. They wished to turn the story into something akin to the popular Romantasy books on the market.

Should the writer take the editor's advice? The author's vision would have been altered in this case. Though not happy with the editorial comments, the writer increased the amount of emotional interiority within the story to portray a truer picture of what the characters experienced. Always be open to feedback that may or may not improve the story.

WRITER MALADIES

Writers consider fear their greatest enemy. Fear of success, fear of failure, fear of ruining the perfect story in your head, fear others will hate your work, or fear of others ridiculing your work. Whatever you fear, it can lead to feeling inadequate. This has another name: imposter syndrome. This illness convinces you that your work is terrible, and the world will expose you as a fraud.

Authors are not alone in suffering this malady. A brief biographical vignette on the life of Caleb Dressel premiered at the 2024 Olympics. Dressel, a world-champion swimmer, expounded on his feelings of inadequacy and his dwelling on the negative aspects of his athletic career. He suffered from imposter syndrome. If this issue happened to a world-record holder, why not with writers?

Most writers experience this malady. Even the best of the best, George R. R. Martin, has mentioned this problem. Initially, your writing will be subpar. It could be higher quality than another writer's effort, but still trash. After achieving success, it's common to feel undeserving. Success takes on many guises; completing a chapter, completing a scene, creating a cool character, or anything else to progress the story. Enjoy the successes and move on. Hopefully, early in your writing career, you won't deal with this fear.

Don't get too entranced by success because that mistress disappears. Avoid arrogance with success and stay focused despite the lows. Embrace lessons from both successes and failures and move ahead. As with any occupation, hunt for ways to improve. Dwelling on the negatives, or positives, only leads to bad things.

Next, we move onto the most famous of writer maladies: the writer's block. Most writers experience this in their writing career. You need to make sure your writing doesn't become debilitated by this dreaded disease.

When faced with writer's block, the first step is to identify the issue. After the pandemic, ensuring you are healthy enough physically, mentally, and emotionally. If you are sick, depressed, or need medical attention, attend to yourself first. Many writers struggled during the COVID pandemic and experienced guilt over not writing, which and only make matters worse. Many suffered through a fallow period of creativity due to the additional stress, sickness, and other pressures in their lives. Dealing with these issues first will help clear the way for your writing. Writing should be enjoyable and a release for you. If writing worsens the situation, something is wrong.

If you don't have a health issue, the straightforward answer to solve writer's block is BICHOK (butt in chair, hands on keyboard). You may handwrite everything or dictates your ideas. Regardless of your approach, the answer remains: start writing.

Despite all the advice above, you may still struggle to write. You have the idea, but all you see is emptiness and freeze. To begin, start with some exercises to catapult your writing over the first obstacle. Use some of the exercises identified below to assist you in working your way into writing your story.

- Write a sentence or two about the subject of the book.
- Write a sentence about the main character.
- Write a sentence about the setting.
- Conduct an interview with the main character.
- Type up a question and answer it how that character would answer it. This will help you develop that character's voice and clarify aspects about that character.
- Write a summary of how your story starts.

Figure 1-2 - Possible methods to begin writing.

Start writing short blocks and build up to writing bigger chunks of your story. Don't stress over the final product at this point. Most of what you write in the first pass won't make the cut. But that touches on revision, and this domino will fall later. The key is to conceptualize your plot, characters, and the other key components of your story.

Another curse for the beginning writer is feeling lost in the story and not knowing what they're writing next. Perhaps knowing the primary objective of the scene, short story, or chapter you're writing helps begin the process. Jot down a sentence or two about the scene's goal. Note additional details as that objective clarifies in your mind's eye. Type the basic action of those same beats to get the characters moving. The key is to remember everything in writing is cause-effect. If you create the cause, the effect flows in a logical pattern. The prior action should dictate a reaction of some sort. Start with simple components of the scene and expand from there.

Focus on the elements that help you write. Overthinking hampers creativity and disrupts storytelling flow. Action and dialogue are faster paced elements and allow the writer to develop a rhythm; unlike the slower paced elements requiring more diligence at this stage. Early on, many writers emphasize scene action and dialogue, while limiting description and narration. Incorporating description, exposition, and additional narration will follow in a revision stage.

If writers struggle with a scene and are unsure of its purpose in the story, skip the scene and proceed forward. It might prove helpful to look at a known point further down your story path. Visualize the main character's placement at the next key point in the story. What must they do to attain that? Where do they need to go? Who do they need to meet?

This problem raised its head in the development of *The Unspoken Truths of Casemiro*. The author wrote the first ten chapters without an outline. After finishing ten chapters, he was unsure what should happen next. The writer identified what needed to occur for the characters to reach that next key scene. He wrote the scenes to make the logical moves from the end of chapter ten to the next key point in the story.

Another trap is if a piece of information eludes you. A key fact, or an element of world-building, needs explained, but you don't know the details. In that case, conducting the necessary research could stop all your momentum. If you can find the information swiftly, do so and continue writing. If not, leave a notation in your document. Put a reminder in parentheses to research after drafting. Mark the spot with "TK" so you can't miss the notation when you do a spellcheck later. Highlight this point in the story and remember to return and complete the gap. Flag this spot for later changes in the writing process.

If all else fails, perhaps you need a break from the story. If you aren't working against a timeline, this is always acceptable. Deadlines often trump everything else and provide their own pressures and incentives (mostly money). Many writers pause in the middle of their projects to refresh their perspective. They develop fresh ideas for the next story, or even the current work-in-progress.

If you're not involved in a project and having trouble writing, try internet prompts, books, or a writing group. Perhaps having a freewriting session with no boundaries will help. Writers often organize writing sprints, sitting together, and pouring out their words. Another option is to scan for requests by genre magazines for short story submissions. Use these as motivation and attack the deadline. You can chip away at the dreaded writer maladies with effort and patience. All writers experience these same problems, and we'll experience them again. Don't be afraid.

A WRITING ROUTINE

Early in your career, write as often as possible, even if it's only a summary of a book you read. Exercise this muscle. Once you build up those writing muscles, work on a routine. Productivity for writers often hinges on a specific setting and time. A calm, comfortable location allows for focus on the task while minimizing distractions.

Creating this environment involves experimentation. Many writers listen to music playing in the background. Others prefer silence. Some light candles, and some open their blinds wide. You will need to experiment with where this space is and creating the surrounding environment to best facilitate your writing.

The routine for the author of this book involves using an hour between work and when his wife finishes her day. He uses the time to focus on his writing, or related activities (editing, e-mails, marketing, etc.). Devoting an hour to writing activities allows him to repeatedly produce a thousand words with coherence. Establishing a routine and discovering a distraction-free workspace are crucial.

In the beginning, you may only write fifty words. Soon, you see that double and then double again until you reach a point where you are making sizable gains on your word count and project completion. Like marathon training, discovering your ideal regimen will require time.

The routine boosts your creativity and will become part of the natural rhythm of your mind. Your routine could involve free-writing, followed by editing. Writers often review their previous day's work, edit it, and start something fresh. Whatever your preference, create a suitable routine for optimal writing. Routines help with discipline and eliminating procrastination. Writing at the same time daily forms a habit, helping your body and mind understand your expectations. Routines work.

"First forget inspiration. Habit is more dependable. Habit will sustain you whether you're inspired or not. Habit will help you finish and polish your stories. Inspiration won't. Habit is persistence in practice." - Octavia E. Butler

One technique to use, if an entire hour of writing sounds daunting, is the Pomodoro Technique. In this technique, you write for a block of twenty minutes (or whatever allotment you wish) and stop when the timer rings. You take a five, or ten, minute break and repeat the process. When you finish three or four blocks (known as Pomodoros), your session is complete.

Once you establish a routine, setting productivity goals becomes possible. It will be difficult to set goals if you don't understand your limitations. Do not fear goals. We have goals we wish to accomplish, whether they are at work, home, or in our hobbies. The problem is allowing other things to impede with achieving our goals. You must determine your genuine desire for this. Others won't be aware if you reach your goals, so there's no pressure from outside. You motivate yourself.

Many writers set specific goals around word count or pages completed. Whatever your goals, make sure they are measurable, controllable, and attainable. Ambiguous and unrealistic goals sink people continuously. Start small and build up to larger goals. These goals might include writing a blog post or a certain number of words each day. Perhaps a chapter a week. You don't want to get discouraged early in developing your process. Many writers develop goals to keep their focus on revision timelines, or some other aspect of the writing process. You will learn where you need help and set goals. Building up to these goals shows significant growth as a writer.

Writing can improve through accountability. Connect with fellow writers and take part in a writing group. The group might provide assignments you must prepare for the next meeting. You might have to critique someone else's submission. This experience will expose you to other writers and provide inspiration for ideas and opportunities for your writing. Collaborating with writers at your level fosters mutual growth.

Always remember to foster the writer inside you and your projects. If overwhelmed, pull back to fit your writing into your life.

You can browse for other opportunities to write stories. Search for writing contests or submission opportunities for short stories, flash fiction, or even fan fiction. These will help you learn to write toward deadlines, a potential benefit later in your career. Don't fear attempting other genres or formats. You can become a better writer by writing various types of stories and learning new techniques. The important thing is to keep writing.

BUILDING YOUR PROCESS

An undervalued form of storytelling is stand-up comedy. It's the world's toughest storytelling form. First, you are in front of people. The number one fear often cited in studies is the fear of talking in front of crowds. And to be honest, we all share this fear to an extent.

Second, comedy is difficult. Making jokes or comments that tickle people's funny bone is an extra challenge. Humor is subjective and varies from person to person. That is tough stuff to master.

Stand-up performers develop their skills and routines through time and process. They have a process around joke development, joke testing, revision, and timing the punchline. Comedians don't blurt out their idea. They develop the joke, their form of story, over time until they release it into the world. Like comedians, writers should use a process.

Quotes from Stephen King or Anne Lamott lead you to think they just spit out their work. They don't. They use a process. Every writer does. You can take the various elements you learn from this book and work them into your process. Over time, you will try techniques

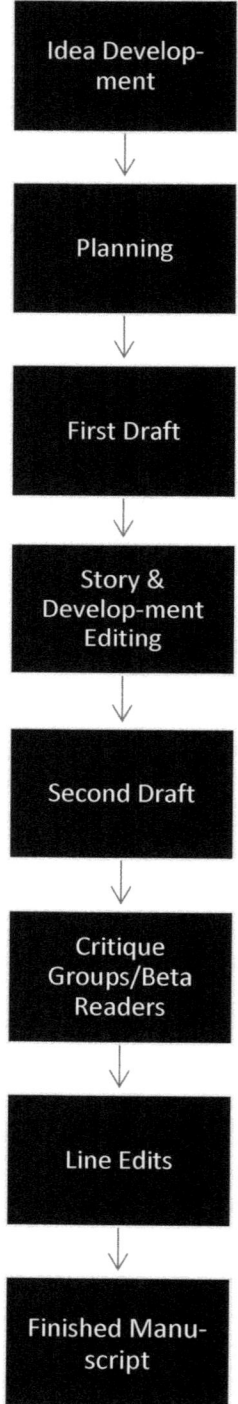

that work, tricks that don't, and you will tweak your process. Creating your own unique process is important and eventually you will build it up enough to take on a marathon, or your magnus opus.

This process encompasses your writing routine, the concept creation process, and every other component of writing a manuscript through the revision phase. The process should work for you. And once you figure it out, the process should be repeatable and measurable. That measure can be word count, time, responses from readers, or anything else. Determine what your measure of success is for your process and the components within. Measurement informs you of where you are falling short. Document your process and update it as needed to compensate for any measure in which you fall short.

Once you develop your process, certain tendencies within your writing become evident. Perhaps using words like "that" and "just" too often. Perhaps you overuse pronouns while trying to let the words flow. Once you document those problems, you pay attention to them in your writing. Attention to these habits will reduce those tendencies.

Documenting your process makes it concrete and more than an ephemeral notion. You can visualize how changes affect other parts of the process, either positively or negatively. Every business in the world documents processes. Do you believe they find enjoyment in doing this? No, they document their processes because the action provides a measurable and material benefit. You don't need to do a full-blown Microsoft Visio treatment, but a simple flow chart might help you visualize your process. When you are ready, memorialize it. Frame it and put it on the wall. Refer to your process with each project to ensure you don't miss a step. A checklist is a wonderful way to ensure you aren't missing a necessary component.

Internalization will occur without your notice after time and practice. You will trust the results and write without wondering if you hit a specific plot point or introduced a character element. Defining a process will be a key sign you are conquering that marathon.

The recommendations mentioned are not actual rules. You can do this however best works for you. You can scrap the process altogether for a specific project. As an example, my current work-in-progress was an experiment on my part at discovery writing the first draft. Planning for the rest of the book came after reaching chapter ten in the project. The usual process was abandoned in this instance. Whatever your process, change the formula whenever the need arises.

Do not hold yourself accountable to unrealistic measures. Sales figures are things you cannot control. Coveting what other authors achieve will only feed negative emotions. Avoid the world's definition of success. People might ask if you've received a movie deal yet, or if you've hit the bestseller list. Chances are the people asking haven't achieved that level of success in their profession, either. Don't fret. Turn the question around and discuss your latest project and get their reaction. Do not let the expectations of others create a roadblock in your writing.

You started this journey because you wanted to write. Keep this in mind. If you only chase financial success early in your journey, writing will disappoint you much more often than not. Embrace the joy of writing and the creative outlet. Developing the muscle of writing, creating effective habits, consuming media, and studying your craft will lead to a rewarding career as a writer, regardless of the number of books you sell. Keep in mind the reason you are writing.

Writing always comes back to you and the blank piece of paper or computer screen in front of you. We return to the same thing you had when you started this book. Do you want to write? Do you enjoy it? Begin by writing the first sentence. Then the first paragraph. Then the first page. Keep doing that until you complete the first chapter. Keep plugging away, even if you scrap an entire chapter, rewrite a character arc, or even kill a couple of your darlings. Every writer does this. These steps may not create the path you envisioned, but every step gets you closer to the goal of writing your first story, poem, novel, screenplay, or whatever your project. Now go write.

EXERCISES

1. Observe your world. Make notes about something you see out your window. Use only one sentence, or a paragraph, or a page. Describe it, depict its motion, or imagine some sort of dialogue and put that on a piece of paper or type it into your computer.
2. Study the craft. Go to your local library and check out a copy of one of the books mentioned in the reference materials section of this chapter. Read it and take notes on what you find fascinating about it.
3. Defeat the block. List what prevents you from writing and identify the primary fear behind it. Then write about to resolve that problem.
4. Begin your story. You probably have a story in mind already. Write a one or two sentence description about it. Write more if you wish. Write about the setting, the characters, or the plot.
5. Subscribe to a word of the day service. Start building your vocabulary.

REFERENCE MATERIALS

- *On Writing: A Memoir of the Craft* by Stephen King
- *Bird by Bird: Some Instructions on Writing and Life* by Anne Lamott
- *Publishing 101: A First-Time Author's Guide to Getting Published, Marketing and Promoting Your Book, and Building a Successful Career* by Jane Friedman

These three classics examine the challenges and advantages writers face in and outside of publishing. King's discussion of struggles as a writer resonates with several readers. King is perhaps the seminal genre fiction writer of the late twentieth century and the early part of this one with over fifty books to his name.

Lamott brings humor to the table when it comes to most of these struggles, especially the ones involving her inner demons. Lamott, an acclaimed writer, received a Guggenheim Fellowship in 1985 and is known as the "People's Author" with a substantial online following.

Friedman's voice as an industry insider and speaker at writing conferences around the country provides a unique view of the publishing industry. Friedman has served as an executive at Random House and been on boards of various other literary and publishing organizations.

All three writers demonstrate a specific viewpoint about writing and the publishing industry. Heed their words, even if you find only limited practical application for your writing. These three books are successful in the writing craft market for a reason.

2 – CONCEPT DEVELOPMENT

When we speak of developing a concept, we refer to everything in the pre-work stage leading up to drafting the novel. We will explore various levels of this development of a writing project. Let's start by discussing how to develop your ideas.

This development stage varies depending on where you sit on the discovery writer (pantser) and planner (plotter) scale. True discovery writers will jump into the project and begin writing to explore their topic. Plotters may go the entire world-building and outlining route. The information presented in the following paragraphs should offer suggestions to help anyone on that scale early in the planning process, or if they run into an issue early in the writing stage of their project.

One thing many writers look for is an idea that creates passion. If you cannot sustain your own interest, you won't be able to convince the reader to do that either. Many writers have "trunked" several projects on this point alone.

Once you identify this passion, you might identify possible beginnings, endings, and other elements of your story, but perhaps you can't quite envision the entire picture. These ideas start you down the mental road of developing the idea into a workable concept. To advance the idea, there are multiple methods and processes you might use, depending upon your process. Most variations form off the same basic premise: expanding on a single, initial conceptual nugget.

Let's assume you wish to test your basic idea and determine if anything is usable. An early episode of the *Writing Excuses* podcast espouses the concept of attractive depth. More than likely, your initial idea lacks this. How will you gauge if your idea is significant enough for a complete story? This is where the term "high concept" comes into play.

High concept ideas are often believed to be massive thoughts that encapsulate everything within a story. It is quite the opposite. High concepts today are simple beasts. These specific points center around a concept hoping to provide the initial framework for an entire story.

- A familiar setting from your life experience or your world-building.
- A character the audience identifies with from the beginning of the story.
- Problems, internal and external, that powerfully resonate with the audience and you.
- Well-written dialogue through well-defined character voices.
- A consistent theme that runs throughout the story.
- A memorable set-piece scene that reinforces the other elements of the story.

How do you turn ideas into a story? The next several paragraphs provide several methods for this task. Remember, this tome provides various tips, techniques, and tools. Try them and test which works best with your storytelling process. At times, you may use more than one tool, or switch them from project to project.

IDEA DEVELOPMENT

There is one thing every writer experiences: the onset of a story idea. It stems from observing people on the street from your window, or watching a movie with a terribly wrong ending, or anything else in your surroundings. We all get these brilliant ideas, these AHA! moments. Developing them into a story is the problem. There are no rules in this space, but the following paragraphs walk through a few usable tools, along with examples from the author's writing career.

One of the most common tools in developing ideas is the brainstorming method. In this approach, you catalogue the additional thoughts attached to the initial idea that attracted your attention. Doing this builds depth into the idea and takes it beyond the initial concept. As an example, a short story titled *The Flight of Nevada Lee* involved a spaceship named the Menagerie. While contemplating the ship, the author considered its name's implications for the crew. These additional layers provided the depth to develop the beginnings of a story concept.

The word menagerie projects an image of a group of unwanted individuals; people outside the law, maybe pirates. Perhaps they are outcasts, or black sheep, from their society or family. Menageries provide homes to those without, or family to the lonely. The ship from that short story proved to be the major inspiration to develop a complete novel called *Argent's Menagerie*.

Another approach called a mindmap is often used in business environments. The mindmap is a modified version of the fishbone diagram. You build specific aspects of your idea by branching off with new thoughts and add depth to the initial concept. Begin by putting your initial idea in the center of your workspace (whiteboard, screen, or paper) and begin building branches off that to flesh out the idea even further. This visual tool appeals to many creatives because the mindmap puts the idea in front of them artistically. As an example, your idea may center on a particular character. You can add elements pertaining to a specific character and tie those elements to some sort of plot or setting components of the story. A variation on the mindmap is available in the Vibrant Prose Toolbox.

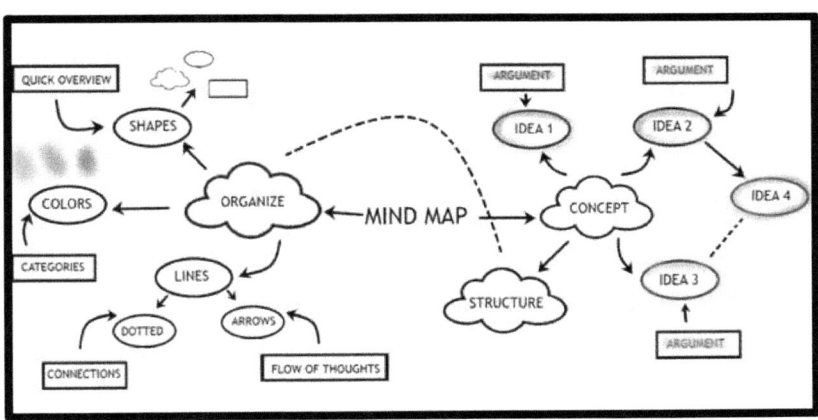

Figure 2-1 - Example of a Mindmap

Another approach to extract this quality is synthesizing; the act of taking one idea and melding it with another. For example, let's say your idea involves telling the story of a family of penguins. But you can't figure out how to communicate the concept. Imagine telling the story through dance. Voila! Say hello to *Happy Feet*. Often, your initial idea may not be sufficient, but creates the impetus to generating a greater idea with the addition of another element.

Many writers take an idea for a "test drive." They perform a writing exercise, brainstorming multiple story ideas and crafting brief paragraphs on how those ideas shape narratives. This might spring forward other ideas where your initial idea is a component. The process pushes you to challenge what interests you about your idea.

At this point, some writers stop with development because they don't want to ruin the creative aspect of their writing. These would be your discovery writers, or pantsers. Other writers may choose to undergo a more intensive and formal development process. A set of tools related to this deeper dive follow.

ORSON SCOTT CARD'S MICE QUOTIENT

What is the kernel of your idea based on? Is it a character? If so, what makes them tick? What makes them interesting to you? Can that interesting feature be used to create some conflict? What sets your world and unique setting apart? Is it an event or action that you believe creates an interesting story? Ever considered a novel concept for space travel? All these sparks of inspiration carry value.

There is a tool to mine those ideas deeper, the MICE Quotient popularized by Science-Fiction writer Orson Scott Card. The MICE Quotient is a method of assigning the type of story based on your initial idea. You then layer on additional pieces of the quotient for additional depth. Incorporating all four components provides the basis for a novel.

M - Milieu, a fancy term for place or setting. A character enters the central location and exits to conclude. Jules Verne's classic The *Journey to the Center of the Earth* is a splendid example.

I – The idea becomes the center of the story. Pose a question at the story's start and provide the answer at the conclusion. Agatha Christie's entire career was centered around these stories. Murder mysteries are a notable example of the idea story.

C – Characterization is often at the heart of the greatest and most complex stories. These stories revolve around a few characters and their personal evolution. Romance stories are character stories at their heart. The more characters you add, the longer and more in depth the story becomes. *To Kill a Mockingbird* would fall into this type of story.

E – Event based stories focus on some change in the world. Will the world be saved? The story ends when we get the answer to that question. This is perhaps the second most common story type, behind characterization.

Card's tool nests ideas within the overall story to add complexity. You begin with an idea story (a murder occurs), but then your character gets trapped in a basement and must escape (milieu), then they meet someone and fall in love during the action (character), and the character must prevent a nuclear bomb from exploding and destroying the city (event) before they answer the original question. In theory, the best approach is to answer the questions in the reverse order of their presentation. For example:

(Ask M)(Ask I)(Ask C)(Answer C)(Answer I)(Answer M)

In some sequences, changing the order on the interior questions works. In the above, answering I before C. The opening question, regardless of its nature, should be answered at the end using this tool. If you answer the initial question that hooked the reader too early in the story, they may not finish.

Once you use the MICE Quotient, hopefully, your story is defined. This is all built upon your core idea. The MICE Quotient is one of the most flexible diagnostic tools available to a writer and their process.

JAMES SCOTT BELL'S LOCK SYSTEM

Bell developed his method after reviewing hundreds of novels. He outlines this technique in his writing book, *Plot & Structure*. He also demonstrates the tool in several writing craft books. Bell's system takes the idea and defines key components of what will evolve into a concept, but Bell pushes that idea a little further down the path.

L – Determine the lead character of your story. The lead character drives the action throughout the story. Scout is the driving force in *To Kill a Mockingbird*.

O – Every story has an objective, a question, for the reader to answer or resolve. The lead character either wants something or wants to avoid something. Scout wishes to gain wisdom about life from her father.

C – Great stories contain some form of confrontation or conflict. This is the obstacle for the lead character in achieving their goal. The primary conflict in *To Kill a Mockingbird* involves the trial and Atticus Finch fighting the forces of racism in the town.

K – Bell takes some liberty to create a nice acronym, but wishes to promote a knockout ending. The character resolves the story question, gets through the confrontation, and has an ending that leaves the reader satisfied. At the story's end, Boo Radley rescues Scout and her brother.

Bell also advocates the Hollywood Three-act Structure method of plotting, and his LOCK system aligns with this story telling technique. This method leaves the door open for an unlimited number of plots as the objective, the type of conflict, and the potential endings vary based on the factors you build into the system.

ERIK BORK'S PROBLEM SYSTEM

Erik Bork defined his PROBLEM system in his appropriately named tome, *The Idea*. Bork's tool is much more about the relative qualities of the idea than actual components, as seen in Card's and Scott's tools. Bork uses another acronym and conveys his most elemental qualities of idea development through seven letters. Perhaps the greater number of letters creates additional depth. Let's see.

P – Punishing your main character. Devise a complex problem that only the character can resolve, resulting in a continuous struggle throughout the entire story. There will also be at least one character that is part of the problem facing our hero. The problem must display some thematic resonance.
R – The main character and whatever they are dealing with must be **relatable**. The story must also progress and keep the audience enthralled. The audience should gravitate to one character as the focal point of their journey through the story.
O – Originality is a key. People find comfort in the familiar, but adding a personal twist prevents clichés. Irony should also be present.
B – Believability is necessary. When the audience empathizes with the character, even the wildest world becomes believable.
L – The story needs **life-altering** change to the character. Without character growth or world-altering circumstances, readers question the purpose. There must also be an intense reaction from the character to the obstacle presented.
E – Entertaining. Avoid the boring aspects of everyday life and cater to the audience's cravings by emphasizing the action-packed moments of the main character's journey. Also, you need at least one set piece to blow away the audience.

M – The story requires real stakes if the protagonist fails. It should hold **meaning** for both the character and the reader.

Bork focuses on character in four of his elements, the other three deal with aspects of the storytelling process. Are those points simple and self-explanatory? Sure, but for some reason writers have struggled for centuries to apply those simple guidelines to their concepts. Becoming a successful writer is a much harder dream to chase.

As we examine all seven of these requirements, we see how these all apply to Scout throughout *To Kill a Mockingbird*. Atticus is tried throughout the novel. His beliefs make him even more relatable today. The story's originality and believability are clear through its inclusion of many true-to-life events. The questions around life-altering, meaningful, and entertaining are answered positively. Harper Lee's classic, *To Kill a Mockingbird,* provides a solid concept based on any of these approaches.

THE JOURNALISTIC TECHNIQUE

The Journalistic Technique asks the classic questions of Who? What? Where? When? Why? and How? Answering these questions develops a rounded concept of the overall story. This technique is the first step toward developing characters, plot, and setting in many authors' processes.

- Who — This question pertains to the main characters for this story (protagonist and antagonist) and the key elements of their character (wants, needs, flaws, and motivations). If you identify those elements, that will help identify the core external conflict and the main character arc of the story. For *Argent's Menagerie*, the author identified the main characters of Argent and Grishon early in the process, they represented opposite sides of the same coin.
- Where and when — Both questions relate to the setting of the story and define where and when this story occurs and how the setting affects the saga. Once the author of *Argent's Menagerie* assigned his main character, the next piece they developed was his ship, the Menagerie, which was intended to reflect the character.
- What — This question focuses on the type of story you are writing. Is your story a mystery, romance, or another genre? Each genre carries certain aspects that need to be present. You also want a general idea of the overall plot concept based on the core conflict

identified from the character portion of the exercise. For *Argent's Menagerie*, the author wanted to write a Science-Fiction story and studied the genre's conventions.

- Why —Why do they care? Is the conflict engaging and the stakes significant enough for the reader's investment? Why write this story? Does the story speak to a fundamental thematic truth that we live through in our world? The answers compel the reader to continue.
- How — This question focuses on the narrative structure of the book and your story's ultimate form. What kind of viewpoint will you use? Is there a certain narration structure you wish to use? What kind of tone will you establish in the book? With *Argent's Menagerie*, the story used an ensemble cast with several third person viewpoint characters to account for the various locales where the action occurred.

This detailed process is not something every writer prefers. The important thing is finding the approach you are most comfortable and productive with. If you do not get results with one process, investigate the other processes mentioned.

STORY SYNOPSIS

Once you complete your initial exercise to add depth to your original idea, it would be best to summarize what your core concept is for the story. Writers often call this the synopsis or logline. There are many templates available online to provide you guidance on how to develop your synopsis. With our core pieces defined, summarizing the story pitch becomes easy. Let this be the driving force to write your story. The key elements of the synopsis would include the following:

1. A quick sense of who the main character is.
2. The catalyst that launches the character into action.
3. The importance of resolving the challenge and the difficulty involved.

A well-written summary has long-term project benefits. It is always beneficial to prepare your elevator pitch for your idea. The summary is useful for submissions, selling books, and discussing the story with other writers. Nothing impresses like a well-developed synopsis. Below is the synopsis of *Dune* by Frank Herbert, a Science-Fiction/Fantasy tale.

> "Paul Atreides, a brilliant and gifted young man born into a great destiny beyond his understanding, must travel to the most dangerous planet in the universe to ensure the future of his family and his people. As malevolent forces explode into conflict over the planet's exclusive supply of the most precious resource in existence, only those who can conquer their own fear will survive."

Once you develop the synopsis, refer to it while writing to judge your alignment with your original concept of the story. Straying can be advantageous, but revert to the original route if unsure.

These methodologies aim to help you decide what to write. Using one or more aids in developing a clear concept and potentially an accurate summary of the story.

You now reach a fork in the road. If you are more of a discovery writer, you may wish to jump forward into the project and start drafting. Or perhaps you are a plotter and want to start character development, world-building, or plot outlining at a deeper level. Later chapters will discuss all those topics. In the meantime, consider naming your story.

STORY TITLES

You've created the story concept and chosen the type and genre. It's necessary for you to create a working title. Notice the word working. Something better may come along before you finish the story. If you are going to be published via the traditional path, the title will probably change.

Why pick a title now if it might change? Having a title improves the chances of completing a story. A story gains life and power through its name. Don't discount the thrill of telling others you're working on a book and giving them a title. You could attend the weekly social and passing cucumber sandwiches when you drop the news. "Oh, I'm working on a mystery novel called Death by Cucumber Sandwiches." It will stop the crowd in their shoes.

By the time you finish the story, you might change the title multiple times. To provide an example, the Fantasy novel *The Forsaken Protector* had a litany of prospective titles along the way. There was *Rojo, The Dragon Queen, The Nine Nations, The Protectors of Austeria*, and *The Wolf and the War*. The author experimented with the title a lot. Some books come to you quickly. The name *Curator of the Gods* emerged early in the book's writing process.

Ultimately, you will want a title for your story. How do we select that? Consider these points when choosing a book title.

The title of your book is the first piece of marketing the product. A title should only be unexpected if there's a valid reason. Ensure the title is not off-putting.

Intrigue your readers by drawing them in. Make the title exhilarating. A notable example is a book by Lisa Jewell called *Then She Was Gone*. The title draws you in with the name. In this day of hyper-vigilance, titles like this attract our eye. Can we find any comparable stories to this one? What happens? Do they find her? Was she alive? If your title prompts the potential reader to ask questions, you are that much closer to drawing them in and plunking down their cash to buy your book.

Make the title easy to remember. You don't want a bland name that just blends into the woodwork. A fitting example from Stephen King's writing includes *Cujo*. The word has now become part of our vernacular for anytime you engage with an aggressive dog. Spooky, with a rough feel as the word rolls off the tongue.

Find two more components for a book title: main character's name or a summarizing phrase. Famous literature often features books titled after their main character. *David Copperfield* and *Don Quixote* come to mind.

A thematic phrase may be a little harder. Examining the premise of your book is a suitable place to start. Does the book contain a standout phrase for a title? Examine the logline you created for the book for anything that catches your attention. Feel free to come up with an alternative that suits you. *Legends in Addington,* a sports story, took its title from the coach's closing speech.

Is this the first installment of a series? If so, create a connection within the titles as you progress. Genevieve Cogman uses titles with references to books in her *Invisible Library* series. Popular mystery scribe Sue Grafton used letters of the alphabet for her titles, as in *A is for Alibi*.

Once you select something, make sure you research your project title. Go on Amazon or Google and search for your title. Check for books with the same title. If you find no matches, then you don't have to worry. If you find a match, ask a set of questions. How well known is the book? Is the author a household name? No worries if your title matches an unknown 1970s book. If your book matches a title of a book by Charles Dickens, rethink the name. If your book matches a New York Times best-seller, switch to another option.

Also, make sure you check the words in your title to ensure you aren't picking a word that has another meaning in popular slang. You may write a book on elevator carpet choices and call the story *Shags in the Lift*. People might misinterpret your meaning.

EXERCISES

1. Watch the Ira Glass series of videos on YouTube. Write a short essay detailing Ira's ideas.
    a. (www.youtube.com/watch?v=5pFI9UuC_fc)
2. Use a mindmap template to discover various elements of your story and identify key pieces of your story.
3. For your story, write a two-sentence synopsis using the example provided in this chapter or by searching for other models on the internet.
4. Use the MICE Quotient or the Journalistic Approach to expand on your original story idea.

REFERENCE MATERIALS

The Idea: The Seven Elements of a Viable Story for Screen, Stage or Fiction by Erik Bork
Characters & Viewpoint by Orson Scott Card
Plot & Structure by James Scott Bell
Ira Glass video on storytelling from YouTube

Bork's book is a perfect guide to idea conception and developing them into stories. This includes the PROBLEM method, a tutorial on synopsis writing, and other impressive tricks for the writer. Card's book excels in character development and explores viewpoint in writing. It also serves as an introduction to the MICE Quotient. Bell's tome, introducing the LOCK Structure, is a must-read for any aspiring writer. The Glass video series looks at the development process used in much of screenwriting today. Elements of this bleed into fiction writing.

3 – GENRE & STORY TYPES

As you begin the writing process for your novel, if you have done nothing else in the way of pre-work, you should understand what genre your story will fall into. This will be a key factor in understanding what your potential readers expect from the story. The reason genre fiction works so well is people want that expectation met and talented writers deliver the goods in a fresh manner. In many ways, genres speak to the duplicity of the reader. They desire novelty, but readers seek comfort in the familiar aspects of your story.

Familiarity is one of those implied promises. Romance readers want the kiss. Mystery readers want the reveal. Your job is to give them what they desire. You desire to achieve the unprecedented. This is where your creativity comes into play, along with two other tools: subversion and irony.

Subversion is the act of taking a typical scene, trope, or character and doing something different with the trope. One of the best examples in modern media is *Buffy the Vampire Slayer*. Most people would presume a vampire slayer being a muscular and experienced person armed with various weapons, much like the character Van Helsing from Bram Stoker's *Dracula*. But Buffy Sommers is a high school cheerleader. Her character is a subversion in two ways. Being the hunter, she lacks the typical look and background. The other is the role portrayed by a young women is the victim in most horror genre stories. Buffy is no victim.

The key to subversion is finding the trope within your story that you want to make your own and twist it in a different direction. Subverting multiple tropes is even better if you can. Sometimes this requires a skilled hand. Remember, you want to give the trope a distinct flavor, not change the entire meal.

Irony breaks familiarity traps as well. Irony occurs when the character believes something occurs within the story for one reason, while the audience knows the event occurs because of another. An example from the stage would involve *Romeo and Juliet*. Romeo mistakenly assumes Juliet is dead and ends his own life. This is an example of tragic, or dramatic, irony. Irony often appears in comedic, verbal, or situational forms. When using irony, don't undermine your character's credibility or believability. Irony can be used in a multitude of ways to profound effect:

- Allow your character to make mistakes they wouldn't make if they saw the entire picture.
- Allow your character to be vulnerable in circumstances they don't understand or to characters they don't know.
- Add comedic irony when it makes sense and provide levity to break the tension.

WHAT GENRE ARE YOU WRITING?

Modern publishing drives stories into specific genres for marketing and selling purposes. In reality, genre can be divided into two types that shape storytelling: commercial and content. Most of us are familiar with the concept of commercial genres. These are books that fall in line with a stylistic presentation. They feature magical and fantastical settings. They hinge on futuristic technology. Or a body is found.

Content genres concern themselves with the structure and general plot of the story falling within a specific style and format. Heist and Status stories are notable examples of these. These stories possess common characteristics that readers desire. Without these vital components, the reader is let down. Going forward, those will be known as story types.

The two classifications, genre and story type, differ subtly, and many stories incorporate aspects of multiples types of each. Some genres crossover between the two categories. Romance and Mystery contain specific plot points found in many stories outside of those respective genres because their traditional structures provide a flexible format for storytelling. These crossover capabilities make them popular to use with other genres. It also explains why they are two of the top selling genres year after year.

Many writers use multiple genre aspects and will pull elements from Science-Fiction, Fantasy, Myth, and Adventure story types while implementing Mystery and Relationship (an offshoot of romance) plot lines within the larger story to build depth to the plot and the secondary characters. This genre bending is a growing trend and began in earnest when *Star Wars* put the media industry on notice with its cross-genre appeal.

You may have a story that you like, but it needs something else. The desire to write pull from the market and follow trends may arise. Restrain yourself. Better advice is to examine trends and involve a simple concept from another genre or story type and using it within your overall story. Using a mystery to build some intrigue, a love angle to open your character up to more emotional interiority, or an action sub-plot to create some excitement and pick up the pace.

Let's say the trend is noir detective series. What are the key traits of such a story? Research those and determine if implementing one of those elements into your story makes it more intriguing. Truth be told, many of the greatest stories incorporate aspects of various genres. There are very few stories that fall into one genre. Fantasy tales often involve elements of the Mystery and Romance genres. Horror, Thriller, and Science-Fiction elements may cross over in your writing. Understand genres and story types to use them effectively. It is all about you developing your skills and processes to be the best writer and create the best story possible. The following is a list of commercial genre fiction categories you might recognize from your local bookstore:

Literary Fiction – Most consider these stories works of artistic and literary merit. They deal with weighty issues around political and social criticism or reflections on life. Usually these are character driven. These include Coming-of-Age stories dealing with the emotional growth and maturity of a child into an adult.

Mystery – A question is asked, and a detective finds clues to solve the riddle with elements of tension and suspense throughout until the satisfying reveal of the bad guy at the end. The most famous of these are the Sherlock Holmes stories by Sir Arthur Conan Doyle.

Thriller – Dark and suspenseful plot-driven stories. Suspense and tension are the key elements, and they use plot twists and cliffhangers throughout. A popular style of fiction today.

Horror – Horror should solicit primal emotions like fear and terror from the reader. The story often involves monsters or the macabre. Darkness and dread are the general tones of these stories.

Historical Fiction – These stories take place at a specific time and locale in the past. Many of these stories involve historical figures, events, and settings as part of the plot. Extensive research is necessary to assure readers of the world's accuracy.

Romance – Love stories. Usually, the mood is light and optimistic. Conflict won't dominate the story's relationship dynamics. Love prevails in the end. Facets of these stories work in relationship and buddy stories.

Western – Focuses on the stories of cowboys, settlers, outlaws, and Native Americans during the exploration of the American West. Features many genre-specific elements that the story relies on to succeed. Some elements serve as secondary genres in larger stories, such as in *The Mandalorian*.

Science-Fiction – Sci-Fi includes elements that don't exist in the real world but inspired by natural and social sciences, along with technology. Common conventions include time travel, space exploration, futuristic societies, and aliens.

Fantasy – Fantasy is another sub-genre of speculative fiction that focuses on imaginary characters and settings. Mythology, folklore, and magic are key components of these stories.

Speculative Fiction – Speculative fiction includes fantasy and science fiction, along with dystopian and steampunk stories. The stories happen in a world different from ours. Certain stories are founded on altered historical events and emphasize the consequences of those changes.

Realistic Fiction – Novels set in a time and place that might occur in the real world. They depict actual individuals, locations, and occurrences with a focus on authenticity. They stay true-to-life and abide by existing laws of nature and man.

Is this a complete list of genres or story types? No. Research more to explore if your story fits into an unmentioned genre or sub-genre. With this information, you can understand the usual form and market expectations for a story like yours. Don't feel obligated to adhere to traditional formulas, but consider blending genres while meeting reader expectations. For more genre specific information, refer to the Genre Guides available to you as part of the Vibrant Prose Toolbox.

TROPES AND CONVENTIONS

One other aspect of genre fiction is the use of concepts that appear consistently over many stories within that category. Most refer to these concepts as tropes and conventions. Conventions involve presenting a particular character archetype, a recurring type of scene, or standard twist expected by the reader. Many genre fiction readers expect these to be included in the story and not doing so violates your unwritten contract. Tropes are the method in which writers deliver these conventions.

For example, we all know that a mentor exists in the Hero's Journey story structure. The mentor is the convention. The trope is delivering the mentor as an old, gray bearded wizard. The key to fulfilling this contract with the reader and making your writing less formulaic is creating an imaginative twist on the trope. Your creativity will refresh and engage the reader. To contrast against the traditional wizard, in *Avatar: The Last Airbender*, the mentors for Aang appeared in the form of other children he encountered on his adventures; namely Katara, Toph, and Zuko.

Steer clear of clichés when handling these tropes. Is your character the same type of mentor we experience in a hundred other fantasy stories? Has the same type of breakup and reunion occurred in every Hallmark movie you have seen? If you have read or seen the scene before, then trust the genre reader has seen the device more. Try to provide something new. That doesn't guarantee it hasn't been done. At least you provided something unique in your mind and not the standard clichéd approach associated with lazy writing.

From a practical standpoint, imagine story types and genres as a combined resource, allowing writers to open their stories up to wider plot lines and casts. Each of these genres involves certain conventions in the form of characters and plots. By incorporating these tropes and standard plot lines, as expected by readers of certain genres, our stories become richer and more immersive. Let's say you desire a space opera with a mystery and a strong romance plot. You will combine three different genres. If you use mystery elements, you need a sleuth, a dead body, and a reveal. A romance requires the first kiss, the separation, and the HEA (happily ever after). This cross pollination of story types provides three sets of questions, plot lines, and character types to pull from to build a larger and more comprehensive story. As writers, we can develop the story framework before writing anything on the page. It almost makes our job as a writer easier and allows us to focus on writing the story and developing our prose.

GENRE CONNECTED TO THEME

Genre and story archetypes don't just relate to prescribed plot and characters. Consensus dictates that theme belongs to the literary realm, distant from genre. The gatekeepers of the writing world perpetuate that fabrication and untruth. Ironically, theme and genre are inextricably linked. The theme revolves around our acute awareness of life's truths. Genre uses specific story types to explore certain questions that pertain to life and truth. And if you are like many modern writers, you meld more than one genre into your writing. There are multiple questions being asked and truths being explained.

John Truby's latest book, *The Anatomy of Genres*, provides a thorough examination of this question of mixing genres with varied themes and provides excellent keys that each genre writer can use in their quest to draft the best story possible. Truby highlights inherent life questions for each genre.

GENRE	PREVALENT THEMES
Horror	Facing Death and Taking Humane Action
Action	Competing, Fighting, Winning, and Losing
Myth	Self-Searching and Finding Destiny
Coming of Age	Seeing the Value of One's Life
Science Fiction	Recognizing Choices and Creating a New World
Crime	Living by Laws and Fighting for Justice
Comedy	Living with Absurdity and Laughter
Western	Doomed Existence
Gangster	Slavery to False Values
Fantasy	Realizing One's Potential
Thriller	Discovering Guilt and Uncovering Our True Enemies
Romance	Love and Relationship

Life questions, or values, should connect to your story and be your writing's focus. Are these the only themes we will deal with in our stories? No, but they should be part of what our stories address.

To look at those questions, how are they reflected in *Argent's Menagerie*? The main character, Argent, is a representation of a life of freedom. His pursuit is to reclaim freedom (Fantasy) and he will fight for his desire (Action). Through all of that, he wants to create a better world using the technology behind the fusion engines and fusion-charges (Science-Fiction) but opens himself to a destiny different from what he pursued before (Myth). By addressing diverse themes, a writer can broaden their book's appeal and explore profound life questions. Each of those themes overlaps with the dominant theme of Argent's internal story around broken trust and reestablishing long-lost family relationships.

From a practical standpoint, the cross-genre approach opens our stories up to wider thematic through lines. Each of these genres and story types leverage the conventions in the form of thematically driven characters and plots. By incorporating these tropes and standard plot lines, as expected by readers of certain genres, our stories become richer and more immersive and explore more of those truths.

STORY TYPES

What kind of story are you writing? When that question is asked, it doesn't refer to the commercial genre. If you boiled your story down to the overarching story plot, what kind of story is it? Perhaps this would serve everyone better if we conducted a quick overview of story archetypes and how those are used to define whatever story you are writing.

There's a common belief that the number of stories is finite. This reinforces the concept of existing story types and the continuous argument over their limited number. Story type refers to an established story pattern with certain plot points to create a structure similar as other stories. The best stories blend elements from various categories to create better tales.

Now, some will argue over the number of true story types. Writing snobs claim only two genuine stories exist: one where a character desires something and one where they aim to retain something. Oh, if it was only so simple.

Christopher Booker, a noted British writer, premised there were only *The Seven Basic Plots* in his large tome. His theory has gained traction over time. Others attempted to quantify the raw number of basic plots. Ronald Tobias wrote *20 Master Plots*. Georges Polti wrote about *The Thirty-Six Dramatic Situations*. William Wallace Cook beat them all with his book *Plotto: The Master Book of All Plots,* where he identified 1,462 different plot scenarios in a research project that impresses even the worst stricken OCD victims. The story types number is unobtainable and irrelevant, except for demonstration. The following paragraphs examine nine categories with examples of each story type's hallmarks.

Overcoming the Monster – This type of story involves the protagonist defeating the big bad at the end of the story. The Monster may either be an actual monster or the wicked villain. Other key story points include the hero using a magical weapon, the monster guards some sort of treasure or princess, and defeating the monster in their lair. The hero escapes with the Princess at the end. Prominent examples, like *Clash of the Titans*, are immediately thought of. However, this may encompass stories like James Bond or Westerns with the hero rescuing the damsel in distress.

Rags to Riches – This is an obvious story based on the title. The poor, down-on-his-luck, hero leaves their miserable life and becomes rich, famous, and/or powerful. The main variations on this involve the ending of the story. The character may fail to achieve the goal, or they achieve the goal and find it is a hollow victory. *Cinderella* is perhaps the best-known example of this type of story.

The Quest – A hero embarks on a journey to obtain a glorious prize located far away. This story may overlap with the Monster story type, but the goal sets it apart. The goal is getting the prize, whereas in the earlier story, defeating the monster is the desired outcome. Some variations lead to a less happy ending. The aim of *The Lord of the Rings* is to surrender the prize.

Voyage and Return – This story bears some of the same characteristics as the Quest and the Monster. Again, the objective is the key. The aim is to return home. The character journey emphasizes the protagonist's growth. One key story point is a fantastic escape. Some versions see the character return, but he leaves happiness behind (and often sets up a sequel). *The Hobbit* is a classic version of this tale. The sub-title itself mentions the goal, "There and Back Again."

Comedy – This is a lighter-hearted story where the character achieves their goal and resolves an inner conflict. The story can be humorous or satirical. Common convention attaches a romantic relationship to the story, and the story ends with a happy couple. Writing these stories is challenging, as mastering comedy is difficult. The greatest examples of this category are often Shakespearian dramas.

Tragedy – Tragedy is the opposite of comedy in outcome and tone. These are the greatest of Shakespeare's dramas. They end with achieving the goal and, most times, the death of the main character. They carry a great thematic message as well. Examples include *Hamlet* and *Dr. Faustus* (for those not wanting to only hear about the Bard).

Rebirth – These stories involve the hero being trapped by the villain. The hero is saved by another character, a love interest. One issue with these stories is the main character requires someone else to resolve their issues. This creates additional tension within the storyline. Dickens' *A Christmas Carol* is a variation with Scrooge trapped within his desire for wealth.

Mystery – Often an investigation into the death of an innocent character. It involves a sleuth, perhaps an assistant, and multiple suspects. There are specific aspects of mysteries that are deemed necessary for the audience. Ultimately, a question arises, and the objective is an exhilarating unveiling of the antagonist. See anything written by Agatha Christie.

Rebellion – A hero rebels against an all-powerful enemy, perhaps the state or a dictator. The hero must preserve their status, defeat the enemy, and lead a rebellion. Modern literature often reflects a global discontent with the government. This is the basis for much Dystopian literature that proliferates the market today. Orwell's *Animal Farm* is a classic example.

Are these all the story types? Others could be named if given time and space. You have heists, romances, white room stories, underdog sports, buddy cops, war, and coming of age stories. Realize that each story type has its own baggage. As a writer, you must grasp the story components and their relationship with the genre.

Which category does your story fall into? Are there components of other story types you carry in the story? Most literature overlaps to a degree between various buckets. Obvious examples would be Fantasy stories that involve a Monster, Quest, and a Return motif. Whatever your favorite, or whatever group your story falls into, having a solid understanding of the components of each story will be beneficial to you as a writer in the future.

OTHER TOPICS

Genres contain many traditions that provide further structure and guidance for the writer. The story's length is a primary consideration. Most novel categories fall within 70,000 to 90,000 words. The exceptions to that; Fantasy, Science-Fiction and Historical Fiction consist of stories exceeding 100,000 words and even larger if you are dealing with Epic or High Fantasy tomes.

Another item that varies by genre is the use of viewpoint. Sleuth mysteries often use a first-person point of view. Romance stories often contain multiple POVs as both of the romantic leads need their thoughts and emotions available to the reader. Once dominated by the omniscient viewpoint, Fantasy stories now employ diverse first, third, and even second-person perspectives. The dominant viewpoint is third-person limited, but most genres have a customary norm for their devoted readers.

In the prior paragraphs, the discussion has focused on these broad categories of genre and story type. Truth is, it's just the external face of genre. Every genre has numerous subgenres, with detailed conventions for plot, characters, and settings. Steampunk, for example, uses technology using steam or clockwork mechanisms, takes place in a Victorian-inspired locale, and is a social commentary on some facet of life. Though the story falls within Science-Fiction, it pulls on many genres to make that story type work. You can dive as deep as you want into your genre, subgenre, and sub-subgenres to find a place that fits with your writing.

The last aspect to consider regarding genre is the audience's age. This text assumes the audience is primarily adult in age. The writer must adjust specific elements of the story depending on the age range of their audience. For example, Young Adult stories contain a lower word count. Also, Young Adult is considered a commercial genre of its own that tells stories with protagonists in the teenage range. Violent and sexual scenes are toned down for age appropriateness. For middle-grade readers, writers tone down situations involving those extreme scene, or only allude to them, in the story. For smaller children, avoid intense situations almost universally. It is best that you research how to deal with your specific story within the genre parameters.

Understanding the unwritten rules of genre and story types is crucial for writers to succeed. Using these genre conventions and tropes to create a better story is the sign of a shrewd writer.

EXERCISES

1. Think about which genre or story type your story falls into and document the tropes or conventions your story will use.
2. Identify typical elements of another genre that a reader would expect in your story.
3. Write an essay on your favorite trope or convention from your favorite book/movie.

REFERENCE MATERIALS

The Anatomy of Story: 22 Steps to Becoming a Master Storyteller by John Truby
The Anatomy of Genres by John Truby

John Truby has written two excellent tomes on storytelling. The first, *The Anatomy of Story*, is perhaps one of the essential craft books that every writer should own as it details the entire story development process. Though the book skews to the side of being a plotter's dream, it contains information beneficial to every person who considers themselves a writer. *The Anatomy of Genres* covers the topic in excessive detail, but if you're interested in Truby's genre elements, this book provides abundant information.

The Seven Basic Plots: Why We Tell Stories by Christopher Booker
20 Master Plots: And How to Build Them by Ronald Tobias

Though most might disagree with the categorization by Booker, the effort deserves recognition and respect. This book has seen a climb in popularity, and some consider this the defining book on story types. *20 Master Plots* has been in the public space for longer and provides a wider perspective of the same idea. Both books are worth a read, but unnecessary for a writer's personal library.

The Trope Thesaurus by Jennifer Hilt

Hilt has done an excellent job of crafting herself the niche of a trope/genre expert. She has a general resource on tropes and has books dedicated to specific genres such as Romance, Horror, Fantasy, and Science-Fiction.

4 – THE READER

Our concept development process is impacted by three influential forces. The first is, of course, the writer. Without your input, passion, and knowledge, the idea is nothing. You will shape the largest part of this concept. The second influence is the genre your concept falls under. The concept adopts normative attributes to succeed in the eyes of readers, publishers, and writers. The third element that influences your concept is the reader.

You may ask, "How does the reader influence the idea if they only read the story after publication?" The reader is going to bring expectations, experience, and knowledge to the table. You must tailor your story to fit them in a fashion that doesn't destroy your intent. How do you do that? That process begins by trying to develop an image of our ideal reader. Without knowing the reader, how will we know their effects on our concept?

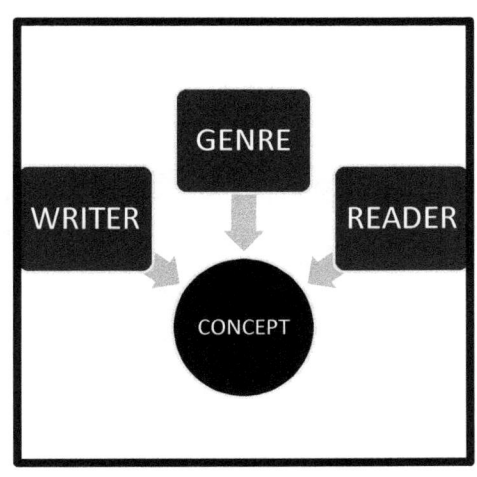

Figure 4-1 The Influencers on Concept

THE IDEAL READER

Let's define the ideal reader for those unfamiliar with the term. At a high level, the ideal reader personifies the writer's and the story's core target market. Understanding what this person looks like, where they live, and other fundamental aspects about them provides clarity to your story's composition, marketing, and the focus you apply to certain aspects of the story. You are attempting to pinpoint the specific person who would buy your book, as if you tailored the story to them. The theory suggests that others like your ideal reader would want to read your story. Once you understand this concept, the benefits become quite apparent. How do we go about that? How does this fit into my writing process?

Both are excellent questions. Let's tackle the second one first. Performing this task fits best in one of two spots within the writing process. Some writers attempt this early in the story, developing that knowledge from the outset. The second, and probably best time, is after you complete the first draft and begin your revision process. After completing this exercise, hopefully, you'll grasp your story and its potential readers.

Defining your ideal reader takes on the form of an interview in many ways. You will identify and compile a composite "sketch" of your ideal reader. To many writers, this may sound odd. We want our stories to appeal to as many people as possible. But your story won't appeal to everyone. Your ideal reader is not one person, but a representation of many similar readers who will be thrilled by your story. What are some of the key items we should know about our ideal reader? The following are a group of qualities to identify.

- How old are they? — This is the one element you should define early in your process. It makes a difference in the story you write if your ideal reader is a middle grade student or a 40-year-old. The content, style, and format of the story will be different depending on the age of your audience.

- What does your reader read? — Do they read a specific genre? Do they read the genre of your story? Which subgenre are you targeting? If these elements don't synch up between your reader and the story you are writing, you are looking at the wrong person as your audience. Do you think a 40-year-old male steel factory worker would be into a dragon-shifter romance?

- What other books is your reader reading? — Identifying what other books your reader consumes will provide you with comparisons to use in marketing your book to attract the reader's attention, assuming your story exists in the same genre and subgenre. Perhaps your story shares a concept with their favorite book. Or you might write the antithesis of what interests them. Keep in mind that if you are writing a time travel Science-Fiction story, the tale may not appeal to the reader of high-tech espionage thrillers, even though both fall under Sci-Fi.

- Where do they live? Where do they vacation? — Perhaps your story takes place in Seattle. People love reading about their familiar places, even if the book is of a different genre. Using a real location provides additional pressure on the writer. The reader understands the context your setting imposes on the story. They will love seeing local slang, landmarks or historical events in your story. They will bring contextual understanding that will allow for subtext in your story.
- What are their demographics? — Are they male or female? Yes, that matters. What is their occupation? Is there a character in your story with the same occupation. This might lead to an immediate connection? Is your reader politically motivated? If so, which party? This might reveal if they'll agree with your thematic message. Do they have a family? This could be a key part of your story and perhaps they can relate.
- Then we ask deeper personal questions. — Do they partake in any hobbies? What is their personality type? These might determine the intensity of certain scenes. People who were abused as children tend to avoid such narratives. Are they jovial people? Then they may enjoy witty banter or humor in their stories. What are their fears? Their dreams? What keeps them awake at night? Tying your story to these deep-seated items could open up a new audience for you.

Once you answer these questions, develop a detailed picture of who your reader might be. You will understand the pieces of your story they will attach themselves to. You will understand where they lack the context surrounding a situation and can build that into the story. This exercise provides clarity for developing characters and settings on the page, rather than leaving it as subtext. It should help determine what to leave out to build tension within the story. You do this by working from their expectations and contextual knowledge on the story elements they are familiar with. A detailed look at your ideal reader allows you to understand who you are marketing too and points to where you need to push your promotion efforts.

READER EXPECTATIONS

So, you created a profile for your ideal reader. What does that do for the story? How does this reader information impact our concept, as was mentioned earlier in the chapter? Writers should grasp that when readers engage with their story, a contract is formed. There are unwritten promises you make to them because the reader is entering this transaction with certain expectations. Will this book be like others within the genre they read? If a particular city is the setting of your story, are you portraying the setting properly? Are you giving the reader everything they want from a story of this type? Janice Hardy explains the conundrum well in the following quote from an article on her website *Fiction University*.

"There's a fine line between doing what readers expect and satisfying reader expectation, and the trick is to skirt that line. When we do it well, readers anticipate what's to come and eagerly look forward to seeing it happen. When we do it poorly, they know what's coming and the story feels stale and predictable. If you can get a sense of what readers expect as you write (or in an early draft), you can play with those expectations so they're satisfied by what happens, and surprised because it's not the way they thought it would be."

Yes, your readers create a paradox in wanting to know what you will do while being surprised. How more human can they be? What creates these expectations? Three things you, as the writer, provide to the reader create numerous expectations.

Genre incites the first set of expectations. Each genre, as we learned in the prior chapter, creates the opportunity to use certain conventions and tropes. The reader expects and desires innovative use of these story elements. If you're writing a Fantasy story, is the mentor the tried-and-true gray-haired wizard or do they take the form of a cricket that sits on the protagonist's shoulder? All these elements are expected by the reader, and you better deliver them.

The next set of expectations comes from the story world you use. Is your story set in a derivative of Middle-Earth? Then you better provide elves, orcs, and dwarves. Are we on a spaceship? We anticipate either interstellar travel or contact with aliens. Or is the story set in New York City? If so, use the subway, Statue of Liberty, or Times Square to your advantage. When the reader sees where you set your story, they expect you to do something that creates a sense of familiarity with their world or other stories they have read.

Plot delivery is the third element shaping expectations. You are creating promises and asking questions as you progress through the opening section of the story. Is there a dead body? You better identify the murderer, their method, and motive. Imagine two strangers, from different cities, meeting at a ski resort during a snowstorm. Bring those two people together and ensure everlasting happiness. Your story, more than anything else, creates expectations.

Having said that, the reader also brings in their own expectations. In Historical Fiction, readers usually comprehend what happened in history. If your story involves Pearl Harbor after Thanksgiving in 1941, your reader will anticipate the impending events and the resulting suspense will glue them to the story. They want to witness these people respond to their impending doom.

The reader brings with them context that fills in holes that you, as the writer, don't include. Their familiarity with the situation or location can help fill some of that subtext in for you. They may know that a certain park has a reputation and if you did your job right you will implement that and that will create suspense for the reader. But you as the writer must also account for people that might not be familiar with that setting. If the story needs that information, you must provide it. But when possible, appeal to your ideal reader's knowledge base.

You, as the writer, remain in control. You identified your ideal reader and know what they comprehend about your story. Use this to subvert what they expect in the story. If they are expecting a story like *The Grapes of Wrath*, on the trail to California, force your protagonist and his family to peel off from the convoy and stop in Las Vegas. Transform the deviation into a narrative of fresh beginnings that leads to the creation of something completely surprising for the reader. Most readers give you leeway to shape the story if you captivate them. Even if the new direction veers off the path a bit they will enjoy the journey more often than not. The key is understanding your reader's expectations and a writer's role in controlling the story for impactful and entertaining reading.

HOOKING THE READER

At this point, you've determined who your ideal reader is, modified your story to account for this, and lured them into reading your story. You're halfway through the battle. Now, how do you keep them hooked and craving more of your story? What actions will you take to prevent them from being another lost opportunity?

First, make sure you truly engage them in your story. There are four basic questions the reader is searching for you to answer. They want to understand whose story this is. Introduce your main character and make that first image impactful for the reader. Create an opportunity for the reader to become interested in them. The reader also needs to realize there are some stakes in this story. Early on, introduce the first question of the story to give the reader a sense of direction. Without direction, they'll abandon the book. Next, allude to the type of change we are going to see in our main character quickly. It may not be in the first scene, but evidence of the required change needs to happen early.

We have the reader interested in our opening sequence and they haven't jumped yet. The reader staying hooked to your story depends on how well you create narrative tension. This means asking the questions and presenting obstacles for your protagonist. Keep readers intrigued by varying the intensity of questions and obstacles. They *need* to turn the page. We appeal to the reader's interests to engage them in the story. We are using their expectations to illuminate the aspects of the story they desire to see come alive. Use the excerpt below from *Argent's Menagerie* and identify elements that draw in and set up reader expectations.

"The thud of a Terraxian body hitting the floor filled the aggrieved party's quarters aboard the warship known as the Hurricane. An electric shock knocked the large male of the ridge backed and heavily scaled race unconscious. He still breathed deeply even after an attack sufficient to kill most others.

Argent Aquilus Second-Feather, Argent to his small crew and even smaller number of friends, stood over the body with the crackling shockspear. To verify unconsciousness, Argent kicked the body with his right lower dactyl. The ugly cuss might be faking.

Argent mumbled to the nonresponsive body. "You are lucky I'm a mercenary with a conscience. Anybody else in my crew would have killed you without a second thought."

Argent killed only when no other alternatives existed. Even though a mercenary unfitting of his family's rank, he held an unspoken moral code. He was entitled to hold himself to a standard, especially if others did not.

A beep from his sci-watch brought his attention back to the mission. The device identified a particular energy signature, hopefully from his desired prize, emanating from a corner armoire with a full-length mirror.

Argent warily walked to the piece and caressed the armoire like a newborn pet. His sensitive talons and feathers searched for imperfections or hidden latches, finding none. No keypads or locks prevented him from opening the cabinet. Argent swung the door and discovered the reason he boarded the Hurricane, a Phantori requiem cube.

Ah, the rush of stealing something precious.

Argent admired the intricate white runes carved into the black, porous block. He traced his feathered fingers over the surface of the artifact from a lost world. Heat, pressure, smoothness, and grit on the surface of the cube, remnants of its previous owners, teased his senses. Argent pushed the cube into his breast pocket and zipped it closed to keep the prize safe.

I hope she appreciates this.

Argent closed the cabinet and peered at his reflection in the mirror. The image revealed how ruffled his silver feathers were and his lean nature testified to his recent diet. Thoughts drifted to a possible trip to Aviara, his home world, to enjoy home-cooked meals and regain a semblance of good health.

The sci-watch beeped and refocused Argent on the job at hand."

Dan Brown's *The DaVinci Code* is a master study in how to do this. Brown knows his audience intimately by this point in his career. He knows they want the action and tension of his rollercoaster stories. They don't care for flowery description or long infodumps or immersive story worlds. They crave the intrigue, suspense, and mystery of the investigation. They want to feel attached to the protagonist, Robert Langdon, as he unearths the massive hidden stories of the world.

Every page provides an obstacle or question that Robert Langdon must resolve to move to the next stage. The reader also desires progression as Langdon works through the traps, clues, and information. Each new element exposes Langdon's character and facilitates his personal growth. These obstacles also hearken back to the thematic drive of the story. All of them assist the plot's progress, but introduce complications that cast doubt on Langdon's eventual resolution. The story thrives on tension from start to finish.

USING THIS IN YOUR PROCESS

How does knowing this information change your process? That depends on when you wish to implement these steps. For plotters/planners/outliners, a research-based element is a natural addition to the analysis in the initial stages of the pre-writing work and incorporating your information into the first draft. If you're a discovery writer/pantser, you will take the task into consideration when you go through the revision stage of your process.

How does this impact the final product? Your first concern is staying true to your story. If adjusting for the reader's expectations outweighs the story you wish to write, you identified the wrong reader. Or you need to draft a different story. There's a disconnect. You must choose a way forward. Regardless, the ideal reader is not the only audience for this story. Provide enough context to prevent the story from falling flat for others. Not everyone has visited Oxford, England, but R. F. Kuang provided enough context in *Babel* that anyone picking that book up understands the environment of the university and the surrounding community.

How can you incorporate this into the story? Fantasy writers have known the answer to this question for decades. Use a prologue. How else will the writer prepare readers for a unique story world without giving them a taste? Another approach involves gradually revealing relevant information and context as the story develops. The third option is to provide context through the use of the characters. Either they provide the information to the reader through their daily life, or they explore the world to show the locale to the reader.

How do you evaluate if you did this effectively? That is where critique groups and beta readers become important. Have them provide feedback on these elements. In the real world, people who fit your ideal reader profile can tell you if you missed, were heavy-handed, or hit the mark. Then take their feedback and implement any changes to enhance the story.

The goal is to benefit your story through the reader. Try aligning the story to their expectations but add a surprising twist for entertainment. Give them what they want, but something different, a paradoxical joy.

EXERCISES

1. Create an ideal reader interview form from the Vibrant Prose Toolbox and complete it to find the ideal reader for your story or your favorite story.
2. Identify an aspect of your reader interview and edit an aspect of your story to reflect the impact of that item.

REFERENCE MATERIALS

Wired for Story: The Writer's Guide to Using Brain Science to Hook Readers from the Very First Sentence by Lisa Cron
Hack Your Reader's Brain: Bring the Power of Brain Chemistry to Bear on Your Fiction by Jeff Gerke
Fiction University website by Janice Hardy

Cron and Gerke wrote very reader centric craft books that provide a lot of information on how to implement this information into your writing. They each have multiple books out there that can be useful for your writing, some of which are referenced later in this book. Hardy provides a great deal of information for every writer through her website and her multiple writing guides about finding your ideal reader.

5 – DEVELOPING CHARACTERS

Across the spectrum of writers, we all hold beliefs that certain elements of the story are key. Authors differ in their answers to the question of the three key elements of story development. Some might say setting or structure. Several reply with theme. Most will mention the plot. But we all agree that characters are integral to developing your story.

While your plot and setting may be exceptional, a prominent character is crucial for your writing's greatness. Characters resonate with readers more than anything else. The reader relates to the story or escapes reality through the character's experience. The main character is so important to stories that many authors feel the need to define this lone element before starting the writing process.

You may wonder, how do the prominent writers figure out the details of their characters? Shakespeare, Dickens, and King wrote dozens of them. Their characters resemble ordinary people, but with a twist, intensified to the extreme. They are often exaggerations of these character traits, at times to a comedic level.

How do we decide who our characters are? What techniques help us come up with those details?

Great questions. Numerous techniques exist, but they are variations of the same theme, merely packaged differently. The upcoming paragraphs will discuss these techniques. Perhaps a quick walkthrough of the qualities we are dissecting would be the best primer for your thoughts. We need to dive into what makes your character unique and drives their innermost thoughts and emotions.

People have preferences for different methodologies - outside-in or inside-out. The method is irrelevant if you focus on the character's essence. Remember this one question as we explore defining character elements. How does this inform the character's mindset and their story? Perhaps it drives a piece of their backstory and is a key to defining their path. Knowing this information at the outset of your project is critical to drafting your story and the direction it will take.

NAMING YOUR CHARACTERS

We will start with the first thing we learn from everyone: their name. No fixed rules exist for this exercise, but general guidelines apply. These will help you keep the characters straight as you write them, but also make it easier for the reader. You want to avoid confusing the reader as much as possible.

- Keep in mind the last name infers the ethnicity or lineage of the character. A name like Mancini implies Italian heritage. A name like William Harrington III implies an importance to the name. Jane Austen did this with one of her prominent characters in *Pride and Prejudice*, Fitzwilliam Darcy.
- Try to avoid names for the main characters that begin with the same letter. If you have several characters with first names that start with "B" they will blend together.
- Vary the lengths and sound patterns of the character names. Avoid having all one or two syllable names.
- Use flamboyant names, or names that depict the characterization, on non-major characters. *As the City Burns* contains a character named Malachi Connett. If you shorten it, his name is Mal Connett, a play on malcontent. J K Rowling used this to enormous success in the Harry Potter series.
- For potential international concerns, don't use the foreign word for villain or another role as it will translate to villain or that role in that other language. Plus, it's a little on the nose.
- Maintain consistency in referring to the character throughout the story, unless there's a valid reason to change. The main character in *As the City Burns* refers to the characters he likes by first name, the ones he dislikes by last name. You can track his opinion of the character in the story by how he refers to them.
- Use alliteration to make names memorable. Dickens did this with many characters, the most famous being Nicholas Nickelby.
- Layered names suggesting something are excellent. Uriah Heep from *David Copperfield* would be a primary example of this.
- Names can also be tied to language components, especially in Fantasy or Science-Fiction stories where language is a key driver of the culture of the society.

Sometimes you just haven't decided on the perfect name for your characters. You could leave the names as XXX or YYY as you write the story and create the names later when they occur to you. This becomes a revision nightmare if you don't maintain a character list. You must track how you use the codes throughout the story. This also causes problems if you use full names, last names, or just first names at various points in the story.

EXTERNAL QUALITIES

Designing a character's external image can be one of the easiest aspects of writing. As you imagined the character, you developed a visual in your mind. Other characters' perception of them, and even their self-perception, may hinge on this image. We will focus on character description in a later chapter, but knowing what this person looks like is important, even if you never mention it in the story.

A technique referred to as the Casting Call helped many writers develop the physical image of characters in their stories. You cast an actor or model as a stand-in for the physical attributes each character possesses. This aids in developing the description of the characters when they are introduced. Sometimes, you tweak those physical attributes to give them a quirk. Something that either draws the eye or subverts the normal thought. Perhaps the guy is a typical surfer dude but has a rare skin disease that causes him issues in ocean water. And perhaps he is self-conscious about it.

As an example, the goddess Hera appears in *Curator of the Gods*. She appears as an attractive redhead in her late 30s-early 40s. Hera's physical inspiration came from an internet photo used by the author. Marcia Cross was the author's initial choice for the actress.

After forming a mental image, add character-defining details to their voice. What they sound like, where they have lived, how they were educated, what type of jobs they held, who are their peers. These components fill out the depiction of their voice. These elements shape the way the character thinks, the thoughts they have, and how they speak. This will inform us of any possible accent, their diction, and possible slang they use.

If they are from Boston, perhaps they have a hint of the stereotypical accent, but they use wicked too often for your liking. Perhaps they are a botanist, and their thoughts have a plant-based lean in description and word choice. Perhaps they are a teenager with a classical liberal private-school education, but their friends in the neighborhood go to an inner-city school and that influences them more than the 8 to 5 gig. Know your character's voice will be influential in how you present that character to your reader.

These choices of looks, address, and educational background play a part in the character's development. Only focus on the external character elements crucial to plot and theme. The key is inside the character.

INTERNAL QUALITIES

Now we get to the stuff that makes your character tick, their psyche. The first aspect of this is developing their personality. Perhaps you know what you want their dominant personality type to be, let's say sarcastic.

Personality profile tests provide amazing inspiration and material. Meyers-Briggs is a popular version of these tests and classifies personalities into sixteen distinct categories. Use these distinct types to build your various characters. Each of these core personalities have strengths and weaknesses. This technique is heralded by Jeff Gerke in his book *Plot vs. Character*. Explore personality types to find a match for your story's character. Use these details to spark conflict in your story. Going beyond identifying the personality, Linda Edelstein goes into more detail in her *Writer's Guide to Character Traits*.

Psychological details established, now we detail the things that inform the story and plot, the deep stuff. Wounds, lies, secrets, and foibles are the things that make the character interesting. The words imply a negative connotation, but that may not be the case. Some may not be recognized by the character. David Copperfield has a mental block, perhaps dyslexia, which prevents him from reading to the level expected by Mr. Murdstone in his eponymous story.

The wound, often called the shard of glass, is a defining event that has shaped the character's present identity. This wound could have been physical, but it must affect their mindset. And it should impact the plot. For instance, suppose the character had an abusive father and now they vow to never repeat that behavior with their own children. But one day, they react and hit their child. What do they do next?

Secrets are juicy fruit ready for the harvest of plotlines. There are two types: the innocent and the not-so-innocent. The innocent are things like a person secretly watches *My Little Pony*. The not-so-innocent, a struggling father watches teen pornography. We can't use the former except for a quick laugh. The second option could be used as a significant plot point.

Flaws are the key factors you will leverage throughout your story. The character flaw ties to the character's false belief and faulty worldview. The story's end sees the main character's arc shift from lie to truth. Perhaps your character believes he can work through difficulties in life by himself, but he needs help from others.

Fears drive your character to act. What is your character's greatest fear? How does it interact with their fatal flaw and motivations? In your story, you should have your character face their fear. Reactions vary with the story and desired outcome, but confronting fear drives conflict.

Virtues are also important. What redeeming qualities does your character have? Perhaps they are hardworking, loyal, or compassionate. We want to see these qualities. Building connections with readers is crucial for long-term success. Visualizing the positive attributes of your protagonist will help keep them in the story. Demonstrating these qualities early and often will build that bridge to your audience. At its heart, these redeeming virtues are the chief inspiration for the phrase "save the cat" and its association with character development. Jo Boone does this early in her story, *The Magnetar*, about a young girl named Charlie who has the virtue of bravery. She shows this virtue repeatedly through the story and it grows until she performs a heroic feat at the end of the book.

The desires of your character are also key. All character arcs involve getting your character from where they start the story to where they desire to be. Some writers believe the entire idea of fiction is having characters pursue something they don't have or attempting to regain something they lost, including relationships. These desires may involve entering a magical world, pursuing a specific job, or leaving a job. The character's desire motivates them and sets the stage for conflict in the story.

Having the goal is not enough. We need to understand the reason behind it. Maybe it relates to their childhood wound. Perhaps it involves eliminating their source of fear. Knowing the goal and the motivation behind it is critical to your story. This is why David Copperfield's desire for a new life seems so genuine. He comes from simple means but wishes to provide a good life for Dora Spenlow.

To what extent will the character go to achieve this desire? Are there boundaries your character believes they won't cross? What would it take to cross those lines? Batman refuses to use guns because that was the weapon used to kill his parents, but how often has he been tempted? Creating moral dilemmas and having the character face those imaginary lines is a central tenet to developing internal conflict.

These internal qualities and conflicts are also the key to the character arc of the story, the internal struggle. The plot shifts as the character turns. We desire a character evolution from page 1 to the final page. Readers expect your characters to grow and learn. This transformation is important. A later chapter dedicated to plot will cover the details of the character arc.

Once you flesh out characters, where do you track this information? A character bible is useful if you have a larger cast. This file contains references to various aspects of the characters for consistency throughout the story. This includes character voice, motivations, or any other facet of the character.

RELATIONSHIPS

After you determine the details of your character, there are two major categories of information you still need to determine: the relationships and backstory of your character. The relationships of the character involve status and hierarchy. The character's status varies depending on the relationship's location. Let's say a character is equals with his friend on the basketball court, but they work together, and their friend is in a higher position in the company. Putting your character into the correct status and defining these relationships and their accompanying roles is critical to their world. Those relationships influence the decisions the characters make and the way they act.

The character's sexual orientation and gender identity have become pivotal in many stories. How your character identifies might be important, but this cannot be their defining attribute. Their sexual orientation is a fundamental part of who they are, not just a plot device. The central aspect of the story revolves around their struggle to fit into society, specifically regarding their sexual orientation or gender identity. Not the identity itself.

Many stories feature characters breaking away from existing relationships and forming new ones to illustrate life transformations. This often ties to the character and thematic arc of the story. We need to demonstrate the impact of past and future relationships on the main character's life and story. Is it through conflict or tension? Or is it in another manner that impacts the story?

You could use a character map to document the connections between your main character and others in the story. It encompasses the physical, emotional, social, and mental impact on the lead. It involves their family, co-workers, friends, and enemies. And if the secondary character isn't connected to either the main character, or the chief antagonist, then you should reconsider why they are in your story. You must establish how characters connect to the story and the main character. Perhaps your story centers around two strangers. Either way, a map will help you establish these connections in your mind. It will then be easier for you to show them in the story. These relationships may also drive the backstory of the character.

BACKSTORY

The backstory details the character's life before the story begins. The reader only focuses on story-related information. If you develop a series, you can dive back into the character's history to pull out fresh stories. The comic book industry has depended on this approach for years, as original ideas seem to have vanished. By reseeding the backstory of these characters with nuggets of information we didn't know existed, they create new stories.

Relating backstory is an essential technique for any writer. Backstory is essential to develop any character unless you begin the story at the time of the main character's birth. Still, an incredible backstory may precede their birth. Using backstory helps identify such things as the motivations for the character and the character's fears and other obstacles standing in the way of achieving their objective. The backstory must show how it informs the story of that character.

Your character may have had an incident that formed their beliefs, self-opinion, or other motivations. These events store emotions and fears that, if triggered, could create obstacles for the character or prevent them from achieving an objective later in life. This creates an inherent conflict. When the character can't conquer this obstacle, it heightens stakes and tension and hooks the reader. The backstory influences the character's starting point in the story. How did that event lead to their flaw of greed, or their desire to house abandoned children, or their blind allegiance to the government?

Though each character has their own origin story, often, a backstory element connects to the story's antagonist. Perhaps the event deeply affected both characters' desires. A connection between the two amplifies the backstory's significance, even if discovered later in the main story. This makes their struggle even more compelling. But you need to create that backstory. The challenge lies in sharing this information with the reader.

Conveying this information is just as important as the event itself and the techniques are many. You can do this through exposition, dialogue, or action. But you need to be judicious in your approach. Avoid information dumps as these slow down the momentum of your story. Withholding information for as long as possible heightens the tension. Slowly revealing the emotional impacts will increase the tension as the story unfolds, prolonging the agony for your character and reader as much as possible. Also, use something to trigger an emotional response from the character that provokes the backstory, forcing it to bubble to the surface.

Ellery Adams mastered this approach in *The Secret, Book & Scone Society*. She slowly reveals the backstory of Nora, the main character, through the novel. She uses sensory impressions, often tied to fire and the color red, to expose memories of Nora's past. After resolving the murder mystery, we hear Nora's entire story and fully understand why she hesitated to talk to men and drink alcohol through the main story. Using that as a cue, below is a guide on how to treat backstory.

- Don't front load or infodump the backstory early in the book. Sprinkle it through the story.
- Don't use "As you know" dialogue to relay backstory.
- Don't withhold information that is relevant at a point in the story. At best, it confuses the reader; at worst, it completely removes them from the story.
- Don't let the backstory stall the main story
- Backstory must be concrete and clear and illuminate something important about the story.
- Tie the backstory to the plot and trigger the use through the story.
- Only use flashbacks when an in-depth look at the moment is required.

Here's an example from *Ember in the Ashes* by Sabaa Tahir, illustrating backstory integration in the main text. The backstory elements are in italics.

"My big brother reaches home in the dark hours before dawn, when even ghosts take their rest. He smells of steel and coal and forge. *He smells of the enemy.*

He folds his scarecrow body through the window, bare feet silent on the rushes. *A hot desert wind blows in after him,* rustling the limp curtains. His sketchbook falls to the floor, and he nudges it under his bunk with a quick foot, *as if it's a snake.*

Where have you been, Darin? In my head, I have the courage to ask the question, and Darin trusts me enough to answer. Why do you keep disappearing? Why, when Pop and Nan need you? When I need you?

Every night for almost two years, I've wanted to ask. Every night, I've lacked the courage. I have one sibling left. I don't want him to shut me out like he has everyone else.

But tonight's different. I know what's in his sketchbook. I know what it means.

"You shouldn't be awake." Darin's whisper jolts me from my thoughts. He has a cat's sense for traps – he got it from our mother. I sit up on the bunk as he lights the lamp. No use pretending to be asleep.

"It's past curfew, and three patrols have gone by. I was worried."

"I can avoid the soldiers, Laia. Lots of practice." He rests his chin on my bunk and *smiles Mother's sweet, crooked smile. A familiar look – the one he gives me if I wake from a nightmare or we run out of grain.* Everything will be fine the look says."

EMPATHETIC CHARACTERS

The question then becomes how you know if your character bonds with your readers. Throughout literary history, famous characters, especially protagonists, have consistently exhibited certain attributes. The following paragraphs dive into how to write these attributes for your characters and build your story.

Let's discuss relatability first. If you have built your character, you have a promising idea of their desires, fears, and flaws. You need to show those to the reader early in the story. The character's introduction could mimic a James Bond movie, showcasing their impressive abilities. However, it is crucial to portray their humanity. Readers want to attach themselves to your characters, bring them in by showing how much like them the lead is.

Also, show that your protagonist is more than just an average person. It helps if they are likable. Initially, they portray a jerk, but the character should evolve and become less crusty. This is where the phrase "Save the Cat" arises. You require a moment to showcase the character's inner goodness. Conversely, you need to do the opposite for your antagonist. Yes, they may "Save the Cat" early in the story, but down the line, you need to show their true intentions and their moral failings and victories, depending on which side of the coin they fall.

This reader attachment comes through recognizing a shared trait with the character. Perhaps they share life experiences, perhaps a disease, perhaps a family circumstance. The character requires an enticing element for the reader. Earlier, the text mentioned providing your character with a unique trait. This is its place in the story.

Next, give the character an area of competence. It's hard for readers to cheer for a foolish character who bounces around and accidentally saves the day. Yes, Mr. Bean works as a comedic sketch character, but for a novel it doesn't have a lot of legs. The lead could be an auto mechanic, plumber, or have an affinity for birdhouses. Include it in the story. However, avoid making the character excel in all areas. This leads to them becoming a "Mary Sue" type of character. We want to avoid those types of characters in your story.

The lead mustn't be an idle bum. Your lead cannot be lazy. Proactivity defines protagonists. Show the lead being active and persevering against minor obstacles early in your story. The character needs to exhibit agency over their lives through their choices and actions. There may be reluctance early in the story, like Luke in *Star Wars*, but once they commit, they must sacrifice to achieve their goals.

Displaying these traits in the story enhances character relatability and engages the reader. Showcase these attributes early for later story utilization. Character establishment is crucial prior to introducing significant plot elements. This leads to creating a sympathetic character for the reader. If the reader becomes invested, then when you turn the lead's life upside down, they will feel compelled to read to the end of the story.

To prevent a flat character, consider all these elements. Characters should not be completely aligned in every aspect. That just isn't human. Humans have complexity. There are elements of our being in constant conflict with other aspects of ourselves. This helps to create what many people term gray characters. We want those desires within the character to be at war; their wants and their needs cannot align. Having these differences within the character provides the kindling to start the fire of conflict, at least internally, in every story.

We also want our characters to be credible. The character's presentation is crucial for credibility. If our lead is from New York City, they will behave much differently than someone from the Midwest in various situations. They also need to be bound to the core beliefs that create the complexity within them. When we see characters betray these parts of themselves, it breaks the story and creates a problem for the reader.

There's always one family member perfect for a story. The key is not using the whole character, just a part. Use one aspect of that person and meld it with another character. Hide who the character is. While your inspiring person depicts the character's struggle, be mindful of lawsuits. If a person fears you have defamed them or you have portrayed them in a negative light, they could sue you. They would have to prove the damage, but who has the time or the money to deal with something like that?

After working through these various methods, hopefully you create a roster of characters ready for use in your story. Will you add characters or change things about your characters? Possibly. Will these characters change something in your story? Almost definitely. The key outcome is that you, as a writer, understand your characters. What are their motivations? How do those create conflicts? How will they react to obstacles and other pressures? Familiarity with your characters enhances writing and transforms them into dynamic actors in a well-crafted story.

DEVELOPMENT METHODS

When we develop characters, we need to understand our character from the core to the outside. Attribute assignment for character appearance is the least important. You must assign numerous items that address their reactions to any circumstance. These attributes reveal a character's essence and guide their transformation.

Writers engage readers by avoiding three dismissive statements: "I don't care", "No one would do that", and "That makes no sense." Building characters effectively prevents reader distractions. The following methodologies present numerous ways to dive into your characters and build them to prevent this from happening.

PROMS

Fantasy writer Brandon Sanderson uses a technique that he refers to as PROMS. The acronym is catchy, and the keywords align with his goals. Each aspect reveals character details and uncovers motivations and conflicts. Stick to pertinent information when compiling this data. Minutiae like whether the character likes condiments on their sandwich should be excluded unless necessary.

- Past – Every character has a backstory. This drives the foundations that shape the character. These memories evoke emotions.
- Relationships – How does your character interact with others? Do they require the last word in every argument? Use concrete details on how the character relates to others within the story. These relationships should vary depending on the characters and their status.
- Obligations – How does your character relate to their social constructs? Do they have a job or belong to a certain group? Do they have responsibilities to anyone other than themselves or their loved ones?
- Motivations – Every character has motivations. Present those to the reader without disrupting the story's flow. Show the foundations or those desires early in the work so the emotions displayed later feel genuine. Three things we must know: their greatest desire, their greatest fear, and their greatest flaw.
- Sensibilities – This is more in line with how your character is wired. How do they view the world around them? What are their beliefs? What is their POV on issues in their world? Everything else falls into this category.

CORE

Mary Kole uses a technique referred to as the core technique. Its focus is driving to the core identity of your character to understand how they will respond to conflict in the story. This technique focuses on the central aspects of the character and what will drive their emotions in either direction. This may be the right technique if your story hinges upon emotional factors as it will expose the raw center of the actors in your story.

- Strength – What within your character will give them the strength to keep going?
- Virtue – What emotion resonates with your character? Loyalty, love, or fear?
- Flaw – Flip virtue on its ear and what is the character's greatest flaw. What is it they cannot see or value in themselves?
- Emotions – What evokes the characters' emotions?
- Role – What role does your character desire? Are they forced to take on something greater than they desire? Or less?
- Boundaries – What is the line your character will not cross? What will it take for them to cross it?
- Outlook – How does your character feel about their future? How will that cloud their conflicts in the story?
- Beliefs – What is the foundational belief system of your character? Why do they have those beliefs? How quickly could those beliefs fall apart?

A popular technique to gather information on your characters is the interview, or Dossier Method. You create a series of revealing questions to provide information about your character. The character then becomes more three dimensional as you see their qualities develop through the questioning process. Some individuals go through the process and use separate sheets for character responses.

The Dossier Method could also be useful in providing that information to the reader within your story. An example exists in several films, as they use this method to provide a subtle approach to information dumping. This method was used to develop the character models in *The Forsaken Protector*. It was effective due to the considerable number of characters in that tome and allowed each character space to be expanded on by the author. Various versions of character interview forms are found online. The Vibrant Prose Toolbox contains one of these forms.

The Monologue Method is popular with discovery writers. The writer reveals character information through monologues. This allows the writer to develop the character voice for various players within their mind. Dan Wells is a writer that uses this methodology to develop his characters.

Regardless of how you pull this information together, or if you do it as you write. You need to ensure you are consistent in displaying your characters to the reader. Inconsistency will push the reader out of the story.

EXERCISES

1. Identify a Meyers-Briggs personality profile and build a character from it.
2. Look at a character from your favorite story and document how their attributes were shown by the author in their story.
3. Create a character map to identify the relationships in your favorite book.
4. Use the character interview form to develop your character.
5. Writing a monologue with the main character of your story.

REFERENCE MATERIALS

Dynamic Characters: How to Create Personalities That Keep Readers Captivated by Nancy Kress
Characters & Viewpoint by Orson Scott Card
Plot Versus Character: A Balanced Approach to Writing Great Fiction by Jeff Gerke
Writer's Guide to Character Traits by Linda Edelstein

These works were mentioned in the chapter, and each presents valuable information in this area of character development. *Dynamic Characters* is a perhaps the strongest book on creating the character from scratch and building them in your story. Kress has ample accolades to support her sound advice. Card's book is more comprehensive in addressing viewpoint and is an instrumental tome on the topic. Gerke and Edelstein each authored a book to help you identify specific elements you may wish to focus on in the development of your characters, especially if you have a certain personality type you wish to include in your story.

6 – CHARACTER ROLES

Because few stories lack characters within them, we must define the character types needed for our story. We need to create a cast. In old Shakespearian plays, the playbill identified the characters. Agatha Christie employed this technique in the opening of her books. We will work our way from the main characters down to the bit players.

While reviewing the list, consider the requirements for each role. The protagonist and antagonist have different objectives and, therefore, distinctive characteristics that feed into filling their role. Also, filling other roles depends on how they play off the protagonist or antagonist. It is important that you determine who your protagonist is at their core. If you are still unsure, review chapter 5 once more. Here's a description of the major roles in most stories.

- Protagonist – The character that drives the action of the story. The story's protagonist is frequently seen as the hero. The hero often upholds the morals and upright qualities that we find admirable in the story. Often, we experience the story through the main character's viewpoint. Their story is the focal point of the overarching story.
- Antagonist – The star of their own story and the character providing the major obstacles that block your protagonist and prevents them from achieving their objective. In the current vein of writing, the antagonist often carries as much weight as their opposite number.
- Supporting Characters – These are characters that have the spotlight on them at times within the story, but always fall in line behind the main character. They may have character arcs that are essential to the story. Supporting characters may support the antagonist as well.
- Secondary Characters – These characters are necessary to achieve character arcs of those listed above and could have their own character development. Without them, the story doesn't work.

- Tertiary Characters – This group of characters is essential for prescribed aspects of the story but has no character growth through the story.
- Extras – These are other characters that exist in the story but only serve a function, such as the waitress at a restaurant or the nurses in a hospital. Omitting these roles would hinder reader immersion in the story.
- Point of View (POV) Character – This is the character that tells the story to the reader. The viewpoint may shift between characters throughout the story. More information will be given in the subsequent viewpoint chapter.
- Plot B Character – This character serves a specific purpose in the story and will be one of the above characters. They are pivotal to the protagonist's character arc and often appear at the beginning of the second act of the story.

THE PROTAGONIST

DING! DING! DING! In this corner, hailing from the recesses of your imagination and weighing in with the burden of the plot on his shoulders, is the protagonist. In the opposite corner from parts unknown is the antagonist that will destroy his hopes and dreams. That's the battle royale we pay to see, right?

When thinking of great protagonist/antagonist relationships, many minds jump to the comic books of our youth: Superman vs. Lex Luthor, Batman vs. The Joker, Spider-Man vs. Doctor Octopus. Many of our favorite movies, books, and television shows feature a similar recurring motif. The hero versus the villain, good versus evil. Is there a more compelling conflict in writing? Perhaps, but the best of these are the ones that keep us coming back. All of them, and your novel, hinge on one key component; you must write a compelling protagonist.

The protagonist, hero, and main character are synonymous in certain books. In many, these three roles are split among several characters. In the event where that occurs, you will need to determine where the hero and main character lie in the character hierarchy and build their character along those lines.

Perhaps it is unfair to put the entire weight of the story on the shoulders of one character. It's a burden that comes with the job, but you can alleviate that to some degree if your antagonist, the story, and the other characters carry their own water. Otherwise, your hopes and dreams rest with one character.

The protagonist's role changes throughout the narrative, transitioning from an average individual to a superior being or even an artificial entity. The main character's appearance has no set description, but certain traits are necessary to engage readers. You need to turn this character into your story's superhero. Perhaps we should define what a protagonist should be in more detail.

- **They must become proactive.** Even a couch-dwelling bum can find something that ignites their passion and drives them to take action. The reader hates a lazy protagonist.
- **They must be identifiable.** The plot is seen through the lead. When the lead is compelling and relatable, it impacts the reader. Superman struggles to reach readers while Batman remains popular. One is an alien with extraordinary powers. Who can relate to that? The writer's job becomes harder in conveying the story if the protagonist is unrelatable.
- **They must be empathetic.** This character will face punishment and endure immense physical and/or emotional suffering. Your hero can't just swat everything away and not feel anything. The reader needs to see them as vulnerable and worthy of their empathy and emotional investment.
- **It helps to be likable.** Though it isn't a requirement to start with a likable character, it helps. Your character might be a jerk, but they must undergo a change to gain reader support.
- **They must be competent.** To save the day, your character needs skill in a discipline. Your hero can't save the day unless they have expertise in a field, even if it's just oil changes. You can turn that into something for your story.
- **You must upset the lead character's world and make it worth it.** The reader must perceive the conflict and the protagonist's pursuit as worthy of their time. You need to attract the reader with tension and stakes that compel them to keep reading.
- **Show the character's greatest desire, fear, and flaw.** This shows the reader what the hero desires and paves the way for obstacles.

Once the lead has established these qualities, introduce and *show* them to the reader. Doing this early with a simple demonstration of "show don't tell" is essential.

Since the protagonist drives the story, you need to make them proactive as early as possible. How do we do that? This depends on the style and type of story you are writing. Action-oriented scenes lend themselves to jumping in with both feet with a technique many writers call "late in." The reader is placed in the scene by the author, following the commencement of the build-up and action. You can layer in the background as you communicate what happens. Upon opening the scene, convey three essential points.

- **What is the objective of the lead?** What question is being asked of them? In mysteries, the dead body introduces the riddle for the sleuth to solve. Each scene and the overall story need an objective. Make it known early.
- **What is the motivation of the lead?** The reader must understand the importance to the lead. Why does it matter to the character? Are their personal stakes met if the objective is not met? Does it impact them? Do they have a higher calling or a level of righteousness that makes the resolution a dilemma upon their personal code? As the writer, your response must resonate with the reader and make them feel this cause is worthy of their attention.
- **Does the question prompt action from the lead?** If not, the story falls apart and goes nowhere. What will it take to get your lazy character off their ass? Therefore, jumping into an action scene is a great idea. Immediately, your character's "man of action" trait is apparent and will address the issue.

Once the story starts, the possibilities are endless. Will your lead uplift and transform the world from its lowest point to be a rising paragon by the story's end? This is an option, but remember to keep this protagonist worthy of your reader's support.

- **Instill in your protagonist a personal code.** It is hard to root for a guy that keeps making poor decisions. If they are married, avoid adultery. Readers don't like people that cheat on their spouse. Try to not have them kill indiscriminately. We believe our leads should value life. A code of honor, or a line they won't cross, is admirable. Don't fall into lazy writer syndrome and allow your

character to cross their personal line without sufficient reason. Otherwise, they are no better than the bad guy.
- **Keep their status.** Great characters defer to those they respect but refuse to play second fiddle when confronting obstacles. The writer needs to depict the protagonist as honorable in the face of evil. They can be clever, but they must keep their status as the main man. Avoid the temptation to turn them into an Anti-hero.
- **They must persist and be heroic.** If the lead stops being the lead, the story stops unless you do something drastic. If that happens, you will have a tough time keeping the reader invested. The lead might fail, but they must attempt to face the impossible. Sometimes, it's the bravest act available to them.

In some cases, multiple protagonists exist within a story. The main goal is to ensure the characters remain in their correct position behind the lead. Their stories play second, or third, fiddle and they are below the level of your protagonist. A deuteragonist shares characteristics with the lead but is secondary. A fitting example is a sidekick. Robin, the Boy Wonder, is the secondary protagonist. A tritagonist is a character with a lower status than two others. In the Batman comics, this would be Alfred Pennyworth. Character arcs and subplots center around them, but they must always fall in line behind the lead character.

Another likely scenario is a heroic couple where the protagonist and their love interest are equal. Or perhaps they are siblings. These situations arise in several stories (i.e., Romance), and you need to make clear the motivations and objectives of the characters and prioritize the plot lines and character arcs based on that primary objective. Michael Scott's series, *The Secrets of the Immortal Nicholas Flamel*, featured twin brothers Sophie and Josh Newman and represented them as equal characters.

THE ANTAGONIST

What attracts people to the bad guy? Some believe the hero's worth is tied to the villain's quality. If so, the hero's value would fluctuate depending on the opponent. A little-known character in Batman lore is the Condiment King. Can a character like that define a preeminent fiction character from the 20th century? Whatever the reason, many writers believe the villain is the most attractive character in most stories they read.

Sacha Black devoted a wonderful series to character development. She loves to shine the light on the bad guys. Here is a quote from her book *13 Steps to Evil: How to Craft Superbad Villains*.

"Heroes are interesting. But mostly they're predictable. They save the world and win. Again, and again, and again. If the constant monotony of halo-polishing heroism has worn you as thin as it has me, then you're in the right place...
...Heroes aren't the fun ones to write. It's much more satisfying to craft a character with an evil glint in their eye. Someone who's so unpredictable even you don't know what they'll do next. That's why a villain will always be the most delicious character to write."

Because that belief is held by so many writers, it is equally important to define the antagonist as it is our hero. The following are strategies for achieving that.

- **Develop the origin of the villain.** Show their backstory has a form of trauma. For additional points, reveal a connection with the protagonist. The closer that connection, the more animosity between the two characters will be present.
- **Use backstory to elicit sympathy.** The trauma they faced may have set the character down a terrible road. Convince the reader they are not lost. Show them doing something that appears to be kind to create additional sympathy.
- **Give the villain a sense of right.** The villain believes they are doing the best thing for themselves or society. They think their actions will be beneficial, regardless of the lines they cross. The modern take on Lex Luthor falls into this category. He feels he is doing what is right for humans when he tries to kill Superman.
- **Make the villain attractive to the reader.** They possess a side similar to the reader. The completely evil antagonist only works in certain situations. Make it seem like the antagonist might choose the right path but deliberately selects the worse option, implying no conscience. Hannibal Lecter seems like a charming fellow... when he isn't trying to eat your liver with a nice chianti.
- **Ensure the antagonist is equal or superior to the protagonist.** The antagonist should have favorable odds, but not without hope for the protagonist. Try to avoid antagonists that are too powerful.
- **The antagonist believes this is their story.** Give the antagonist their own sense of objective and motivation. Have the tables

flipped and make it appear to them the protagonist is their obstacle. But always remember, this character arc plays a secondary role in the larger story. Keep the status in check.
- **Always remember the antagonist is not a slave to their history.** Show them deciding to do terrible things and their thought process behind the decisions. Just because they have faced trauma doesn't mean their backstory controls their destiny. Conscious decisions to do evil creates conflict with the protagonist.

THE ROLE REVERSAL

One of the most daring approaches within a story is to flip the antagonist and protagonist. You must make your antagonist a character with which the reader empathizes early in the story. It allows you the opportunity to flip the script and complete a role reversal between the two characters.

Not every story requires this, but if the main characters' motivations shift or if decisions alter their character arc, a dramatic change is possible. In the following paragraphs, three variations on this technique are presented. The crucial contrast between these options is the timing of the switch in the story. The later it happens, the more intense the reversal.

The usual scenario occurs when the expected opponent becomes the main character. In *The Dark Lord: The Rise of Darth Vader* by James Luceno, the book takes place after the movie *The Revenge of the Sith*. Vader's transition to the dark side leads to emotional struggles. He is becoming acquainted with his armor and is recovering from the life-threatening injuries. Luceno begins the story by sowing the seeds of empathy for Vader by showing how he was manipulated, how agonizing his new armor is, and how much emotional turmoil he suffers. The writer does not portray Vader as the hero, but he is the protagonist. Even though everyone anticipates him being the antagonist.

In the second type, a story takes a turn when a significant event occurs, changing the characters' motivations and causing them to switch roles. A splendid example of this occurs in V. E. Schwab's title *Vicious*. Early in the novel, Eli is the primary driver of the story with Victor playing along as his pseudo-sidekick. Eli is the All-American guy, but Schwab puts a flaw into his character that stays dormant early in the story. Through a scientific experiment, Victor and

Eli both gain superpowers. Eli's flaw overcomes him, and he revels in his newfound power. Victor becomes the protagonist of the second half of the novel and acts to destroy Eli. Schwab's early introduction of character details makes this switch feasible.

The third type is where we believe for the entire story one character is the protagonist and, as a plot twist, we learn the other character has been driving the action. In *Thrawn: Alliances* by Timothy Zahn, Grand Admiral Thrawn and Darth Vader are ordered to deal with a deep space disturbance. Zahn portrays Vader as the protector of the Empire, while depicting Thrawn as manipulative with conflicting motivations. At the end of the book, it is revealed Thrawn has manipulated Vader to determine the root of the disturbance and helped protect Thrawn's people and protect the Empire from a threat. As a result, it becomes apparent that Vader was the primary obstacle to Thrawn executing his plan and thus became the antagonist. The technical term for Vader is a false protagonist. As Thrawn's story develops throughout the book, the author reinforces his motivations and objectives.

Character development in the beginning of the story sets the groundwork for these approaches. The writer uses that work to alter the motivations and compel characters to make decisions that shift their character arc. When done well, this is one of the higher-level techniques that writers use to keep the reader engrossed in the story and provide the gripping unforeseen, but inevitable plot twist. All of this comes back to building characters with fleshed out motivations that create obstacles, conflict, and a fitting resolution. The depth of the story lies in its characters, particularly the protagonist and antagonist.

SUPPORTING CHARACTERS

Supporting Characters in fiction serve specific roles and have distinct levels of status. *Castaway* had a group of supporting characters. These other characters can be an ensemble with a core group, an epic fantasy where there are over one hundred characters, or a simple love story of Billy Joe and Bobbie Sue. Almost every story will include other characters.

Supporting characters must go through the same treatment as your main characters. But these characters add facets to your story that the main character lacks. The following are characteristics it would be wise to keep in mind as you fill out your supporting cast.

- Your secondary characters have their own life. That includes a backstory and how they are involved in this story. A connection to the story and one of the two lead characters is necessary.
- Supporting and secondary characters must be three dimensional and add something to the story. They shouldn't be boring characters that only exist to advance the plot. They can contrast with the lead characters for additional tension.
- When they appear, make sure they serve a purpose. When they talk, make sure they add something to the dialogue. Don't use them as filler.
- Name them in a way that makes them memorable.
- Develop something about your character that creates an inherent conflict with the main character. Perhaps their personality stands in contrast. Perhaps they have a job that impedes with being part of the protagonist's story. Perhaps they have their own personal baggage that triggers part of the conflict.
- Introduce them with flair. This will pull the reader further in and add a spark to the story. Use them to provide texture and realism, but don't dwell on them too long.
- Supporting characters might reinforce theme, create additional conflict, or resolve plot lines.
- Keep in mind that supporting characters play a subordinate role to the main character in a story.

Often, it's important to give attention to supporting characters and develop them similarly to the main characters. One of the key things to establish in your character relationships and roles is the hierarchy, or status. It determines the time needed for character development and story involvement. Obviously, your leads are going to be the primary drivers, but your other major characters could be involved in subplots, have character development, and present potential conflicts within the story and have a resonating impact on the major characters.

ENSEMBLES

Story size influences character quantity and development needs. If you are talking about a simple romance novel that is much smaller than *The Lord of the Rings* and requires fewer tiers in the hierarchy of character development.

Ensembles present a trouble spot for the writer. In the popular television show *Friends*, the six main characters appear for intents and purposes to be equal. They each have plot lines and character development and they share in the airtime in each episode. But all the major stories run through the characters of Monica and Ross Geller. Every story creates a situation that puts an obstacle in their life that they must overcome. The plotline of Joey falling for Rachel is a hurdle in Ross' pursuit of her. Rachel, Chandler, Joey, and Phoebe are secondary to the Gellers. They are the glue that binds the group together. Find the main storyline at the center of your story and remember that takes precedence throughout your novel.

ARCHETYPES

As you go through the process of character development, you will run across archetypes. These are standard characters which occur in stories in some form through hundreds of books and movies since the earliest tales dating back to Homer and Hesiod. These archetypes are based on a standard pattern of behavior used in stories. Many of these are recurring symbols of traits seen in characters in classic storytelling or in mythic tales. The number of these archetypal roles varies depending on whom you talk with. Some claim only eight character types exist, others argue for over two hundred.

One of the most prominent sets of archetypes rose from the psychological studies of Carl Jung, a Swiss psychiatrist and psychoanalyst. Jung aligned these archetypes with psychological profiles. Jung identified twelve archetypes that are often pigeon-holed into characters. Often, the best characters span multiple of these archetypes as they grow within their own arcs. These twelve archetypes, even with loose qualifications, somewhat limit the number of character types we see on a regular basis in fiction today.

Over time, more ideas and genres lead to additional proposed archetypes. Many audiences believe that a certain type of novel should have certain characters and plot points to qualify as that type of story. Over time, those character tropes have become expected and carry the same categorization as Jung's archetypes.

Fantasy stories, along with many science-fiction stories, have standard tropes in the form of specific characters. Tolkien's use of character types in *The Lord of the Rings* contributes to this trend. Authors developed the genre and mimicked characters from that influential work. Tolkien used many of the archetypes espoused by

Jung in his story with two chief heroes, one reluctant and one predestined in Frodo and Aragorn, a mentor/magician with Gandalf, and many others. His use of other characters created and popularized new archetypes.

Archetypes are not a new concept. They have existed since the Ancient Greeks and the plays by Aeschylus, Aristophanes, Euripides, and Sophocles. In mythic settings, these characters carried attributes tied to specific deities in their pantheologic society. These writers built their characters to carry attributes tied to Ares, Athena, or Aphrodite. Their actions are driven by audience recognition of these attributes and corresponding expectations which these writers used to develop expectations for the story. A dedicated reference to these archetypes is *45 Master Characters* by Victoria Lynn Schmidt.

Characters were not always associated with gods. They also drew upon heroes like Achilles or other well-known mythical characters to drive a certain attribute they desired for their dramas. Given that all stories were shared orally, it was essential to establish these characters to ensure a shared understanding among all audience members during the presentation.

Out of this mythic tradition, twentieth-century writer Joseph Campbell developed his own archetypal methodology. His seminal work, *The Hero with a Thousand Faces,* applied the ideas of thinkers like Carl Jung to create eight character archetypes found throughout the hero's journey, also known as the Monomyth story structure.

Along with the hero and mentor, Campbell included the herald, trickster, shapeshifter, guardian, and the shadow. The newest concept introduced the shadow, a character standing against the protagonist.

Campbell popularized the idea of character archetypes in modern literature and film. His ideas resonated with George Lucas, who used them to craft the arc of *Star Wars'* protagonist Luke Skywalker. Luke became a more "classical" character. The undeniable success of the *Star Wars* franchise then opened the movie industry and genre fiction to the ideas of Joseph Campbell.

Today, archetypes populate much of our fiction. As a writer, your job is to utilize them as tools and create something beyond the traditional roles mentioned. Many more options are available for selection. Need character ideas? Google character archetypes for instant inspiration.

STEREOTYPES AND CLICHÉS

Don't let your characters become stereotypes or clichés. What does that mean? And how do you stop it from happening? There is an overlap between archetypes and the categories of stereotypes, stock characters, and clichés. As a rule, archetypes provide the base guidelines for characterization. You then expand on those base characteristics to build characters. Stereotypes and clichés are negative labels used to describe characters that either stay at those base levels or become melodramatic tropes that occur all too often. They have nothing that distinguishes them from the crowd.

- An archetype does not imply predictability or intellectual laziness. It suggests a character will speak to a universal truth. Familiar archetypes can still be unpredictable.
- A stock character is between an archetype and a stereotype. These characters fit a narrow description. Well-selected stock characters serve as foils for a main character, particularly in comedy. Stock characters originated in classical European dramas wearing masks and performing exaggerated versions of themselves.
- Stereotypes are simplified characterizations, such as the dumb jock, the dizzy blonde, or the innocent child, but all are considered simplistic and undesirable in literature.
- A cliché is an idea that's used so often that it becomes predictable and boring.

A surplus of goodness can be detrimental. Various types of cliché antagonists have appeared throughout history. Unless you put a fresh twist on these, avoid them.

- The evil twin – A character just like the protagonist, but with an evil bent has become cliche. The Superman revival by Zac Snyder, titled *Man of Steel,* had many flaws. One of the greatest was the villain, General Zod. Zod, as is his tendency, mirrored Superman, but wanted to subjugate humanity. We have seen that story.
- The opposite number, or the foil – We have seen it with brains vs. brawn, alien vs. human, evil vs. good. How often have we seen Superman outsmarted by Lex Luthor to only use his amazing abilities to overcome the odds? We should bring a fresh element to the audience.

- The mad scientist – Try to avoid the mad scientist who only wishes to rule the world or watch it burn. Create a character with greater complexity beyond seeking revenge on the world.
- The gritty anti-hero — Distinct from the protagonist and characterized by their willingness to make tough choices and cross moral boundaries. It's a writer's attempt to be gritty and seem connected to the real world. These are characters that lack true moral dilemmas, as there are no real consequences for them. They enjoy the freedom of villains without the morality of the hero.
- The Mary Sue (Gary Stu if a male) — A character who is flawless in every aspect. Building in a character flaw is necessary for every character. An overpowered version of the Mary Sue character grew into the Girl Boss persona and has been used in many Disney and female centric stories in the last decade. Female versions of outdated overpowered male characters are no longer in style.

To avoid clichés and stereotypes, try taking the character in an unexpected direction. A modern example of this is the popular DC Comics villain, The Joker. Though he has the typical garish appearance of a jester type character, he is anything but comical. The Joker is one of the greatest homicidal serial killers in American literature. He also stands as a symbol of the opposite traits of his nemesis, The Batman, who stands for order and justice.

Another tactic is to ensure your character has a sufficient reason to break away from their tendencies. Comprehending their motivations and decision-making criteria is necessary. As a writer, reaching the breaking point is crucial for authenticity and reader engagement.

Considering character roles and hierarchy enhances your storytelling. This order establishes a framework for the reader to follow the story's flow and guides you, the writer, towards a successful outcome.

EXERCISES

1. Write a character sketch of your protagonist. Go into detail about their appearance, their speech patterns, their backstory, and their goals and motivations.
2. Identify the antagonist in your story and make a list of the attributes that appear opposite of the attributes of your protagonist.
3. Expand on the character map from the previous chapter to identify the roles that each character has and their status in the story hierarchy.

REFERENCE MATERIALS

Dynamic Characters: How to Create Personalities That Keep Readers Captivated by Nancy Kress
Characters & Viewpoint by Orson Scott Card
45 Master Characters: Mythic Models for Creating Original Characters by Victoria Lynn Schmidt
The Better Writer Series by Sacha Black

Schmidt's tome on archetypes is the recognized source for using identifying archetypal characters. Sacha Black has an entire series dedicated to writing specific character types, including the protagonist, antagonist, and side characters. Each of those volumes conveys excellent information on how to approach the story through those characters' eyes, including sub-plots and side story development.

7 – PERSPECTIVE & INTERIORITY

When writing, the foremost question for any writer is determining the proper narrative perspective to communicate the story. You may have the greatest characters, a plot that grips the reader, the most immersive setting, tension for days, and a resonant theme. But if you tell the story incorrectly, the rest means nothing. Your narrative perspective, also referred to as point of view, or viewpoint, is the part of the story that opens the lock to finding the full potential of any story. Deciding on the best way to tell your story allows so many other elements to shine their brightest.

This chapter will also dive into the topic of using perspective to characterize the people within your story through interiority. To fully develop a character, it's important to convey their interiority to the reader. This is where the reader connects to characters and story.

To start, we will discuss viewpoint and perspective. Viewpoint comprises two factors: perspective and tense. Each point of view type has strengths and weaknesses. Understanding and working around these weaknesses may determine if your story gets published or stays in the trunk of your car.

VIEWPOINT TYPES

First Person – The story is communicated through one person's eyes, and they refer to themselves as I, me, and myself throughout. First person is primarily reserved for the protagonist's perspective, but it can apply to other characters too.

First person is best at putting the reader at the center of the story. The POV character's mind reveals genuine emotions and reactions to the reader. This viewpoint biases the narration to how the POV character sees events unfold. This color-driven narrative creates a tighter connection between the character and the reader. First person creates a sense of immediacy with the reader. Perhaps the best consequence of first person is "telling" becomes much more difficult to do, compared to "showing."

Cons exist for this viewpoint as well. First person limits the reader to only experience what the viewpoint character witnesses in the story. It is difficult to withhold information from the reader. Also, this type of narration, if in past tense, immediately informs the reader that the POV character survives the story and eliminates one of the potential ways to incite tension.

One workaround, if first person is used, is to shift the viewpoint character. Removing the need for consistent characters in every scene allows readers to experience diverse viewpoints. This also solves the problem of revealing events that occur when the POV character is not present. In *As the City Burns*, Marco Flynn, the main character, watches newscasts or reads news articles to gain information not witnessed in person.

First person creates the potential for an unreliable narrator. Unreliable narrators withhold information to influence the reader with bias. Readers don't like this due to overuse unless you use the viewpoint in a fresh manner. The best-known example is *The Murder of Roger Ackroyd* by Agatha Christie. The viewpoint character (spoiler alert!) withholds key information about the murder. Hercule Poirot, the sleuth, discovers this and solves the mystery.

One other point to consider is first person narration works well in shorter stories. You have fewer characters to introduce and less scope to cover. The longer the story, the more likely you will want to consider another option. Below is an example of first person narrative from *As the City Burns*.

"I expected this day to begin much different. The frigid canal water, cold from the prior night's unseasonably low temperatures, blurred my vision, filled my ears, and froze my arms. The first day of autumn should not be this cold. The chill and remaining darkness were the least of my dilemmas.

A mural of a girl blowing bubbles was my compass in the early morning dawn. The image my lighthouse, a beacon, as I pulled the limp body to the side of the man-made waterway. The slight undercurrent and the inability of my cargo to help made it doubly difficult to get back to the cement border. My mouth kept going under as I paddled to the side and my torso slowly succumbed to the icy temperature. My sock-covered feet slipped on the algae coated slope and I wondered if success was possible. Then I felt the edge and knew safety was within reach.

"Hold on! Don't die!" I yelled over my aching shoulder through the crisp, frosted air as I stretched my arm for the solid masonry, a stark contrast to the liquid muck with which I grappled."

Second Person – This least common style is communicated by a narrator as if the reader embodies the protagonist of the story. The narrator communicates the action in terms of "You walked. You ran. You killed the leader of the Sharks." Second person singular is where the story is told to one person, second person plural is told to a group.

Genre fiction seldom uses second person viewpoint, but when used, second person creates a profound effect. N. K. Jemisin used this viewpoint with her first Hugo winning novel, *The Fifth Season*. She then used second person in the two remaining books within *The Broken Earth* series and won two more Hugo Awards.

Second person is much more popular with literary fiction which tries to push boundaries in technique. Perhaps the best use of second person in our culture is within video games and role-playing games where the story is told through a character that the player controls. Second person draws the reader close to the story.

Second person works well in short bursts to depict certain mystical or out-of-body type of experiences within the story. Because this viewpoint is seldom used in genre fiction, second person seems awkward for the reader. The challenge for the writer is to establish second person viewpoint in a transparent manner to the reader. The difficulty is in developing characters and working around the limitations on story options. There is a reason second person is the least used viewpoint. Experimenting with second person would be advised before committing to a complete story in this point of view.

Third Person Limited – The characters are referred to as he and she. The story is conveyed through a character's mind, as if you're right there. This perspective allows some intimate knowledge of the viewpoint character's thoughts and provides the flexibility to switch viewpoint characters or become further removed from the scene to provide more information to the reader. This is the most popular style in commercial fiction.

Third person limited has similar advantages to first person but allows the reader to experience the thoughts and reactions of various characters as the viewpoint shifts, which provides different perspectives. Another advantage is third limited makes withholding information from the reader easier and increases the mystery within the story. Third person limited is easier to deal with larger casts and stories of greater scope.

The major disadvantage to third person limited is the narration often takes longer and is less succinct than the omniscient point of view or first person. Another disadvantage is that shifting viewpoints breaks the momentum of the story unless you use certain techniques. Too much movement becomes a problem, known as head hopping. For newer writers, another problem with third limited is the increased opportunity to slip into an omniscient narrative voice. Below is the same passage as before from *As the City Burns* rewritten in third person limited. Note the differences in referring to the character.

"Marco Flynn expected this day to begin much different. The frigid canal water, cold from the prior night's unseasonably low temperatures, blurred his vision, filled his ears, and froze his arms. The first day of autumn was generally not this cold in Indianapolis. The chill and remaining darkness were the least of Marco's dilemmas.

A mural of a girl blowing bubbles was his compass in the early morning dawn. The image was his lighthouse, a beacon, as he pulled the limp body to the side of the man-made waterway. The slight undercurrent and the inability of his cargo to help made it doubly difficult for Marco to reach the cement border. HIs mouth went under while he paddled to the side and his torso slowly succumbed to the icy temperature. Sock-covered feet slipped on the algae coated slope and he wondered if success was possible. Then he grasped the edge and knew safety was within reach.

"Hold on! Don't die!" he yelled over his shoulder through the crisp frosted air as he grabbed the solid masonry, a stark contrast to the liquid muck with which he grappled."

Third Person Omniscient – The story is communicated through an all-knowing narrator not involved in the story. This is the old standard of the speculative fiction genre. It allows for consistent storytelling but lacks some of the intimacy of first person and third person limited.

Omniscient reveals information pertaining to all characters, providing more information in less time. It works well for large scope stories containing several characters with the multiple perspectives required for the story to work. In many ways, this allows the omniscient narrator to become a character within the story. When the omniscient voice is objective and formal, the narrator remains unbiased and neutral. A non-biased, informal omniscient voice will enhance the presentation by influencing the story's mood and tension.

Omniscient viewpoint might not create the necessary connection between the characters and the reader. Omniscient is a more distant view of the action and adds difficulty to withholding information. If the objective narrator knows something, they will tell the reader.

One undervalued aspect of Omniscient is the viewpoint allows the writer greater freedom to control the pacing and the tension within the story. Because omniscient is used best in larger stories, the viewpoint provides the reader natural valleys within the story to break from the book. This is not a concern for shorter tension driven fiction like Thrillers. The same passage is shown from an omniscient perspective. Note the perspective change in describing the world around the action.

"Marco Flynn expected this day to begin much different. The frigid canal water froze everything it touched inside and outside his body. The first day of autumn was generally not this cold in Indianapolis. The chill and remaining darkness were the least of Marco's dilemmas. His flailing in the water was oblivious to a passerby as music blared through their headphones.

Below the bridge, a mural of a girl blowing bubbles was his compass as he pulled the limp body to the side of the man-made waterway out of anyone's view. The slight undercurrent and his cargo made it doubly difficult for Marco to reach the cement border. He nearly gagged on water as he paddled to the side and his torso slowly succumbed to the icy temperature. He slipped on the slope until he grasped the edge and knew safety was within reach."

Third Person Cinematic - Another, but newer, approach to third person is labeled as the third person cinematic. It shifts between limited and omniscient perspectives, resembling a movie camera lens. You observe the action from a greater distance, rather than being in the characters' minds. You resolve the distance issue of omniscient viewpoint, but you lose the emotional connections to the characters. Sometimes, combining the cinematic and limited viewpoints provides the balance that many readers cherish in their storytelling experience.

The cinematic viewpoint is perfect for certain situations, sizeable crowd, or battle scenes. You may use the cinematic approach as a transitory mechanism. Cinematic is perfect for panoramic views of your setting to express tone and establish mood, and then zoom in from there. It allows you to zoom out of a scene and finish with a wide-angle image to provide a larger viewpoint of the story. Cinematic viewpoint provides a great tool to bridge between limited and omniscient viewpoints within a story but should be used in small doses.

Third Person Deep - Deep point of view is a recent phenomenon in fiction and has become an accepted form of the third person style. It is described as a mix of first person and third limited. It retains the positives of both point of views, but tells the story with a lean toward third person, using he/she instead of I. This viewpoint provides the immediacy of first person, along with the access to the direct thoughts of the viewpoint character but also provides that separation from the character that third person limited provides. Deep viewpoint excels in a story with sustained tension and a tight focus on a single primary character.

Deep point of view is driven by the intense reactions of the character. Hiding information the character knows becomes difficult. In deep viewpoint, you will have a lot of character thoughts and internal dialogue, which builds a connection to the reader. The other major benefit of deep viewpoint is the style eliminates "telling" in most stories.

Some disadvantages exist with this viewpoint choice. The character's knowledge encompasses the story and its world. Anything that happens away from the character is outside of the reader's knowledge. If the information is relevant, find a method to share it with the reader. It may prove difficult to maintain multiple deep viewpoints if additional viewpoint characters are introduced. *Argent's Menagerie* balanced one character with a deep point of view, with many other limited viewpoints. Using a deep viewpoint instead of first person allowed the narrative to shift to a more limited viewpoint without nearly as much shock to the reader.

The key in using the various third person viewpoints is narrative distance. Understanding how the distances vary and knowing when to shift between them will help eliminate any issues with implementing these various viewpoints.

Multiple/hybrid viewpoints - There are several ways to meld multiple viewpoints. In *Elantris*, Brandon Sanderson used a method of rotating the viewpoint characters in a standard pattern. The problem arises when readers skip an unlikable character's narrative to reach their preferred characters' story.

Multiple viewpoints are beneficial when working on a project of significant scope. Robert Jordan's *The Wheel of Time* covers hundreds of characters over a long time span. A story of that size requires several viewpoint characters. Tom Clancy used another technique to cover enormous distances but to continue with the same action. A rocket is fired at one end, then the viewpoint switches to another character at the opposite end of the line of fire.

The problem with having multiple viewpoint characters is always one of losing the interest of the reader and losing momentum in the story. Based on the story, find the optimal way to avoid those issues. When switching viewpoints, remember to anchor the reader somehow. Move to the next scene by using a chapter, line, or hard break in the story. You want to avoid head hopping in every circumstance. Getting the thoughts of more than one character into the scene is an error unless you are writing in an omniscient viewpoint.

Another mechanism to provide multiple viewpoints is to use a frame story technique. The story begins with a distant narrator, then transitions to a different perspective, typically third person limited. The best example of this is perhaps *The Hobbit*. The story is narrated, but the viewpoint occasionally shifts to another character.

A quick note on using viewpoints of non-human items, such as animals, machines, or objects. When choosing to do this, do so sparingly and briefly. Readers typically dislike extended periods of this in a story. Snippets or short stories work, but the usage becomes tiring in a novel.

VIEWPOINT TENSE

Tense may not sound like an enormous concern regarding your storytelling, but the tense makes all the difference. There are three options. The following paragraphs will examine and identify the largest concerns in using each.

Past tense is the most used tense in writing and the standard in most genre fiction. Most writers find past tense the easiest and default choice. The key is to be consistent in the usage of past tense throughout your story. The one disadvantage to using past tense in first person writing is past tense conveys the impression that the narrative character lives to the end of the story and eliminates some of the tension of the story. One other thing to watch for is slipping into past perfect tense in your sentences while using this past tense narrative. It's not a crime to use "had" but overusing the past participle will annoy readers and cause problems.

Present tense is not used as often but can be used to significant effect. Present tense provides a greater sense of immediacy and implies the conclusion of the story is possibly open-ended as you progress. Tense consistency for present is more difficult if you drop into backstory or situations reliant on prior events in the story. Some stories shift from past to present tense to provide increased tension and suspense for the reader. Be careful in doing this to not create inconsistencies within the same scene.

Future tense is difficult to use in genre fiction. The most practical uses for future tense are using it in flashforward scenes, or in a situation surrounding the fulfillment of a prophecy or some other future based event. It could be used with foreshadowing, but the use of future tense may draw too much attention to that element. Subtlety and small doses of future tense are the right prescription.

Nailing viewpoint is a tough skill for new writers to master. Grasp the mechanics and challenges of each type through scene creation or reading. Mastering multiple viewpoints in a story is a skill that requires practice.

HOW TO CHOOSE

Viewpoint strives to bring readers closer to the story's action and emotion, crafting the ultimate tale. According to Janet Burroway and her masterpiece *Writing Fiction*, determining the proper viewpoint should answer the following questions. A version of this grid is on the next page and is included in the Vibrant Prose Toolbox.

We discussed the first and last questions in that list in the prior paragraphs. Who is speaking relates directly to the character sharing their perspective to the reader. And the tense was discussed in the prior section.

Let's discuss the middle three questions. To whom refers to the audience the narrator is speaking to. In second person, "to whom" usually refers to you, the reader, as a character. Third person and omniscient are almost always to you as a reader. The first person narrator may speak to themselves or another character, but mainly to the reader through their thoughts. Sometimes, the character breaks the fourth wall by talking directly to the reader.

WHO IS SPEAKING?

TO WHOM ARE THEY SPEAKING?

IN WHAT FORM ARE THEY SPEAKING?

FROM WHAT DISTANCE ARE THEY SPEAKING?

IN WHAT TENSE ARE THEY SPEAKING?

The question of form often relates to a structural type of tool. Is the communication done in the form of letters or a journal? This worked for greats like *Dracula* or *The Martian*. A chronicler plays a significant role in *The Name of the Wind*. Some writers incorporate alternative forms of communication to deliver specific messages. Frame stories are another popular method, such as with *The Princess Bride*.

The other significant question in determining the proper narrative perspective is the distance you wish to maintain between the narrator and the reader. If you want intimacy, you are going to gear toward a first person narration, or third deep. For distance, choose third person narration, perhaps omniscient. As a rule, the greater immediacy of the connection means less distance between the reader and contains fewer viewpoints.

These are not the only concerns. We haven't discussed the tradition of specific POV in many genres. Countless mysteries are told through a first person lens. Dr. Watson relayed most of the Sherlock Holmes' stories. Hercule Poirot novels are told through the viewpoint of his associate, Captain Hastings. Readers of specific genres have expectations around certain aspects of the stories they read.

The number of characters is another concern in the selection process. The main concern is determining the focal point in the scenes. In *Argent's Menagerie*, several viewpoints told the story across many locales and required specific characters relaying specific emotions to the reader in certain situations.

> **PROS AND CONS OF TRADITIONAL VIEWPOINTS**
>
> - First Person works if the following circumstances are met.
>   - If the story is solely about the main character changing.
>   - If the main character can tell his own story.
>   - If the main character has access to all the information.
>   - If the main character lives to the end of the book.
> - First Person Observer and Unreliable Narrators would be acceptable if the main character cannot tell the story.
> - Third Person Limited functions like first-person, but with added capability. Works best if other characters provide some of the information for the story.
> - Third Person Omniscient works best if there is information and experiences not accessible to the main character or other supporting characters and if there is a larger story world involved.

Once you decide on a central character, determine the type of viewpoint. If that character can convey the events of the entire story, you are shooting toward a first person or third deep viewpoint. For a grounded perspective that incorporates multiple characters' experiences and thoughts, opt for third person limited. For conveying events and reactions at a higher level, choose omniscient.

Before selecting a viewpoint, the advantages and disadvantages listed should be a concern. In the end, the story's best interest is paramount. Experimenting with various viewpoints aids in determining the optimal approach. Choosing the correct viewpoint to use will establish a relationship between you, your characters, and your readers and, if done well, makes your story great and one they will talk about for years.

Once the narrative viewpoint and viewpoint character are determined, you can focus on characterization and presenting the story through that character's eyes. Building the character in your readers eyes is critical in making the emotional connection that will pull your reader into the story.

GUIDELINES FOR PRESENTATION OF VIEWPOINT

- Anchor the reader into the mindset of a particular character. Make it clear which character's POV the reader is experiencing.
- Avoid head hopping, especially within the same scene. Head hop only if needed but anchor the reader if you do.
- Switching POV characters at chapter breaks is preferable, but at scene breaks is fine.
- Make each POV character's voice unique. Align this with their voice in dialogue unless there's a specific reason for the story. This ensures the reader's immersion in the story.
- Unless there is a specific reason for the story, make the POV character an active character in the story. This will help with pacing and keeping the interest of the reader high.
- The POV character will probably be the one most affected by the events of the story.

CHARACTER INTERIORITY

Understanding the story's perspective allows for richer characterization of the main and supporting characters. Whether the perspective be first person, third person, deep, or omniscient viewpoints, we run the story through the eyes and minds of these characters. While doing so, the story gains undertones of the characters' world interpretations. This will add depth to the characters through which we experience the story. This is known as character interiority.

The writing world has embraced character interiority as a new buzzword, despite its long-standing existence. Austen, Dickens, and Shakespeare all explore interiority in their writings to some extent. Remember that many older works do not focus on developing interiority. This is a primary reason that many traditional "classics" no longer interest many modern audiences. This points out the obvious need to accept different styles within the literary world.

With all due respect to the other chapters of this book, there is one thing that trumps everything else: writing effective character interiority. This tool is a key component of many top selling novels of the current age. Writing effective interiority invites the reader into your character's mind and opens their thoughts and emotions, but also allows the reader to follow along as the character processes what is happening to and around them. Readers observe the character's responses to life's stimuli. Well-written interiority requires a deep and intimate viewpoint lens. This creates an instant benefit to using first person and third person deep viewpoints. While helpful, close interiority may not suit every story.

Interiority can be written in a variety of ways. Many writers "show" the reader their character's emotional state. Some incorporate physical beats to accompany the emotion. Who hasn't tried to get away with only showing anger by having a character slam their fist on a table? These physical actions help convey the message but remain vague. We also want the character to show the reader their emotions and a reaction within their interior thoughts. This process can also be seen in this brief excerpt from V. E. Schwab's wonderful *The Invisible Life of Addie LaRue*.

> "She (Addie) licks her lips, expecting to taste blood, but the mark left by the stranger's teeth is gone, swept away with every other trace of him."

The author shows Addie reacting to the stimulus of a bite, expecting to taste blood, and then realizing the bite vanished. Then the emotional connection to that anticipated trace of the stranger disappears. If you've read the story, you understand the thematic impact of someone fading from another person's memory. This brings up one of the key aspects of interiority. The interior aspects of the character are always shown within the context of the character's situation. Thoughts and emotions are linked to stimuli, eliciting reactions.

Writing interiority is a key aspect of your narration. In some ways, you split your writing into three categories: dialogue, narration, and interiority. Interiority has specific qualifications. First, it isolates the character's perspective and their own mind. Within this interiority, the reader resides in the character's head, encountering a blend of free and direct speech with indirect thoughts. Second, the interior thoughts are always biased based on the character's perspective. The character's reasons for feeling that way are subjective, often explained through their backstory.

VIBRANT PROSE

Interiority is the key to understanding your character and providing solid characterization. This element of writing provides the reader insight into the characters' motivations and goals, their fears, their wants and needs, their thoughts and emotions. We require a true sense of how the character's emotions change over a story or scene. It unlocks their private thoughts and shows us the character mentally bared naked for readers to see and makes the character vulnerable. This vulnerability pulls in the reader and makes the connection between reader and character easier to establish.

Actions, like pounding a fist, convey thoughts, but revealing characters' interiority to readers is essential. Below is an example.

"A long braid pulled the woman's red hair away from her apple shaped head. A yellow sundress revealed a little more cleavage than Tasha was comfortable seeing in the office, even though it was attractive to her eye.

"Is he ready for me, Marcie?"

"Just a moment, Dr. Raines. He's in a briefing with someone else and then you can go in." Marcie pressed a button on the telepad to inform Dr. Samuelson that Tasha had arrived. She filled the time with small talk. "How was the drive this morning? I heard about the backup on 70. By the way, love the shoes." She winked at Tasha and lifted the corner of her mouth to produce a sly smile.

Tasha giggled off the subtle gesture and the supercilious compliment. "Yeah, the drive was brutal. And thanks for noticing the shoes." Tasha wondered why Marcie was so congenial, knowing the flats she wore today were nothing special. An idea flashed through Tasha's mind, and she smiled back at the red-headed woman and shot a glimpse at her chest again. This time Marcie caught her looking and turned with a knowing closed-lip grin sliding across her face. Tasha tried to cover her tracks and panicked. "Hey, you doing anything Wednesday night? I've got an extra ticket to the Etheridge tribute concert at the White River Amp, if you're interested."

Marcie's eyes brightened. "I love that show. I went a couple years ago." She took a post-it note and wrote something on it. "That's my telepad number. Give me a call tonight and we'll firm up the details."

Tasha smirked, now realizing she was stuck in a situation she was unprepared for. Shit, I just asked her out. What am I doing? "Sounds good." She put the paper in her pocket. Can't believe I did that. And that it worked.

A buzz came through the telepad near Marcie, and Samuelson's voice followed it. "You can send in Dr. Raines now."

> *Marcie raised an eyebrow and pointed Tasha to the door. "Knock him dead.""*

Throughout this scene, we experience Tasha's emotions and thoughts. The scene includes internal monologue and reveals Tasha's conflicting emotions about her attraction to the woman. We understand Tasha's character and where her mind is.

FORMS OF CHARACTERIZATION

Interiority, similar to perspective, takes on different forms or even a combination of them. Every level of interiority reveals character and clarifies the world and events around them. The question is, at what level do you wish to expose your characters to the reader? The answer depends on the situation and the character's role in the scene.

Obsessive/Immersive is the furthest you can go within a character. At this level, the characters' thoughts nearly drown out the world around them. It reflects stream-of-consciousness writing and occurs in the works of William Faulkner and James Joyce, along with Thomas Pynchon's infamous *Gravity's Rainbow*. You're immersed in the character's mind, where thoughts surpass the narrative.

Full/Rounded is perhaps the version of interiority most preferred and is now considered core to the literary establishment and to genre writing across the board. This view provides the thoughts, feelings, emotions, and everything else that helps the character come alive and become a "three-dimensional" entity to the reader but falls short of Immersive style. This level is preferable for engaging with the main characters in the story.

Partial interiority is perhaps the most used level in modern fiction. This level reveals some characters' thoughts and emotions, but not as much as Full. Most supporting characters in your story will be at this level. This level of interiority provides a character a little more mystery. An unreliable narrator might frequent this space, the optimal level for characters with specific roles in your story, ensuring depth and avoiding flatness.

We see an excellent use of partial interiority in Gillian Flynn's *Gone Girl* when the police search for clues to help solve Amy's disappearance. Every time evidence turns up and they ask questions of Nick, he holds something back. If the character had full interiority, we would uncover his secrets from the police. Because this is a Thriller, we wonder what he isn't telling them. This heightens the anticipation and mystery of the story, thus increasing the tension. The cracks become apparent as the story progresses. We suspect he's hiding something to spare his or his wife's embarrassment. He might lie to the cops, but deep down, we don't believe Nick would lie to us. Right?

Flynn lulls us into a sense of trust earlier in the story through interiority by presenting Nick's naked thoughts. Thoughts we would never expect to hear from anyone. She opens his consciousness to allow us in and, by seeing these thoughts, we trust him. We believe Nick because we saw into his mind. We don't notice when the veil slips back over, and we no longer see the nakedness of his thoughts. So, we accept this falsehood until the truth hits us. Then we are shocked we missed he hid the truth all along.

The last level of interiority pertains to flat characters. Flat characters should fulfill a plot dependent role and are often characters you must include for a specific reason. It is encouraged to remove this representation, if possible.

In reality, every story has a bit of everything, except possibly the Obsessive level. Balancing these levels of interiority focuses the story on the characters that matter to the reader. Certain characters should embody the Full category, and prioritizing their interiority should drive your revision cycle.

Characterization is the toughest part of writing, as the technique requires finding the right perspective and level of interiority. There is no scientific approach or methodical step-by-step manual on the matter. It is as much based on feel and experience as anything else. But once you have mastered the technique, you have mastered something quite special, and your stories will be elevated because of your skill.

EXERCISES

1. Use the viewpoint grid and chart the answers to the questions using either your favorite story or your own story.
2. Take a passage of your story and re-write it from past tense to present tense, or vice versa, and identify the differences made by switching the tense in this passage.
3. Take a passage of your story and re-write it in first person, third person, and omniscient viewpoint. Identify the differences of using the various viewpoints in the story.
4. Take a passage of your story and re-write it with a full level of interiority for each of the characters, then repeat it to produce a partial level for each character. Observe the scene's transformation and combine the two passages to form a final version.

REFERENCE MATERIALS

Characters & Viewpoint by Orson Scott Card
Deep Point of View by Marcy Kennedy
Writing Fiction: A Guide to Narrative Craft, Chapter 7 by Janet Burroway
Fiction Writing Made Easy Podcast by Savannah Gilbo
Who Says?: Master Point of View in Fiction by Lisa Zeidner

Many writing craft books cover viewpoint, but these sources stand out for exploring unique aspects. Card discusses varied viewpoints in storytelling, including cinematic viewpoint, a tool used so well in visual media but often ignored in fiction. Kennedy offers a perspective on deep point of view that reveals a tool for shortening the narrative distance in a story without the issues of first person. Burroway provides a unique viewpoint on objectivity and around the decision-making process. Gilbo's podcast preaches the benefits of interiority and how to use it as a secret weapon in your writing. Zeidner covers the basics but also provides a chapter on viewpoints from a non-traditional source, such as animals and machines.

8 – THEME, THE NARRATIVE FULCRUM

We often talk about the necessary elements of a great written work. Character and plot are often the top two elements in almost every discussion. Setting and drama are also two primary components that rank right up there. One other element every writer should account for early in their writing process is theme.

Many writers consider theme part of a triangular relationship with character and plot. Each piece works off the other two components to further build the story. For example, if you write a scene meant to progress the plot and meet the character's external goal, you must consider how the scene impacts the thematic character arc. The three interact in the story's progression from start to finish.

Imagine a teeter-totter, with theme as the central pivot. If the plot gets a little heavy by overexerting your theme, the story becomes unbalanced with the lack of character development. The same goes the other way. Also, if you downplay the theme, plot and character fall and remain rather flat. However, if they work in unison, we see a balanced story throughout.

What is theme? Themes are simplified expressions of humanity's life pursuits. Common examples of theme revolve around greed, generosity, and genuine love. Though themes may seem pithy, they are qualities that hold sway over our lives. Theme is the focusing central concern the reader derives from the overall story and is a common thread throughout the work. The character exemplifies the theme by moving from their Big Lie to the Truth of the story. Donald

Maass claims theme is important for three reasons in his essay titled "Something to Say."

1. All stories are moral and have underlying values.
2. Readers seek out stories that align with their beliefs.
3. Fiction is the most engrossing when it pulls in readers with varied points of view.

Incorporating themes into a novel appeals to our higher selves, our ideals, the person we aspire to be. We wish we lived in a world with upright morality, and we can exhibit that in our fiction. Authors shouldn't fear expressing their stance and opinions via characters. Freely expressing our thoughts is part of our internal design. Sharing stories is a cherished human tradition. How does theme enhance your favorite story? How does theme manifest itself in storytelling?

- Theme is the main idea of a literary work. It is an abstract concept that registers as an underlying current and focuses your story.
- Theme helps the reader understand an idea the writer wishes to convey on a subject—the writer's view of the world or a revelation concerning human nature.
- Theme helps to connect with the reader on a deeper level than with just plot, characters, setting, and dialogue. It provides an extra dimension with an underlying message to the reader.

Each author approaches theme differently. Theme is pushed aside by some authors, particularly new writers, to be addressed later in the writing process. Others tackle theme early in their process and spend as much time on the subject as they do their characters, plot, and world-building. The resulting product must have a significant theme at the end of the process.

The writer may incorporate theme in either an overt or covert manner. If theme is a driving force within the work, it will be more obvious. Herman Melville's *Moby Dick* is often seen as a thematically driven story. In other works, theme is implied. The theme of reinvention is subtly hinted at in *Legends in Addington*, yet never directly addressed.

Some works include multiple themes that provide key messages on various components of the story. These works often feature complex stories. *To Kill a Mockingbird* is an example. It explores the issues of racism in the American South. It also is a Coming-of-Age story for Scout as she watches her father deal with these issues and forms her own internal code. The story of Atticus Finch is also theme inspired as he develops personal courage to take on the fight he knows he will not win.

As we dissect theme, ask yourself how does theme impact the story you are writing? How does the main plot impact the theme? What is the thematic significance of the character arc? Your story may carry certain expectations from a thematic perspective based on the genre. Let's examine how these additional story elements affect the theme in greater detail.

CHARACTERS AND THEME

Symbolizing your theme through a character is the easiest approach to putting your message for the story front and center. Make the motivating force of the character align with your theme through the novel. Passionate characters come through on the page. The use of three scientists to criticize the use of genetic reanimation makes a good argument in *Jurassic Park*.

In most stories, the protagonist reveals the theme of the story through interaction with other elements and characters that elicit thematic thoughts or emotions through an overt or covert presentation. This interaction with theme may occur internally or externally. William Golding's *Lord of the Flies* demonstrates using external pressures on the characters throughout to reinforce the theme of the story.

"Roger stooped, picked up a stone, aimed, and threw it at Henry — threw it to miss. The stone, that token of preposterous time, bounded five yards to Henry's right and fell in the water. Roger gathered a handful of stones and began to throw them. Yet there was a space round Henry, perhaps six yards in diameter, into which he dare not throw. Here, invisible yet strong, was the taboo of the old life. Round the squatting child was the protection of parents and school and policemen and the law."

Another significant way to attach theme to your character is through the character development arc. How does theme impact the character? As mentioned in an earlier chapter, your main character should have a prescribed set of desires, flaws, and fears. One of the flaws might be a false belief in the character's life. The character's worldview will evolve as the story unfolds and they will discover the truth. The story's theme emphasizes the character's shift from falsehood to truth. The movement of the character exemplifies that theme.

View theme as a two-sided coin, one side negative and the other positive. The elements of our protagonist's life created a negative influence which led to them trusting a relative falsehood. Conversely, there are positive aspects for individuals who have the chance to experience a new life.

One potential problem we need to raise a red flag over is making sure your characters have flaws and virtues that tie into your theme. Theme becomes muddled if character flaws don't align with the intended message. For instance, what if your character has a gambling problem but your theme revolves around global conquest? At first glance, they don't align. This gap creates conflicting elements and an incoherent message. Your characters should mesh with the theme and vice versa.

PLOT AND THEME

How relevant is the theme to the main plot of your story? When the theme and plot align, the result resonates with the reader. Theme is best exemplified through the actions of various characters in the story. The simplest way to use plot to create theme in your story is through the character arc. The internal struggle of the character ties to the theme. Characters' actions reflect their motivations, which revolve around the thematic questions of truth in the story. Character, plot, and theme are interconnected and elevate each other. Theme must be reinforced in each scene throughout the story. Layer theme in, but avoid a heavy-handed approach or overshadowing the main story.

Some treat theme as if it should be additive. To convey a message, writers often integrate the theme as a subplot, add vivid imagery, or present the message overtly. In *Argent's Menagerie*, a particular scene involving Argent and River on his home planet deals with the thematic message of familial bonds and trust as they discuss their past relationship and how that impacts other relationships going forward. This scene becomes key to the two of them resolving the subplot of their relationship dynamic prior to the last act of the story.

The plot of your story could be impacted by the thematic principle of metaphor. A metaphor can occur at a micro-level, a sentence or paragraph, or at a macro-level, an entire story. This metaphor uses the details of the external plot to exemplify the internal elements of theme. The three best forms of metaphor used in storytelling are the allegory, the docudrama, and the fable.

The allegory is the most obvious. A good example of this is *Animal Farm* by George Orwell. The farm animals are a direct and obvious comparison to Communist Russia. The underlying theme is easy to pinpoint as the animals assume the role of the workers rising up to unseat the farmer from the head of their society. They then begin the process of becoming the same elitist society they disposed of originally.

The docudrama takes actual events and molds them to demonstrate a theme. Building a cohesive theme without being heavy-handed is a challenge for any documentary. If the events seem too forced to fit a theme, the story loses its impact. It becomes propaganda.

The fable is the most used form of metaphor in our lives. These use a non-reality to underscore the thematic tones of our real world. Mother Goose and Aesop started us down this path as little children and many successful stories have used those as inspiration.

TYING THEME TO PLOT AND CHARACTER

The preceding paragraphs are still vague about how you connect theme to your characters and plot. In this section, we will dive into that in greater detail. To set the stage, we need to define a few terms. These terms are sometimes interchanged in error. That is often a mistake and leads to further confusion by the inexperienced writer and hinders their effort to develop their theme.

- Ghost – The motivating factor of a character's backstory. An abusive father that abandons the character as a child.
- Wound – The psychological pain created by the ghost that creates personality dysfunction.
- Lie – A flaw that has been propagated in the character's worldview. The character's Lie worked until now, but the Lie won't let them evolve in the story. This Lie results from the Ghost.
- Weakness – A flaw the character must overcome if they are to achieve their goals. The story may feature multiple character flaws, but the central weakness must be conquered.

- Wants – The goal of the character at the beginning of the story based on their understanding of the Lie. This will exist coming into the story.
- Desire/Goal – This is the goal of the character within the main context of the story. It is the plot goal and drives the story. In every scene, the character's goal should connect to the main plot goal. This may change if the context within the story changes.
- Moral Intention/Motivation – The moral reasons for pursuing the goal.
- Needs – The representation of the relative Truth of the story that stands in opposition to the Lie. The story's change arc relies on accepting this Need.

Having covered these terms, let's review a methodology developed by combining the character web concept promoted by John Truby with the methodology from *GMC: Goals, Motivation & Conflict* by Debra Dixon to demonstrate character elements. These results will then be carried forward to be used with other tools developed by K. M. Weiland and Robert McKee to tie the theme back to our plot.

For simplicity's sake, below are the character summaries for the main characters of *Argent's Menagerie*. After reading these summaries, the conflicts between various characters become apparent. If your character web lacks conflict between specific characters of your story, then review that relationship to identify a potential source of tension.

- Argent is a mercenary/pirate pilot that is the outcast of his aristocrat family and has issues with the law. Has a romantic relationship with one of his crew. Has a strained relationship with his twin brother, who sits on the primary law agency in the solar system. These issues date back to the death of their father.
- Grishon is the chief antagonist of the external plotline and has some philosophical leanings similar to Argent, but will destroy lives to establish a tyranny. Has already destroyed multiple planets, including the home of Fen.
- Preus, Argent's twin, has philosophical leanings that stand between him and Argent truly joining forces and trusting each other. He is for a diplomatic resolution but supports bureaucratic society instead of a tyranny.
- Fen, Argent's girlfriend, believes that joining forces with Preus is the best approach but also has second thoughts on her

relationship with Argent. A secret within the story reveals a hidden connection to Grishon.
- River, Argent's former girlfriend and ex-wife of Grishon, is the heir to the throne of her planet.

John Truby's character web is a diagram which shows the connections between characters in the story. You place the characters around the web and add notes on what creates tension between the various characters on the map. There should be at least one source of conflict between each combination of characters. Perhaps characters have a shared history, perhaps they are entwined in a romance, or perhaps they hate each other. Those relationships drive a specific type of conflict to fuel a story. Knowing the relationship dynamics between your main character and the other major characters provides a primary driver of your storyline. These relationships provide the first indication of how wide your story will become (the more characters, the thicker the story).

The theme square, made popular by Robert McKee, is a tool that works with the four-cornered character web. You can align your main characters from a thematic standpoint. This tool will identify degrees of negativity from the truth of your story. These degrees shift from the positive to contradictory to negation to the contrary. In looking at *Argent's Menagerie*, we place the main characters in their respective corners, with Argent being in the positive corner. Grishon becomes contradictory while Preus takes the negation standpoint. This highlights the thematic aspect of lost trust being the focus of the internal conflict within Argent, which aligns with the main external conflict of the story.

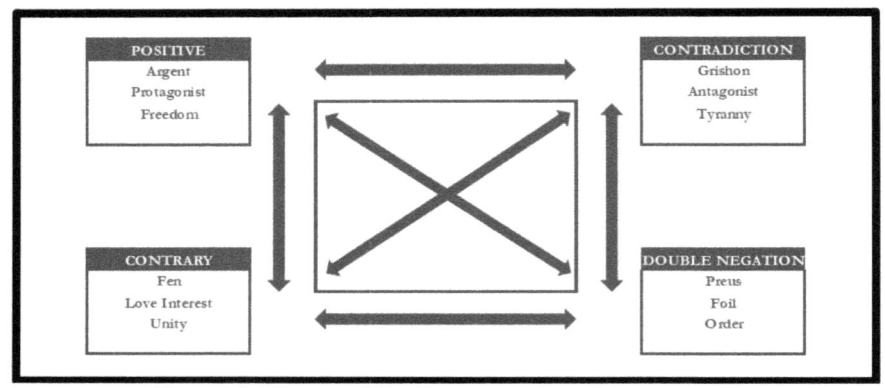

```
┌─────────────────────────────────────────────────────────────┐
│   ┌──────────────┐                      ┌──────────────┐    │
│   │  POSITIVE    │ ◄──────────────────► │ CONTRADICTION│    │
│   │   Argent     │                      │   Grishon    │    │
│   │  Protagonist │                      │  Antagonist  │    │
│   │   Freedom    │                      │   Tyranny    │    │
│   └──────────────┘                      └──────────────┘    │
│        ▲  ╲                              ╱  ▲               │
│        │    ╲                          ╱    │               │
│        │      ╲                      ╱      │               │
│        │        ╲                  ╱        │               │
│        │          ╲              ╱          │               │
│        │            ╲          ╱            │               │
│        │              ╲      ╱              │               │
│        │                ╳                   │               │
│        │              ╱      ╲              │               │
│        │            ╱          ╲            │               │
│        │          ╱              ╲          │               │
│        ▼        ╱                  ╲        ▼               │
│   ┌──────────────┐                      ┌──────────────┐    │
│   │  CONTRARY    │ ◄──────────────────► │DOUBLE NEGATION│   │
│   │     Fen      │                      │    Preus     │    │
│   │ Love Interest│                      │     Foil     │    │
│   │    Unity     │                      │    Order     │    │
│   └──────────────┘                      └──────────────┘    │
└─────────────────────────────────────────────────────────────┘
```

Figure 8-3 - The use of the character web and theme square

The GMC methodology requires you to identify the goals, motivations, and potential conflict for each major character. That conflict will be what might keep the character from achieving their goal. To continue with the example of *Argent's Menagerie*, Argent's GMC information is identified, as well as the same attributes of the antagonist, Grishon. Both characters agree on the need for changes in the space system's administration but differ on the desired outcome. The contrast in opinions reveals the story's external conflict. Expanding this tool to other major characters would reveal additional conflicts and plot possibilities for the story.

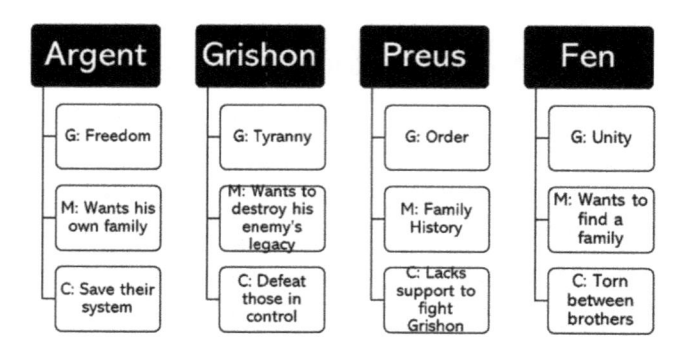

Argent	**Grishon**	**Preus**	**Fen**
G: Freedom	G: Tyranny	G: Order	G: Unity
M: Wants his own family	M: Wants to destroy his enemy's legacy	M: Family History	M: Wants to find a family
C: Save their system	C: Defeat those in control	C: Lacks support to fight Grishon	C: Torn between brothers

Understanding the character's limits in pursuing their desires is crucial. Are there boundaries your character will not cross? What would force the character to cross those lines? For example, Argent refuses to kill unless no other options exist. Creating moral dilemmas and having the character face those imaginary lines is a central tenet to developing internal conflict and exposing the characters deep seated tenets.

Also, all your major characters have a flaw. Perhaps they have an addiction. Perhaps they are workaholics. Perhaps they grew up in abusive situations. These flaws shape their interactions with other characters. Leveraging your character's flaw to create internal conflict is at the core of writing great fiction. We all struggle to overcome our flaws, often tragically. Your characters are no different. This delivers thematic heft to the story.

Another tool to help develop the thematic aspects of your story is the Truth Chart. This tool uses the Big Truth and Big Lie of the main character to develop specific plot points within the character arc. The tool illustrates the transformation of the character and their journey towards the eventual conclusion of the story.

With this tool, you take the attributes of your character and develop portions of your story to ensure the thematic point ties into your character and the plot. You may dive even deeper and look at other flaws and virtues your character carries with them.

THE CHARACTER'S MOTIVATION	THE CHARACTER'S GOAL:	THE CHARACTER'S TRUE NEED
Sense of Betrayal from his father years before.	To live a life free of the world his father intended for him.	Resolution of the conflict with his brother to live in peace.

THE CHARACTER'S LIE:	THE STORY'S BIG LIE:
That he can live his life outside of the legal structures that his brother represents.	That freedom and the law are not dependent upon each other.

MANIFESTATION OF THE BIG LIE:
Argent believes his life as a mercenary is fulfilling and provides everything he needs to live.
SMALL INTRODUCTORY TRUTH:
He is reluctant to have a relationship with his brother because he represents the security that Argent needs to have a relationship with Fen and to have a family of his own.
MOMENT OF TRUTH:
When it becomes apparent that Argent can't resolve the problem of Grishon without the aid of Preus, and vice versa.
REMAINING CHUNK OF THE LIE:
When Argent fears that Fen is dead after trusting her safety in the hands of Preus.
CLIMACTIC TRUTH:
Argent realizes the truth about what his father did for him and how he and Preus were both victims. And that he believes his own faults were as muc to blame for her demise.

THE CHARACTER'S TRUTH:	THE STORY'S BIG TRUTH:
His father loved him, but that took a form of love he didn't understand as a child. He now sees the impacts of that were beneficial for him and his brother.	Love can take many forms, and he needs his brother and the structure he represents to live a full life.

SYMBOLISM AND MOTIFS

Theme can be presented through the prose of your story via many devices. Symbolism and motifs are essential literary devices in fiction writing. They enrich narratives by adding layers of meaning and enhancing thematic depth. While they are often used interchangeably, they serve distinct functions in storytelling.

Symbolism involves using objects, characters, or events to represent abstract ideas or concepts. Symbols can be tangible items, such as a rose symbolizing love, or more abstract, like a storm representing turmoil. The power of symbolism lies in its ability to convey complex ideas subtly, allowing readers to infer deeper meanings and engage more profoundly with the text.

In *Moby Dick*, Melville uses the interaction with multiple ships through the story to provide repetitive opportunities to reveal Ahab's growing anger and obsession with the white whale. The following passage shows how Ahab has affixed his emotions to the leviathan's demise, as if the whale's defeat would eliminate all evil from the world.

"All that most maddens and torments; all that stirs up the lees of things; all truth with malice in it; all that cracks the sinews and cakes the brain; all the subtle demonisms of life and thought; all evil, to crazy Ahab, were visibly personified, and made practically assailable in Moby Dick. He piled upon the whale's white hump the sum of all the general rage and hate felt by his whole race from Adam down; and then, as if his chest had been a mortar, he burst his hot heart's shell upon it."

Motifs are recurring elements, such as images, phrases, or structures, which reinforce the themes of a story. Unlike symbols, which can appear once, motifs must recur to underscore the central themes. They create a pattern that helps to unify the story and highlight its key messages. The green light in *The Great Gatsby* is an oft-cited example of a recurring element that hearkens back to the underlying themes of that classic American novel.

Symbols often work within motifs to create a cohesive narrative. For example, in William Golding's *Lord of the Flies*, the conch shell is a symbol of order and civilization. The recurring motif of the boys' descent into savagery is demonstrated by destroying the conch. Presenting symbolism and motifs occurs in numerous ways through figurative language. This can happen through metaphor, simile, allegory, or even in character archetypes. Another popular method of representation is through the use of specific colors that carry a symbolic meaning.

Symbolism and motifs are crucial tools in fiction writing and allow authors to convey complex ideas and themes subtly. By understanding and employing these devices, writers can create richer, more engaging narratives that resonate with readers. Whether through a single powerful symbol or a recurring motif, these elements help to weave a story's thematic fabric, making the message more memorable and impactful.

OTHER METHODS

Theme is the component of your storytelling that is easy to lose track of or forget about in your implementation. There are basic elements to keep in mind throughout your writing. The first one involves theme and genre. As mentioned in an earlier chapter, each genre carries its own implied thematic message. Consider embracing the anticipated thematic message in your story, as subverting expectations may leave the reader unsatisfied.

The second facet of this is the premise of your story. Look at that and draw out the underlying theme of your story arc. The Big Lie of your character will drive the key theme of the story. Marrying a thematic message to this character arc will always be successful. Once you solidify the central thematic message, you can then work to drive home other themes you wish to express in the story through your main plot arc.

Theme is shown through the descriptors, verbs, and nouns that depict the setting and vivid imagery. Perhaps graffiti in an urban setting presents messages pertaining to injustice. Perhaps the style of homes and their surroundings in a suburban setting conveys just as much meaning. Or a jungle intending to replicate a prehistoric rainforest. It worked in *Jurassic Park*, so perhaps we should pay attention to the message our setting sends.

The tone of the work also greatly influences the presentation of theme. Creating an atmosphere that is conducive to the theme is paramount. If your tone opposes the theme, the story won't resonate with the reader. It's hard to portray happiness in a dark, noir-themed story.

You should present your story as either explaining your message or exploring the world to discover that theme. If you force the theme, your reader will know. The force that you use to drive home the theme influences the story and changes the way the message comes across to the reader. R. F. Kuang writes her stories in a way that the themes are apparent throughout. In *Babel, the Necessity of Violence* the author delved into anti-colonialism, violence acceptance, and power usage, and was perceived by some as heavy-handed.

To contrast, Moniquill Blackgoose addresses many of the same themes in *To Shape a Dragon's Breath*. Through her character, Blackgoose gently reveals new realities in a different world. Both stories take place in British Empire-dominated worlds, with the main characters challenging its culture and dominance. Kuang's story presents the themes in a way that explains her stance and the character's fall in line and reinforce the messages through extreme situations. Blackgoose explores the world's impact on characters through interactions and daily events. Balancing tactics enhances the reader's experience more than relying on just one approach.

If theme is not a primary part of your story, determine what the theme of your story is and layer theme into the writing with subtlety. Include a sentence or two, an image, or a symbol in each chapter and scene.

THEME TRACKING TOOLS

We have discussed the theory of theme. Now let's get into the actual practice of implementing theme. How do we assure ourselves we are building enough thematic elements in our story to get our point across? This depends on your style of writing and the tools you wish to use.

The number one tool many writers use to help with implementing theme is an outline. Outlining each major scene with a one sentence blurb identifying the major action, the main character, and the thematic impact. The thematic impact may involve confidence in the Lie, realizing the Truth, or other possibilities. If you can't identify the thematic elements of your scene, your reader can't either.

A scene tracker captures scene aspects and facilitates the analysis of story elements via reporting. Thematic elements are a piece of that puzzle. The tracker is an Excel schedule with a row for each scene. The columns denote various components contained within the scene. The Vibrant Prose Toolbox provides a variation of this type of tool.

Two thematic drivers are what Shawn Coyne, writer of *The Story Grid*, denotes as the story values. These story values consist of the relative mindset of the character against their pre-existing worldview and the standing of the character against their thematic truth. The method's effectiveness may be debated, but tracking thematic drivers is a solid concept.

The preferred technique for many writers is to build in their thematic elements during the second pass of the story and the revision stages. If unsure of your story's theme, start writing and revisit the message later when the theme becomes clear. Then add the thematic elements throughout your story to provide a cohesive feeling from start to finish.

But don't abandon or overlook the idea. William Shakespeare, considered by many as the greatest writer ever, mastered the use of theme in his works and layered theme into his characters, dialogue, and plot better than anyone else to date. His basic storylines still impact the way we tell stories today.

EXERCISES

1. Write out a summary of what your theme is for your story and how it pertains to the main character. Compare with the genre grid in chapter 3. Look for any overlooked themes that could enhance the story.
2. Take the character map you developed in an earlier chapter and use that to create a theme square to identify how your main characters are aligned with your major.
3. Use the Truth Chart to identify key aspects of the character arc for your protagonist.
4. Share a story where theme, character, and plot are intertwined.

REFERENCE MATERIALS

Writing Your Story's Theme: The Writer's Guide to Plotting Stories That Matter by K. M. Weiland
GMC: Goal, Motivation, and Conflict: The Building Blocks of Good Fiction by Debra Dixon
The Story Grid: What Good Editors Know by Shawn Coyne

Weiland's series on author assistance provides a rare gem among books on theme. Her book dives into detail how writers implement theme into their writing and how theme impacts the other aspects of writing the story.

Every writing teacher out there alludes to Dixon's book. The formula was known to the writing world, but Dixon wrote it down. She dives into the heart of character development, and by extension, developing plot and theme in great fiction. If you are interested in purchasing, go directly to the publisher, Gryphon Books, and get the hardcover version.

The Story Grid is the foundation of several tools incorporated by Coyne to develop a methodology to evaluate stories. This methodology is widely adopted in the editorial world and shapes experts' perspective on storytelling. Coyne based this information on his extensive experience in the industry and it influences many well-known industry experts.

9 – PLOT

Plot is often assumed to be a prescribed story type like Overcoming the Monster, or the Quest. It involves much more than that. Plot happens around the characters in the story. Plot acts on the characters, forces a reaction from them, and then pushes the story forward with their actions. It always moves forward toward a conclusion through narrative momentum. Without plot, your story is a bunch of static settings and characters. Before we delve deeper, let's clarify the definition of plot to distinguish it from the other writing component associated with it: structure. Structure is addressed in the next chapter.

- Plot involves the events that tell a story. It encompasses the actions and the forward progression of the story through a cause-effect sequence towards the conclusion.
- Structure is the sequencing of these events to best present the story in a manner best consumed by the audience.

Before delving into the chapter's subject, it's worth mentioning that some established writers view plot unfavorably. Do not believe those quotes by Stephen King denigrating the topic. Has a writer ever written a great fiction story that lacked a plot? No! Plot walks hand in hand with your characters to create a full and enjoyable story for your readers.

The concept of plot often gets conflated with other elements, but plot is its own animal in the storytelling universe. What are the key traits of Plot? There are certain concepts around plot that you should keep in mind as you write, the six Cs of plot.

- Causality – The writer should write a story from start to finish as a succession of cause-effect events unless you have a good reason to deviate from that method. Every event feeds off the prior events. Every decision feeds off prior decisions. Make sure you keep the cause-effect status in mind as you progress.

- Context – One of the core concerns of the reader will be if something is believable. If not, you kick them out of the story. Everything needs to be believable within the context of the story. To do that, you need to set the table for everything before you drop it on your reader and assume they will suspend disbelief. For example, are there special laws of physics in your world? If so, explain that early in your story. Ensure your characters behave believably within the story's context.
- Celerity – Plot is always moving. If the plot of your story even appears to stop, you are in trouble. You must always keep the story moving towards the conclusion. Control your pacing of the story. Moving too fast is also a bad thing. Expect changes in pace, but don't halt it.
- Continuity – Everything matters in a novel, and it needs to feel like a continuous journey. Do nothing to upset that smooth flow. Readers want unity in tone, mood, and story. Give it to them.
- Closure – Answer your questions, close your loops, and fulfill your promises. All those breadcrumbs you leave through your story lead to questions from your reader. The reader expects to get closure.
- Creativity – This is why we are writers. We desire to be creative and wish to encourage and foster our creativity. If you have ideas, pursue them. Go down those rabbit trails and produce amazing surprises. Creativity is great, but don't sacrifice the story. You must come back to the items we mentioned earlier within the other five Cs.

PROMISES, PROGRESS, PAYOFFS

Plot can be seen as steps to solve a problem. You first entice the reader into the story by providing an interesting question or offering a fascinating journey. Some prefer to call these promises. Your first chance to lure your reader begins right at the start with the hook. From the first line, you want to grab their attention. Action prompts the reader to ask questions. Tolkien has one of the best opening paragraphs in fiction and it involves the character sitting and eating, supposedly in great comfort. It promises that this character will not be comfortable much longer. And we, in turn, ask, "How?"

"In a hole in the ground there lived a hobbit. Not a nasty, dirty, wet hole, filled with the ends of worms and an oozy smell, nor yet a dry, bare, sandy hole with nothing in it to sit down on or eat: it was a hobbit-hole, and that means comfort." – The Hobbit, J. R. R. Tolkien

A group of dwarves create havoc in Bilbo Baggins' home, disturbing the comfort we all know he values. They sing songs, drink his ale and wine, eat most of his food, and trash the place. But as recompense, they offer him an adventure. We begin the story with comfort and progressively experience more tension as the adventures become bigger and larger; with Bilbo becoming less and less comfortable. All hoping to find the Lonely Mountain of Erebor.

At first, the wild spooked us, and Bilbo. Then Tolkien moves from escaping a band of trolls to the wonders of Rivendell. The danger growing ever stronger. Following this, they travel through the Misty Mountains and run into a pack of goblins and a nasty creature named Gollum. They then survive the dangers of the forests of Mirkwood and the Wood-elves. This whole time progressing through the world toward their goal. They reach Lake Town and glimpse the distant mountain. Then the danger becomes even greater.

Now the goal isn't just finding the mountain, but reclaiming the treasure held within. That means battling Smaug, the great dragon. We think we have the ultimate payoff when the dragon is killed. Yet, that's when the danger escalates. Thorin has claimed the treasure, but it brings out the worst in him. And that launches an even greater danger, war.

Do you see how Tolkien took a simple group of bumbling dwarves and a comfortable halfling and moved us from that promise toward the ultimate payoff with a grand story that becomes world changing? Even as we read the story and realize the grand payoff of finishing the journey exists, Tolkien plants the seed for an even greater adventure with a simple, small ring Bilbo takes back to his comfortable environs at Bag End.

Though plot should encompass all six of the earlier mentioned traits, it also holds promises and progresses the reader to the conclusion while providing the payoff for their diligence with an ending that satisfies the reader. A plot, similar to Bilbo's adventure, cherishes its start and finish, as well as the journey in between.

THE MAIN PLOT

As we covered in the character section of this book, there will be core internal and external conflicts. These conflicts should align with external and internal plots. The larger overall plot of the story almost always aligns with an external antagonist. Most people grasp the external plot, the A Plot or Archplot. But there is often more than meets the eye, as the writer often layers in multiple plot lines within the story. The main plot must do more than just hit the major beats. The following paragraphs walk through the most common plot elements you might see just beneath the cover of the large, overarching story.

THE PURPOSE OF THE BEGINNING

At the beginning of the story, there are concrete objectives tied to the plot. The beginning includes everything leading up to and including the decision by the main character to tackle the challenge set in front of him.

To begin, Hook the reader. Bring the reader into the story immediately. Use the first scenes to provide tension and present the main story question to the reader. You should provide the objective and motivation of the lead character early and identify the major conflict of the story.

Introduce the antagonist and their motivation. Establish the story's conflict and the lead's obstacle. Give the bad guy sympathetic characteristics if you want to provide moral grayness. The character believes in their righteousness and considers themselves the protagonist. Make the stakes clear to the reader.

Also, address any story type and genre conventions that exist in the first part of the story. Your readers expect certain things to fall into place based on their experience with the type of story you are writing. It's not a good sign to ruin those early expectations.

Kick off the Inciting Incident. This is the event within the story that starts the action. It may occur during the Hook, before the Hook, or late in the first act, and our Big Event, the transition point from the first to second act, builds off this incident. The formal term is the first plot point.

All the prior events setup the Big Event. Those who've seen *Star Wars* recognizes this as when Luke realizes his uncle and aunt are in trouble. He goes back to their place and finds their burned corpses. Luke has nothing left on Tatooine. He decides, begrudgingly, to accept Kenobi's offer and to help him get to Alderaan. This decision is the first time Luke takes his destiny into his own hands. He claims his agency. Luke and Kenobi follow this decision by jumping aboard Han Solo's ship and leave Luke's normal world and fly into a new world.

ENTERING THE MIDDLE

Why do we worry so much about the middle of our story? The middle of the novel comprises a significant portion of the piece. The reader must push through this part, regardless of how amazing our hook and climax are. Most writing craft books lack direction for this section. *Save the Cat!* calls the first part of this section "Fun and Games" (which no writer believes is true) while providing little guidance.

The second part of your book is about presenting opponents, obstacles, and opportunities to your protagonist. The goal is to show the progression of our plot lines, including the shift in the main character toward their internal goal. We present a new perspective on the setting, dive into other characters, reinforce the theme, and ramp up our tension through this part of the story. Our goal is for the reader and character to explore this new world together as we approach the Midpoint. As the antagonist gains prominence and stakes rise, the main character comprehends the shifting world.

What happens at the Midpoint? We see a marriage between the A Plot (the external plot) and the B Plot (the character arc). The Midpoint holds significance for your character's journey. Two popular choices to depict this point include a hollow victory or a defeat that provides a bit of hope at the end. If you choose the victory, your scenes from the Big Event forward will uplift the character and create a false sense of confidence until they get to the Midpoint and achieve a pyrrhic victory, only to realize how hollow the win was. This begins the precipitous drop for the character. If you choose a defeat, the scenes prior to the Midpoint will pile punishment onto the character until they get to a low point and then, they have hope that launches them to the next part of the story.

For an example, we look at the Harry Potter series. The major scene at the end of *The Goblet of Fire* serves as the series' midpoint. Harry and Cedric win the contest, but are transported to a graveyard. Harry witnesses the death of Cedric and the full reanimation of Voldemort into his actual body. Harry escapes back to Hogwarts through his cleverness. All seemed victorious for Harry until everything crashed down. Now he is despondent and sees the rough future before him, which impacts the next book in the series.

EXITING THE MIDDLE

You have just moved beyond the centerpiece of your story, the Midpoint. Your characters are a mess, but now they must move toward the resolution. Begin with a swift reaction right after the Midpoint event. One, maybe two scenes if you need to see the reaction from multiple characters. Seemingly, incredibly short, but it needs to happen.

In *Star Wars*, this reaction occurs when the Millenium Falcon exits light speed into what they believe is an asteroid field until they realize that they're surrounded by the remains of Alderaan. Once reality hits them, they pause, and the question is on their faces. What do we do now? For that brief instant, we are uncertain what happens next. It depends on what you did with the Midpoint.

This section of the story emphasizes the character's empowerment in shaping their own destiny. The protagonist responds to the antagonist and attempts to defeat them through a series of try-fail cycles. The protagonist suffers various levels of defeat until they take a blow that appears too much to overcome. This moment is the Crisis and leads to the Dark Night of the Soul.

At this point, the protagonist believes they have lost. It must be their worst day ever. The more you crush the protagonist, the better. Harry assumes his mentor cannot be killed and never suspects that Dumbledore will leave him. His enemy is figuratively standing above him and gloating. We end *The Half-Blood Prince* devastated, along with Harry.

The character must move on. Therefore, the Crisis is the most important point in the character arc. It is where the hero transforms into the character they must become. They are compelled to move away from the Big Lie. They are free from the Big Lie's hold. The lie, in Harry's case, is the guarantee of constant protection at Hogwarts. He knows that isn't the case anymore. He realizes he needs to go after Voldemort instead of sitting back behind Dumbledore's protection. The character turns, both literally and figuratively, and attacks to end it all.

CLIMAX AND RESOLUTION

In *The Wizard of Oz*, Dorothy and her friends have been captured by the flying monkeys and stand before the Wicked Witch. In *The Avengers*, the heroes face imminent destruction from a nuclear bomb. The tension rises, but they overcome the odds and defeat the villain. Here is when we transition to our Climax, where our character discovers their truth.

All the movies mentioned in the previous paragraphs involved conscious decisions by the protagonist to take action. Dorothy tried to help her friend. Iron Man made a sacrifice. Harry decides to go after the killer of his parents. It is imperative to observe these moments and the corresponding details. These moments should refer to the fatal flaw and great fears identified when you created your characters. Dorothy feared to be alone. Iron Man feared he would bring about the destruction of his team and the world.

What type of ending are we going to present? Positive endings are the classic. The character gets what he wants or needs and achieves his objective. The lead defeats the villain. Perhaps, the lead fails and doesn't achieve their aim and we have a negative ending. Both are excellent options if we answer the questions asked in the story. The reader can live with either option if the obligations you have set in front of the hero were fulfilled. The one we want to avoid is the ambiguous ending where the story ends somewhere in the middle. The reader feels unfulfilled, and their time is wasted.

Many endings require one additional facet, sacrifice. The lead sacrifices something in pursuing victory. Moral sacrifice means giving up their objective for a greater goal. You present this in the form of a moral dilemma. We must make sure the result is due to their choice. It gives the lead a moment of truth to prove their worth. With Iron Man, he was willing to sacrifice his life to destroy the aliens and save New York City from the nuclear explosion.

This climactic battle needs one more thing. We must see the true difference between our hero and the villain. Push the hero to their limit, toward the boundary they have sworn to never cross. Harry Potter defeats Voldemort, but his spell doesn't kill his enemy. The evil one's own spell backfires on him and does the deed. Harry could have done it, but he holds true to his beliefs and proves the Big Truth.

Authors use the denouement to wrap up loose ends and establish the new status quo. This last element of the story provides a great opportunity to allow the action to fall slowly instead of an abrupt ending. The awards ceremony at the end of Star Wars is a perfect example of this type of moment. It also allows the writer to pull these unresolved threads together for a satisfying ending. Or to capitalize on this opportunity to set up any potential sequels.

CHARACTER ARCS

In *Argent's Menagerie*, the story involves the efforts of Argent and the rest of the crew stopping Grishon from achieving his goal. Below the surface, a disconnected internal plot pertaining to Argent's lack of trust in his brother exists. Most successful stories weave the internal and the external plots together so that resolving the external plot requires the main character to resolve their internal struggles.

This internal plot line is often referred to as the character arc. Every substantial character should have an internal arc within your story, often inviting the use of sub-plots. For example, in *Argent's Menagerie*, there were ten significant characters within that ensemble book, with a character arc for each of them. Arcs differed in size, but each character evolved from start to finish. The Character Arc revolves around the story's theme, Big Lie, and Big Truth.

Most of the grand stories provide multiple conflicts for the main character. In *The Wizard of Oz*, the external conflict has Dorothy trying to get home from Oz. The internal conflict involves her being close to her family. The character arc relies on genuine growth, a change we as readers desire. Our characters' goals require them to evolve beyond their previous state. If it doesn't happen, why bother pursuing it? A simple tool to track these various arcs is the Character Arc Table, which identifies the desire of the main character, the obstacle to achieving it, and the resolution in a grid.

DESIRE	OBSTACLE	RESOLUTION
External	**External**	**External**
Find the wizard to return home.	Wicked Witch and the flying monkeys	Finds the wizard but finds out he can't help. Glenda tells her to click her heels to get home.
Internal	**Internal**	**Internal**
She longs for a place to call home.	Dorothy, an orphan, feels out of place.	Realizes she has a home after she wakes from the dream.

Character arcs are just like many of the external arcs we discussed earlier. The arc's success depends on specific elements, similar to the mentioned plot beats, with the six principal components aligning with many of the previously mentioned external plot beats.

The characteristic moment provides a sense of the character's motivations and desires early in the story. This is followed by a triggering incident that then leads to clearing a doorway for the protagonist. Who, in turn and often reluctantly, agrees to undertake the journey. Incidents occur to prompt them to agree to a course of action, which often meets a major blow at the Midpoint. The experience changes lives, guiding them through the rest of the story. The character undergoes a profound change after a disturbing event and experiences an epiphany. At this point, the character faces the decisive moment of truth. That is the character arc in one paragraph.

The Character Arc has two essential components that require further explanation: "the knot" and the moment of truth. "The knot" is a term for the complex obstacle that prevents your character from resolving their emotional issues. For your character to experience the growth necessary to have a character change, they will have to unravel this knot. It might require multiple sessions at a therapist, a visit to their estranged mother, or running a marathon. A great example from Dan Wells' novel *I am Not a Serial Killer* involves John Cleaver trying to overcome his abnormal obsession with serial killers and trying to be a "normal" member of society. He struggles with this when he taps into those obsessive emotions and thoughts to defeat a monster, but he wants to keep those compulsions in check to function in his daily life.

The moment of truth is where the protagonist makes their fateful decision. The writer brings them to the brink, and they decide how to proceed. Obviously, in most movies and books, this moment is when they defeat the enemy. It's the perfect time for a game-changing plot twist. Frodo Baggins' choice to keep the Ring of Power instead of destroying it was unexpected, but the writer foreshadowed this eventuality with his previous actions and statements. Throughout, indications pointed towards this being a sensible resolution. Fortunately, Gollum intervened and fell into the lava and the world was saved. The writer's task is to reveal the characters' true nature and demonstrate the power of such decisions. Below are three pieces of advice to handle the story's ending.

- The writer must create compelling options for both choices. Not every story must have a happy ending or the one you originally planned. Perhaps write out several options and the results. You may discover a better idea for a conclusion. It took Hemingway nearly 40 attempts to finish *A Farewell to Arms*.
- Make the options viable by showing the negative aspects of the character as well. Show, along the way, glimpses of both sides of the coin. Frodo's temptations to wear the ring were indicated by his weakening state as the journey progressed.
- Include the cost and the consequences. Show the character deciding and understanding the impact of the decision and the aftermath. This displays character depth beyond impulsive actions due to uncertainty.

The reader can accept the character's decision, even if negative, if the author shows the deciding steps. Perhaps the negative option makes an even greater impact. After carrying the Ring of Power through those trials, could we pass up the lure to carry it forward? Perhaps not. Maybe Frodo chose as we would.

Character arcs are the development of a character and documenting their change as they encounter obstacles to their objective. They relate to the plot and showcase how the character impacts the overall story. Through trials and tribulations, the character emerges transformed, altered in an emotional or physical manner from their previous self. There are four possible character responses in a story arc.

Status quo – This type of character sees no real growth over the length of the story. Perhaps iconic characters like James Bond or Superman do not change. In long stretches of time, they stay the same while their world and enemies shift.

Progressive motivations – This type of character embodies virtues the author wishes to explore but their motivations change because the world around them is changing. They must decide how to respond based on this change in their life. As an example, a company shutting down a plant requires your character to seek new employment. These new obstacles complicate their life.

New outlook on life – This type of change is where the character changes even if the motivation remains the same. There must be an emotional response by your character. This type of change needs to be demonstrated through action and must remain intact after resolving the story. Think of someone overcoming an addiction and is sober by the conclusion. Their objective of sobriety remains the same, but they have changed.

Life and motivations change - A character without stability in the story changes to stay alive or preserve oneself. Again, these changes require dramatization. They are complex characters that create an amazing story.

SUBPLOTS

You've dined out, perhaps at a steakhouse. You get your bread and your salad. Then your dinner arrives. You get the main course, but there is nothing else on the plate. No asparagus and no potatoes. You enjoy the steak but believe something is missing for a complete meal. That is what a subplot is. An accompanying path in the story that supplements, complements, and augments the main storyline to become a fuller story. Subplots have only two rules. They must have a full arc and they must play second fiddle to the main storyline. Beyond that, it becomes a free-for-all.

Joseph Bates does a great job of explaining subplots in this paragraph from his book *Writing Your Novel from Start to Finish*.

"Subplots are another way of structuring and unifying your novel. These occur in the novel intermittently and with a cumulative effect... Subplots are raised in some early part of the book, forgotten about as we turn our attention back to the main plot, and then

reintroduced at intervals throughout, but each time the subplot comes back in, our understanding of it, and thus our understanding of the main plot and characters, grows in a way. If the plot of a novel moves in a straight line, then we might think of the movement of subplots as being circular, hitting a certain spot in the main plot and then disappearing from the linear plot, only to circle back around at some later time."

The story of Peeta in *The Hunger Games* by Suzanne Collins is an excellent example of a subplot. We know Katniss is the main character and her story dominates the book. But what if she hadn't formed the alliance with Peeta and the author withheld other facets of his story? The story would have lacked depth for the sequels.

In an earlier chapter, we discussed the various genres and story types. You are probably asking if there are subplot archetypes. We should talk about the key variations of the sub-plot in fiction and film.

- Parallel – This can be called the mirror plot as well. The story has two simultaneous plots, one for the main character and the other for a supporting character. At some point, usually the climax, the plots come together and dovetail into one final resolution. The plot of Aragorn in *The Lord of the Rings* is a prime example. His pursuit of the throne of Gondor does not tie to Frodo taking the One Ring to Mordor, but Aragon's path links to Frodo's success.
- Contrast – This is a subplot where a supporting character walks along a similar path to the main character, but at the critical juncture, they decide to make a different decision from the main character, and it creates additional conflict that impacts the main plot.
- Complicating – This is a similar subplot to the contrast, but the details of the subplot do not follow those of the main plot. The subplot's purpose is to conflict with the main character's storyline.
- Romantic – This is a subplot that involves the main character and a supporting character. A romantic attraction is present. Perhaps it isn't returned. This creates tension in the path of the main character.

As a writer you may ask, "Why would I use a subplot?" A subplot is a tool, like others discussed in this book. It might be the greatest multi-tool in your kit and does just about anything your story requires. Here are some of the primary uses.

- A subplot may showcase the setting. In *The Lord of the Rings*, Tolkien created a massive world. He wished to display it, but recognized an excess of information was inappropriate. He created multiple subplots to take the characters throughout his world and showcase it.
- A subplot adds depth to the story. Many novels would become novellas if they did not contain subplots. It adds more interest to the story and helps keep the reader invested.
- Subplots are a great way to communicate themes within the story. In *To Kill a Mockingbird*, Boo Radley embodies the city's desire to hide its unwanted past. Boo's subplot takes center stage as he saves Scout and Jem's lives.
- Subplots develop characterization of supporting characters. They ensure the development in your story extends beyond just your lead character.
- Subplots help push the plot forward. Subplots provide information to the readers, develop mood, and intensify conflict that brings the plot to full resolution.

A subplot is not an unconnected detour. Incorporating subplots into the dominant story uses many techniques. Using each depends on the goal of the subplot and how it impacts the main plot.

- In and Out – This is where the subplot surfaces multiple times throughout the story, either as a separate chapter or scene. These may feature a different POV character to communicate the activity to the reader. Some refer to this as braiding or weaving.
- Bookends – This is where the subplot surfaces early in the story and simmers in the background. At the story's end, the subplot resurfaces to enhance the conclusion.
- The Chunk – This is where the writer takes the reader out of the dominant story and tells an inset story. *The Adventures of Huckleberry Finn* is a great example of this. Mark Twain removed us from the dominant story to help Huck learn something that he then takes back with him to the main story.

The plotlines within *The Hunger Games* demonstrate how to add depth to the story beyond the main thread and illustrate the point of the Bates excerpt from earlier in the chapter. In some ways, the subplots are critical to the main story. Subplots enrich the story and create a more immersive read for the audience you are trying to reach. Many writers worry about sub-plots, but you need to follow basic principles. They should always reinforce the main plot and return the reader back to the main plot with some additional piece that helps complete the puzzle of the overarching story.

COMPLEX STORIES

You have plotted your story and you look at it and smile, but something inside you asks, "Is it enough?" You can do more. You sense there's more to the story and you develop a desire to enrich it, adding complexity. Most novel-length stories pack more in their story than one plot with one character. How can we increase the complexity of the story?

LONG NOVELS

What if your story is so large you don't think the normal plotting techniques we discussed apply? One possible approach is to analyze the story and break it down into smaller segments with a central plot in each, as seen in *The Forsaken Protector*. The larger story was broken it into four complete sections with natural breaks as the division points created multiple novella length sub-stories.

PARALLEL PLOTS

This type of story provides two stories within one that eventually merge into a single plot. The key lies in understanding how the ending works to merge the two stories. Up to that point, it comes across as if you are writing two stories. To focus the writing, consider writing one side of the story for an extended period rather than switching back and forth. Once you have both stories complete, decide how you want to braid the two stories together to create the ending you desire.

DIFFERENT STRUCTURE AND STYLE

The non-linear story is one that is told out of chronological order. A recent example of this was the movie *Arrival*. The story unfolds through the lead character's jumbled memories of alien encounters on our planet. This technique makes it easy to have a convincing plot twist at the end.

Epistolary novels are stories told in the form of letters, journals, or log entries. Bram Stoker's *Dracula* is the classic example often cited. A recent success was Andy Weir's *The Martian*. The author relays the story through various letters (and multiple POVs) and gives the reader access to the inner most thoughts of the characters.

Use multiple POVs to drive the story and present a unique view for the reader. The Jet Li movie *Hero* details an uprising against the Chinese Emperor through four different viewpoint characters. This creates the opportunity to use techniques such as the unreliable narrator and shows how distinct characters see things different.

PLOT PROBLEMS

The hardest thing for a writer to diagnose are plot problems. Perhaps the writer knows something is wrong, but they lack the knowledge on how to address the problem. What are the most common plot problems and how do you fix them? One the following page is a basic list of these problems and the potential resolutions for each.

PROBLEM	SOLUTION
Flat Scenes	Find the focal point of the scene and evaluate if the rest of the scene components help meet the objective. If not scrap them.
Side Quests	Ensure the quest aligns with the main plot/aim of the story.
Character Growth	Does the character growth create a problem with the resolution in the story? Determine if the character growth is believable. If not, rewrite the scenes necessary. If so, change the outcome to accommodate the growth.
Story Slog	Are you putting in too much exposition? Try switching to more dialogue. Move ahead to the next scene where something occurs
Low tension	Examine the hero's trials and determine if the scenes should end negatively.
Illogical Flow	Check the scene tracker for a cause-effect relationship between each scene.
Lack of Cohesion	Assess scene continuity to identify effective transitions and temporal gaps in the story.
Convenient Events	Examine the elements and assess any foreshadowing.
Lack of Character Change	Examine character scenes for necessary plot revisions.
Anticlimactic	Look to potential unfulfilled promises and the tension built through the story. Begin fulfilling promises and ramping tension.
Believability	Examine character motivations and assess for incongruent actions.
Overwriting/Info Dump	Remove excessive exposition from the scenes. Use dialogue to convey information to the reader.
Theme Overrides Plot	Rachet down the scenes and elements of theme. Keep references to make theme apparent in the background.
Inconsistency	Maintain consistency in tense, tone, mood, and setting within scenes.

EXERCISES

1. Write a summary of the main plot of your favorite story.
2. Identify the character arc of your favorite story and identify how the writer tied the external and internal plots together.
3. Identify a sub-plot of your favorite story and identify how the writer ties that to the external plot of the story.

REFERENCE MATERIALS

Plot & Structure by James Scott Bell
Story Engineering by Larry Brooks
Beginnings, Middles and Ends by Nancy Kress
Techniques of the Selling Writer, Chapter 6 by Dwight Swain
Brandon Sanderson YouTube lectures

All these resources would be advisable for an inexperienced writer to read/watch. There is a bounty of information that you will want to hold on to as you develop your writing from beginner to whatever level you wish to achieve. Bell's book gives you a top level of information. Brooks dives into it just a little further. Kress covers how to build a story and sustain it through each section. Swain's chapter achieves the same, but with fewer pages. Then Sanderson's lectures show you how a master uses the knowledge in the world of writing today.

10 – DRAMATIC STRUCTURE

Structure is a dangerous word in writing circles. Everyone has their own mindset about it. Some hate it, some love it, most just carry on and fret about it later. It's like declaring yourself a Democrat or Republican. Before delving further into the topic, an introduction to dramatic structure would be beneficial.

Dramatic structure is essential for every work of fiction, drama, or film. The structure's ultimate purpose is to tell the story in a sequence that best communicates information to the reader, while evoking an emotional impact. Structure is often displayed as a singular, linear, and uninterrupted storyline. This chronological method is one type of structure. Many significant stories present other methods of structuring the story. Listed below are methods to structure your story, including an example of each.

- Number of viewpoints (could produce parallel plots) - *Elantris*
- Time sequencing (could setup flashbacks, flashforwards, time differential, time countdowns) - *Arrival*
- Format (epistolary, nesting stories, or stories the rely on dreams/visions) - *Dracula*
- Mode of storytelling (mix of textual and sensory elements) – 4D Adventure rides
- Linked storytelling (stories around a similar theme or topic that gets us to a comprehensive ending) – *Hero*
- Stories driven by setting (travelogues) – *The Lord of the Rings*

Why do we gravitate to specific sequences? Primarily, it's how stories have been relayed for centuries and we like the familiar. It's a habit.

Good story sequencing works when we feel the ebbs and flows of the story. The right sequence lets readers absorb the story at their pace. Or it can grip them and hold them as they devour the entire story. Developing the proper sequence helps the storyteller with pacing and keeping tension at the necessary level to keep the audience's interest.

Another reason is certain accepted story sequences have become industry standards. Odd sequences create confusion in the publishing world and with the audience. Poor sequencing often comes about because of problems in the story. Having a standardized sequence helps identify problems with your story and how to fix them.

Lately, tools like outlines and beat sheets are receiving more attention. These tools help us plan our story and provide a direction to begin writing. They provide comfort and guidance to unsure beginner writers. Their assistance guides a writer's progress amidst uncertainty. Referring to these familiar structures helps identify what the writer has forgotten or not done in the story. They form a frame of reference to understand other stories and pull lessons from them to help us in our own writing.

EARLY STRUCTURE MODELS

Aristotle's *Poetics*, one of history's most famous works indicates that tragic events should either happen by chance or through inevitability, with a causal link from start to finish. A complication precedes the knot, the problem at the center of the story which the character creates through their flaws and circumstances. Then, once the character encounters the problem, they unravel the knot to create a resolution. The resolution includes a revelation or a reversal of some sort. In tragic dramas, the character flaw leads to the complication and death, or something worse, to the main character.

This simplified explanation of the dramatic structure is the basis of the analysis by German playwright Gustav Freytag in the 1800s. Freytag believed drama could be divided into five acts in a conflict of man against man, protagonist vs. antagonist. Freytag portrayed these five parts in a pyramid design to demonstrate the dramatic arc.

Western writers have used this basic structure for centuries to pattern their stories. The graphical pattern displays a gradual increase in tension throughout the storyline. Numerous stories follow the same structure, with slight adjustments based on objectives.

- Exposition – The setting and mood are established, and introduces characters. Everything is conveyed through the narrative, alluding to backstory.
- Rising action – The inciting incident after the exposition begins the process of rising action that occurs through several stages. This makes up most of the story.
- Climax – The turning point of the story. From here on, the protagonist's fortunes will cause a traumatic resolution. Keep in mind Freytag is focusing on tragedy.
- Falling action – The antagonist beats the protagonist emotionally, and this leads to the resolution as the author puts the lead in the worst position possible.
- Resolution/Catastrophe – This outcome depends on your intent for the work. This is the story's endpoint, the resolution. The result may be followed by a brief reflection (the denouement).

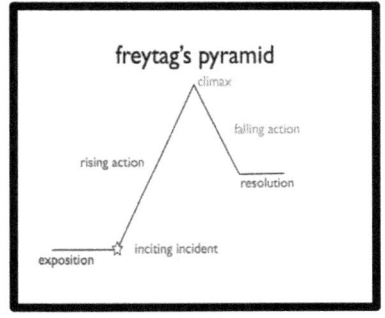

Figure 10-1 - Freytag's Pyramid

Freytag's structure isn't the only one available. Middle eastern culture stories often fall into a parable or fable format. Epic tales of Mediterranean countries often have a pull and hook style with an overarching theme that ties the entire set of tales together. Eastern European countries have Coming-of-Age tales that are very linear in their story development and use a structure called Bildungsroman.

In Eastern storytelling, Kishōtenketsu is a structure used in Chinese, Japanese, and Korean cultures. The Kishōtenketsu structure has four key components. However, conflict does not drive the story. The story presents a problem and resolves it through an unexpected twist to a conclusion. Eastern stories focus on using teamwork and community to resolve the problems presented. These problems center around community benefit, justice, or equality as opposed to the good versus evil conflict seen in most Western storytelling.

Kishōtenketsu's structure affected Western storytelling as people attempted to adapt successful storytelling strategies from other regions. *Inception* and *Arrival* are two movies that follow non-linear storytelling paths. Anime, manga, and Studio Ghibli have played a vital role in recent years.

These examples barely scrape the surface of the unique structures that exist in fiction. In the upcoming paragraphs, we'll delve into further structure tools. This discussion will leverage the Vibrant Prose Beat Sheets presented in the Toolbox to facilitate some of the conversation.

HOLLYWOOD THREE-ACT STRUCTURE

The most popular methodology in plotting finds its basis in the Hollywood Three-Act Structure, with a defined beginning, middle, and end. This method gets its name from the three-act structure of stories in film and television.

Some users split the middle act into two or three components to generate a four-act or five-act structure, but these are just variations of the classic Three-Act methodology. All Three-Act stories have the same building blocks: objectives, obstacles, conflict, and resolution.

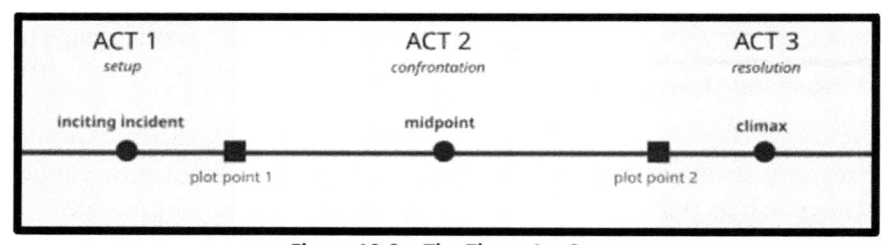

Figure 10-2 – The Three-Act Structure

The three-act structure uses a standard series of plot points. The story's first point is the inciting incident. This begins the action and is what drives the lead character toward the decision to act. The first act concludes with a doorway. This doorway opens when the lead moves forward toward the objective, even begrudgingly.

In the second act, obstacles are placed in front of the lead to create conflicts and raise tension. It can either be a continual increase or a jagged action with continued highs and small lows that relieve the pressure. The problem is solved through a series of events or cycles. The story reaches a midpoint where the stakes rise, and the lead goes beyond the "point of no return."

Act three starts with the story's climax or shows the lead up to the event. After the climax, we reach the resolution and a potential denouement that reveals the characters' future direction after resolving the story's conflict. Act three, usually the briefest, may only be a small portion of the story.

The simplicity of the three-act structure makes it an attractive option for someone desiring to build in a baseline plot structure. "Pantsers" may find this tool useful for screenplay writing or other projects.

MODIFIED SEVEN POINT STRUCTURES

As we approach more complex methodologies, it should be noted the only thing occurring is identifying more plot points, or scenes, to build into our structure before writing. In moving from the Three-Act Structure to the next level, we look at a structure popularized by author Dan Wells, known as the seven-point structure. There appear to be various versions of this stool, along with a close approximation by Larry Brooks in his book titled *Story Engineering*. Dave Trottier and John Truby both seem attached to other versions available online. These all have similar plot points but rely on a central group of ten.

The key to developing this structure is the order of the plot points. This method begins with the resolution of your story. You determine what you want your resolution to look like before tackling the beginning plot points. Once you define the resolution, you develop the beginning, the hook. The hook positions the character opposite to their story's end. This will create a mirroring effect for the story. Below are the various elements.

1. **The Backstory** is part of Trottier's method and encapsulates the events that take place prior to the story beginning. Knowing this information beforehand helps you plot out your story. Refer to the exercises around backstory and GMC development for more information in the Vibrant Prose presentation files.
2. **The Hook** should captivate the reader, forming a bond with the protagonist and the impending conflict. The Hook must present the main character in the opposite place from their story's end. To use Luke Skywalker as the example, he is a farm boy that wishes to be a space pilot like his father. We need to show that yearning within him and make him sympathetic enough that the reader will latch onto him.
3. **The Catalyst** or **Inciting Incident** will come soon after. This is the point that turns the story arc, and we progress down the plot path. In *The Wizard of Oz*, it is when the twister starts. In this case we jump to the Big Event with Dorothy being transported to Oz. In *Star Wars,* the incident is when the secret message appears

from R2-D2. Until then, Luke's life remained unchanged. This incident awakens him to something beyond his current situation.
4. **The Big Event** marks the start of the middle part of your story. This plot point serves two purposes: it compels the protagonist to decide and introduces the antagonist, if not already introduced. Many times, the lead is reluctant to move forward. In *Star Wars,* this is when Luke's aunt and uncle are killed. He goes forward with Ben because he has nothing left on Tatooine. He is still reacting and reluctant. We also see that the Empire is the enemy in this movie. In *The Wizard of Oz*, Dorothy lands in Oz. Despite her reluctance, Glenda leaves her no choice but to proceed. She also meets the Wicked Witch of the West who makes her intentions very clear.
5. **The Midpoint** is the spot in the story where the character turns from a reactionary mode to forcing the action. In *Star Wars*, this is when Luke decides they are going to save Princess Leia. Before this point, he has been a passive participant. Now Luke shows his heroic chops. The Midpoint, a change in the character's mental attitude, can occur over multiple scenes.
6. **The Crisis** point is transitioning from the middle to the end of your story. It is the lowest the character can fall. Their hopes are almost all dashed. In *Star Wars*, Luke's mentor has died. Many stories use a sequence of scenes involving the Dark Night of the Soul, wallowing and reflection, and the decision to launch into the third act.
7. **The Climax** determines the story's resolution, regardless of its outcome. For Luke, the Death Star targets the planet of Yavin, several TIE fighters are destroyed, and Darth Vader pursues him just before Han Solo arrives and gives him the time to trust the force and fire his weapons. For Dorothy, she throws a bucket of water to put out a fire on Scarecrow and it gets the witch wet, and she melts.
8. **The Resolution** is the end of the story and the character achieves their goal. Luke blows up the Death Star. Dorothy finds her way home. We all depart and disappear into the sunset. This leads to the denouement, the ultimate image.

Beyond these points, two **Pinch Points** in the second act emphasize the antagonist's power, intensify the pressure on the protagonist, and set up the Crisis sequence. The Midpoint splits these two points.

The seven-point structure establishes how the character evolves by using specific plot points that also line up with the key events of the character arc. This methodology has found favor because it seems to hit the sweet spot of acceptance for people who are not pure plotters while also allowing for the creativity craved by discovery writers who envisioned key scenes in their early story development.

OTHER LINEAR PLOTTING TOOLS

These two popular structure tools, the 3-Act and 7-Point, are part of a group of linear structuring tools. These tools identify the key story beats in a fashion that runs in a direct path from start to finish. There are several tools in this category that identify a varied amount of key story points. Below are other tools with a similar concept.

SAVE THE CAT!

Based on the screenwriting advice of Blake Snyder, but adapted to novels by Jessica Brody. This tool adapts the process of screenwriting to novel writing for general fiction and for young adult titles. This 15-beat system prioritizes the story's opening and closing acts, as well as giving some attention to the Midpoint. Its weakness lies in ignoring half of the novel's content. It has achieved popularity due to its universal use across multiple genres and the simplicity to implement.

STRUCTURING YOUR NOVEL

K. M. Weiland's system identifies roughly 20 points in her book. Much of what Weiland calls out is similar to the *Save the Cat!* methodology but adds extra depth in the second act with Pinch Points, focus on reactionary beats, and the Dark Night of the Soul. Weiland's approach aligns with the theoretical approach of Robert McKee and draws a great deal from his writings and those of John Truby. Between the three of them, they form an excellent nucleus of understanding the theory of storytelling.

THE STORY SOLUTION

Eric Edson proposes a 23-point system in his book *The Story Solution*. Edson's approach is oriented towards screenwriting, but the principles work for novel writing just as well. Developing 23 crucial plot sequences through the protagonist's actions and viewpoint is the core of this approach. It guides character development and sub-plot placement, with an emphasis on the hero. This makes an excellent guide on how to outline the main plot of your story from start to finish, including a great deal of detail in the middle section of the story. This could be a good starting point for incorporating character arcs, sub-plots, and genre-specific elements.

27 CHAPTER SYSTEM

This system created by Kat O'Keefe splits your story into three equal chunks, unlike the other systems. The concept relies on splitting your story into manageable thirds, while diving into smaller sections for setup, conflict, and resolution, repeated in each three-block set. The technique develops a high-level goal/summary for each of the 27 chapters. Each chapter could be composed of multiple scenes. This rigid approach lacks flexibility for adding story elements like sub-plots or genre elements.

MONOMYTH – THE HERO'S JOURNEY

Apart from linear structure tools, there is a smaller category with just a few examples analyzed in the paragraphs ahead. A group of these tools visually present the story in a circular, or cyclical fashion. The most popular of these tools is the Monomyth, also often called The Hero's Journey.

The Monomyth structure is a classic approach to long-form story telling. This storytelling method achieved recent popularity due to usage by Joseph Campbell and his terming it "The Hero's Journey" in his writings. Campbell's method received notable attention in the 1970s and 1980s as the basis for the story of Luke Skywalker in *Star Wars: A New Hope*.

Some ancient epic poems, like *The Odyssey*, have cyclical story structures within them where the story seems to repeat, but with varied challenges, and contains an episodic feeling. These stories revolve around a thematic through line.

Since the release of *Star Wars*, many writers attempt a similar structure in their stories. The actual number of plot beats involved in the story pattern varies from 8 to 21 depending on the user and the length of the story. Campbell's version featured seventeen key points and is the version reviewed below. The first thing to understand about Campbell's method is it starts with three main acts: departure, initiation, and return. It follows the Three-Act Structure in some respects, but at a much lower level of detail.

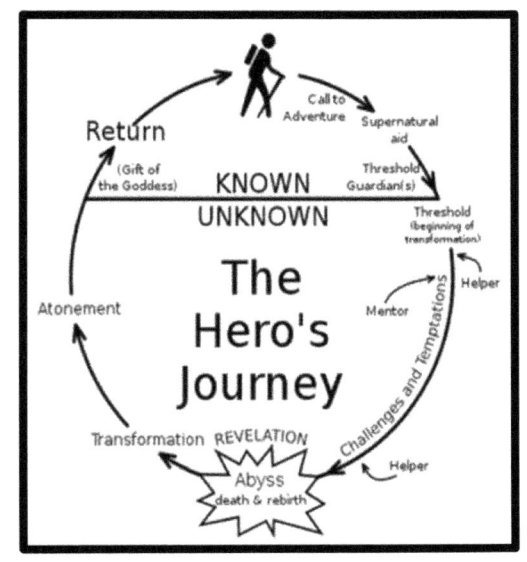

Figure 10-3 The Monomyth

The first stage of the story, departure, involves five steps.

1. Call to Adventure – In *Star Wars*, this is the point where Luke is presented with the chance to go with Obi-Wan Kenobi.
2. Refusal of the Call – Luke turns down the invitation.
3. Meeting the Mentor – This is where Luke accepts Obi-Wan's invitation after the Empire kills his uncle and aunt.
4. Crossing the Threshold – Luke and Obi-Wan enter Mos Eisley spaceport.
5. Belly of the Whale – Luke and Obi-Wan board the Millenium Falcon.

We then begin the initiation stage, which spans over both halves of the second act.

6. Road of Trials – Luke tries to master using the force and experiences the destruction of Alderaan.
7. Meeting with the Goddess – Luke, Han, Chewbacca attempt to save Leia.
8. The Temptress – Luke and Leia seem at odds.

9. Atonement – Luke witnesses the death of Obi-Wan at the hands of Vader.
10. Apotheosis – Luke is told by Obi-Wan's ghost to use the force.
11. Ultimate Boon – The Millenium Falcon escapes but is really a trap to lead the Death Star to the Rebel base.

Then we finish with the return stage and the last act of the story.

12. Refusal of the Return – Luke is disheartened by the death of Obi-Wan.
13. Magic Flight – Luke takes his first flight as a pilot of an X-Wing fighter.
14. Rescue from Without – The Millenium Falcon returns to save Luke from Vader.
15. The Return Threshold – Luke is advised by Obi-Wan to listen to the Force.
16. Master of Two Worlds – Luke turns off the targeting computer in his fighter and relies on the Force to hit his target.
17. Freedom to Live – Luke destroys the Death Star and goes forward as a Jedi trainee and part of the Rebellion.

The key factors to the Hero's Journey involve Luke moving from the normal world to a strange new world of adventure. Then, he transitions to the Death Star, a representation of the dark world. Occasionally, this piece is removed, and the adventure world undergoes changes. In ancient stories, this step included an actual trip to Hades and a return from the underworld. In *Star Wars* it takes the form of a metaphorical journey, the apotheosis, as Luke learns the ways of the force. The Monomyth is a complex and classic story structure dating back to the mythological tales of the Greeks, but it allows freedom to apply the various steps for modern storytelling.

A derivation on the Monomyth is known as the Plot Circle. Dan Harmon has popularized the methodology. Harmon has stripped down the larger Monomyth structure to eight key elements for the purpose of television storytelling. The eight steps are listed below using Charles Dickens's *Great Expectations* to exemplify the steps.

1. Zone of Comfort: Pip, a young orphan, lives a modest life on the moors.
2. But they want something: He becomes obsessed with Estella, a wealthy girl of his age.
3. They enter an unfamiliar situation: A mysterious benefactor plucks Pip from obscurity and throws him into London society.
4. Adapt to it: He learns to live the high life and spends his money frivolously.
5. Get what they wanted: Pip is finally a gentleman, which he believes will entitle him/make him worthy of Estella.
6. Pay a heavy price for it: Pip discovers that his money came from a convict, he drowns in debt, he regrets alienating his uncle, and he realizes that his pursuit of Estella is futile.
7. Then return to their familiar situation: Pip makes peace with his Uncle Joe. Pip disappears to Egypt for years, and once again returns home.
8. Changed: Back once again where the story started, a now-humbled Pip reunites with Estella, who is ready to open her heart to him.

This tool is very similar to the Story Embryo, with one major difference. The Story Embryo pertains to tragic stories that end after plot point 6 due to the sacrifice of the character.

Advanced methods exist for almost every aspect of writing. That includes story structure and plotting. One of the most difficult and effective techniques involves Chiastic storytelling. This technique was used in classical literature from the Greeks to the Holy Bible.

Chiastic structuring is a complex technique that uses mirroring to ensure that plot points on opposite ends of the story have a resonating sameness to them. Opposite plot points connect through characters, imagery, or other features. For instance, the Inciting Incident and the Climax may occur in the same physical location. This technique elevates your writing to a higher level. See the example provided from the Holy Bible using the book of Revelation.

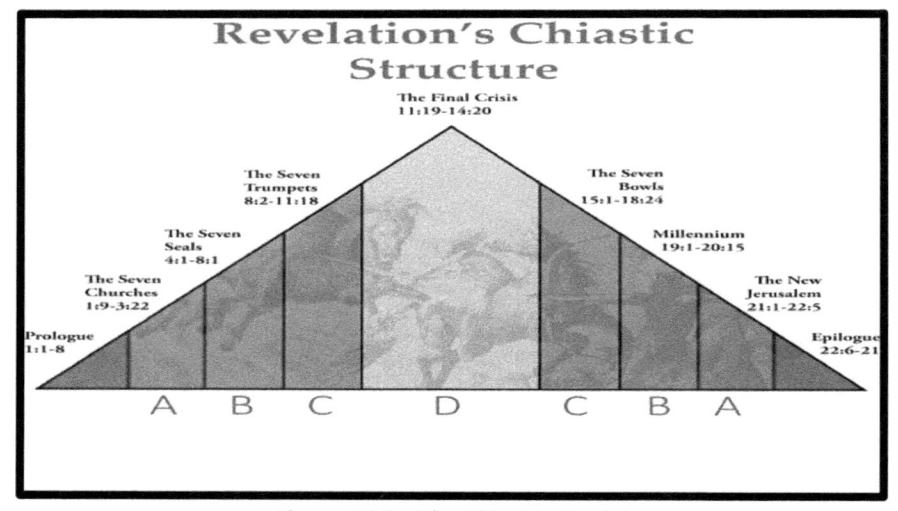

Figure 10-3 - The Chiastic Model

OUTLINING METHODOLOGIES

It is possible to outline at an even lower level beyond the Monomyth structure. This may include beat by beat (points of action) elements of each scene and key pieces of dialogue. At some point, outlining the story will be beneficial even to the discovery writer. Starting at the beginning lets the writer see the story's flow beforehand. It provides comfort that the story works and may lead to fewer rewrites and less time editing.

Many discovery writers feel outlines hinder creative exploration and lead to overthinking. Mindset is a major factor in this. The writer can always push the outline to the side if it feels constraining and begin writing the scenes they need to incorporate into their story on instinct. Also, the writer can make the outline as detailed as they wish.

Developing an outline at the end of the writing process is referred to as reverse outlining. The reverse outline tool is a compromise for plotters and pantsers. The reverse outline works best by focusing on major plot points in your outline. Then, delve deeper into those points to identify any issues, such as plot gaps. Writers like Brandon Sanderson and Dan Wells praise this technique for reviewing their work after the first pass.

Outlining is just one form of breaking down your story into manageable components. Many resources, methods, and tools may be utilized. The following is a list of other ways to apply structure to your writing process.

- Index Card System – Write out key components of scenes and track them on index cards.
- Headlights System – Write out a scene or sequence goal and write to fulfill that point. Then do the next scene or sequence.
- Narrative Outline – Write out a blurb for each chapter that contains the key components of that scene or sequence.
- Project Notebook – Keep notes about your plot, characters, research, ideas, and questions as a reference.

You can use these same tools to develop outlines or plot the events for an entire series. The key is determining the right approach based on the type of series you write. Series often fall into one of three different categories.

- Episodic – The protagonist keeps fighting a new danger in every book. For the episodic series, the character will change very little from book to book. They mostly will engage in flat character. *The Dresden Files*, comic books, or *Doctor Who* are examples.
- Component – The story builds to an ultimate end, and each book is a story within the larger story. The Harry Potter Series is an excellent version, as each book serves as a key plot point in the overall story.
- Continuous – Each book is just a portion of the larger story but separated for publishing purposes. *The Lord of the Rings* is a primary example of this series type.

The primary benefit of plotting out the series to some degree, and even a standalone title, is knowing what elements you need to lay the breadcrumbs to foreshadow future events. Even if you are a discovery writer, knowing a few details through these methods may help steer your writing toward completing the story.

EXERCISES

1. Detail the three-act structure of your favorite book.
2. Free-write three paragraphs of your story without structure.
3. Outline the first section of your story.
4. Write a 500-word essay discussing how your favorite movie fits into a specific structure.

REFERENCE MATERIALS

Structuring Your Novel & Next Level Plot Structure by K.M. Weiland
Save the Cat! Writes a Novel by Jessica Brody
The Anatomy of Story by John Truby
Story by Robert McKee
The Story Solution by Eric Edson

All these resources would be advisable for an inexperienced writer to read. There is a bounty of information that you will want to hold on to as you develop your writing from beginner to whatever level you wish to achieve.

11 – SCENE CONSTRUCTION

What exactly is a scene? A scene is an isolated component of a larger story to show specific action, character interaction, and emotional development. A scene contains a group of characters, in a particular setting, working to achieve a specific goal that is a component of the overarching story. Scenes vary in length, spanning chapters or just a few sentences. Each scene is a micro-story within the larger novel. A novel is a series of interacting scenes that form a complete story.

Imagine a scene this way. Did anyone own clotheslines growing up? Your main story thread is the clothesline. It has a point where the clothesline starts and where it ends. Your scenes are the pieces of clothing you put on the line to tell your story in some sequential manner between the two points.

If you want to break novel writing down to its simplest terms, there are two components: writing scenes and connecting those scenes. If you know how to write a scene, you can write a story. Does that help you feel a little less overwhelmed? If so, good. If not, read that again. Is this easy? More successful novelists would exist if so. Writing is demanding, but possible for anyone if done scene by scene.

What is the purpose of a scene? The first demand on any scene is to move the story and plot forward. Use the scene to answer previous questions and pose new ones. Beyond this, the scene serves many other purposes. It introduces characters and reveals characterization, increases tension through conflict and the resulting resolution, or conveys information that impacts the story world. You should exclude scenes that cannot fulfill these criteria from your final story.

Each scene relies on the preceding one and prepares for the next. We need to understand that our storyline requires a causality relationship from the events that occurred in prior scenes to what happens in the scene you are writing, which affects all the scenes that follow. Adhering to this causality relationship will build the continuity to keep your reader in the story's flow. Only break the continuity of tension for incredible reveals and story endings.

By doing this, the reader will have enough context to adjust to twists, reveals, and cliffhangers. They will realize you set up heightened moments of tension and take them in stride. If you ignore causality and continuity, quick shifts in the narrative will shock the reader and perhaps throw them from the story; an eventuality you wish to avoid at all costs.

In this chapter, we will dive into the various aspects of scenes, including the following topics:

- The type of scenes you may write over the course of your story.
- The components of successful scenes in a story.
- The method of sequencing scenes to tell the best story.
- The various tools you may use to track elements of your scenes.

SCENE TYPES

Scenes perform various tasks in the storytelling process and specific scenes perform specific functions. The scene's objective determines the type of scene you write. Many of your scenes will have similar objectives, progressing the plot with an additional component like introducing a character or a setting. A few are set aside to deliver key components of your story and require additional emphasis.

The opening scene always carries special weight because that hooks the reader. Is your desire to make this the book's finest scene? Perhaps not, but the scene must be extraordinary. The opening scene has specific duties to perform by introducing the central character, asking the initial question of the character, and establishing the setting. It needs to capture the reader's attention. Offer a glimpse and pose a question for readers. We want them to stay with your story until you answer that question. One thing we wish to avoid is infodumps or overloading the reader with backstory at this point. You want them focused on the story's core.

The resolution scene is different because that scene answers all the remaining questions and wraps up the loose threads. All questions are answered, providing closure to the reader. There may also be a separate denouement scene depending on the story being told.

Genre-driven scenes are another category that comes with certain expectations, conventions, and tropes. You can't market your book as a Romance without the kiss scene or the happily-ever-after. No Mystery is complete without the body's discovery and the reveal. You can't write a heist without a chase scene. You have a contract with the reader when you write a specific genre or story type. To satisfy readers, necessary scenes are required even if tropes and conventions are subverted.

Another classification depends on the narrative mode that dominates the scene. You desire this for pacing and scenes that hit all the right notes. Sometimes you will write scenes dominated by dialogue or action. Scenes dominated by dialogue and action will hold to specific objectives. A splendid example is the reveal scene in a detective mystery. The scenes where Hercule Poirot pulls all the characters together to walk through his explanation of the mystery are dialogue scenes. Dialogue and action scenes are also excellent ways to control the story's pacing. If you need to speed the pace up a bit, quick banter and action scenes create forward momentum.

What cannot be lost is that even in dialogue and action scenes, there will be use of description, exposition, and other narrative modes. The key is balancing the usage so as not to upset the pace of the story or to bore the reader.

Continuity scenes are the scenes that fill the rest of the book. They provide the continuity and plug all the plot holes. They often set the context and move the characters from one plot point to the next. These scenes use rising tension and put your lead through the ringer while pulling the reader through the story with read-on prompts.

FLASHBACKS AND FLASHFORWARDS

Other scenes require some special consideration; these include flashbacks, flashforwards, and interludes. Limit your flashbacks to maintain the story's momentum and avoid distracting readers. These scenes provide backstory, or foreshadowing, in a contextually filled environment so the reader captures the full impact of the events being displayed. Many writers avoid these scenes and convey the same information through integrating backstory, or foreshadowing, into the forward moving narrative. Be careful not to disrupt the reader's immersion in the story.

Why would we use a flashback? The flashback often communicates backstory and prior event information more effectively. There are other benefits to this approach. Several writers use flashbacks to slow down the story or change the mood. This is beneficial at times after a very intense and fast-paced scene to provide the reader a chance to catch their breath. It also provides greater clarity about the emotions and mindset of the character. The flashback evokes a mood that carries into the next scene.

Flashbacks take many forms. The simplest is when sensory cues trigger a memory or emotion from the character's past. These are often referred to as recollections. This is a stylish way to flashback without interrupting the story.

The most familiar usage is the actual flashback scene. This scene sets the context for the memory. In the Harry Potter series, using the pensieve always results in a flashback. When using this flashback technique, create a complete scene and imbue it with the same sensory detail and concrete imagery as your normal scenes.

Frame Stories also achieve this effect by using a narrator to pull the reader out and direct them to a new scene. Frankenstein is a popular example of this style. The narrator tells the story as if they are beyond the events being conveyed. Memories of the story's details serve as the bulk of the narrative, unfolding as a flashback.

Another oft-used technique is the dream sequence. The epic fantasy story, *The Forsaken Protector* used these sequences to reveal a different aspect of the story world, the astral plane. These sequences portrayed characters experiencing various forms of trauma. Dreams are effective tools and are often filled with symbolism from the character's subconscious.

Occasionally, you will see a novel with dual story lines, one in the current time and one in the past. The V. E. Schwab novel titled *The Invisible Life of Addie LaRue* deals with a young French woman who makes a deal with the Devil to live forever, but no one remembers her. The story floats between scenes in the modern day and over history as Addie comes to grips with her situation. In using this approach, anchor the reader into which timeline they are reading for that scene.

Remember, flashbacks provide crucial information to readers. Do not detract from the story or interrupt the forward momentum with flashbacks unless they fill in knowledge gaps within the story and reveal a significant piece of the main character's history.

Flashforwards follow much of the same thinking, with one exception. The flashforward (aka prolepsis) takes the reader to a scene expected to happen in the future. The best example occurred in the movie *Arrival* and centered around Louise Bank; a linguist used to communicate with extra-terrestrials. Louise has premonitions of her unborn daughter due to her connection with the aliens, but the viewer realizes the events are out of order only at the end.

The most common use of flashforwards in media involves someone having visions of events, such as an oracle or psychic. *Star*

Wars is littered with these acts from force users. In *The Lord of the Rings*, Frodo sees a vision when he investigates Galadriel's fountain. Stories that use an oracle-type character center their plot around these visions. They're common, but handle them with care to avoid clichés or convenient plot devices.

An interlude interrupts the story's flow. Interludes are often brief scenes that provide information or introduce characters that will become pertinent to the story later. Brandon Sanderson's various volumes of the *Stormlight Archive* use these to significant effect and provide breaks to the reader through those long novels.

THE COMPONENTS OF SCENES

Each scene has specific components and identifies the components using one of two methodologies, the Scene/Sequel approach popularized by Jack Bickham, or the 5 Commandments of Story approach created by Shawn Coyne. The following paragraphs will walk through those necessary elements.

In Jack Bickham's *Scene & Structure,* the scene begins with an identified goal. In many instances, the implied goal is based on earlier information provided to the reader. When looking at scenes, remember the primary objective of the scene: progress the story forward. Every scene should align with the story's overarching goal, have a scene specific objective, and progress the story to be successful.

The novel needs setup to explain the importance of each scene. The setup for one scene could happen several scenes ahead through foreshadowing or some other technique. Two characters in a novel may face each other early on, leaving the scene knowing that their next meeting will end in a deadly fight. Later in the story, when they meet, you can jump right into the action. The setup is done.

In every scene you write, you must anchor the reader within two facets of the story: the setting and the viewpoint. The setting is where the scene occurs. Re-anchoring the reader is unnecessary if the scene follows a previous one with the same setting and characters. However, if the scene shifts locations, introduce the setting somehow. In *Daughter of the Moon Goddess*, to start many chapters, Sue Lynn Tan provides elaborate descriptions of the setting to immerse the reader. Since she does this early, no extra description is needed unless the location changes.

The other important anchor for the reader is the viewpoint perspective of the scene. If you stick to one viewpoint, telling your story becomes easier and requires less anchoring. If you switch your viewpoint characters, you must let the reader know whose eyes they are now viewing the story through. *Argent's Menagerie* has multiple viewpoint characters. In each scene, the author establishes the viewpoint character through an initial action.

The inciting incident of the scene pulls in the reader, a common approach by both methods identified before. You immerse the reader in the scene, minimizing setup. Achieve this by starting *in media res*. You can add to the scene by describing the location, setting the mood, and giving the scene intensified tension. To give good advice, vary your approach throughout the book. Attempt to alternate the entry into your scenes between action, dialogue, and exposition.

If you defined the goal of the scene, provide an obvious obstacle. This sets the conflict in motion. The obstacle can be anything - people, nature, or other factors. Obstacles exist to create conflict and increase intensity in the scene. Intensity of the scene comes from increasing the tension through conflict. If you want to add more tension, raise the stakes somehow. You can move the character from a dire situation to an even deadlier one.

In *Raiders of the Lost Ark*, Indiana Jones assumed his captors were going to kill him or throw him into the tomb. Instead, they made the situation worse by throwing him into the tomb with his greatest fear: snakes. If you give the character some hope by providing a positive result in the scene, immediately give them another obstacle they must overcome to raise the tension.

When the conflict escalates, the action creates the scene's turning point, as identified by the 5 Commandments. This is where the character no longer pursues their original goal. The prompt could come from the character's real world or newfound knowledge. Perhaps an unforeseen circumstance has hindered their pursuit of the first goal. If that is the case, their motivations and goals must change. If your character wishes to pursue a different goal, the character must acknowledge the change to their motivations.

The three major aspects of the sequel are the reaction, dilemma, and decision. The reaction is critical to the character development path. As they progress through their transformation, the character's mind and emotions reveal the thematic movement from the Big Lie to the Big Truth. Action is important, but the reader's connection to the character is through emotions and thoughts. Those take center stage in the reaction. The writer must ensure these emotions and thoughts appear reasonable based on the previous action. If betrayed by a confidante, we can't have the protagonist brush it aside like their morning newspaper got damp from the dew. They need to be angry, sad, heartbroken, something powerful. Then we need to allow the character adequate room to process these emotions. Don't turn the reaction into a melodramatic mess that takes an entire chapter. Keep the reaction in proportion to the event.

After the reaction comes the dilemma and our character must show some aptitude. The dilemma consists of three pieces: review, analysis, and planning. Without repeating the disaster that befell them in the prior scene, force the character to review the events. This is a great way to use summarization, whether through dialogue or monologue. Analysis of the problem is necessary, followed by a plan to rectify the situation. The sequel is a key component of Deanna Raybourn's *Veronica Speedwell* mysteries. In almost every chapter, there is a quick sequel as a response to the events of the chapter as Veronica and her cohort Stoker stop and repeatedly analyze their case. This type of passage is critical for most traditional mystery novels, as the investigator must reset their bearings.

As a result of the dilemma, your character must decide. In reality, we tend to choose the safe option for our dilemma. In writing, we don't want that. Create a state where the character lacks the simple choice. They must make a tough choice, or one that has little chance of succeeding. Let it be their choice, another noteworthy thing. They must be proactive. Also, the choice should present two equal choices with equal consequences. Perhaps they must choose between a job or romance, but can't select both. After deciding, ensure its clarity and inclusion in the story. Then we need the character to act.

After making the decision, the character must act, which is the climax of the scene. This provides the character agency and makes them proactive. These decisions define your character and show how they are transforming, the character change we desire.

The resolution follows. We see the outcome of the decision building forward momentum to the next scene. This result is a mix of victory and defeat. Withholding victory from the main character through complete obstruction is always a fine way to build frustration within the character and increase the intensity of the story. Partial obstruction works many times as well. The "Hollow Victory" is often a fantastic way to end the scene. Harry Potter emerged victorious in *The Goblet of Fire* tournament, but Cedric's demise and Voldemort's resurrection followed. Ending scenes with a clear victory would break the story's tension.

To finish the scene, give the reader a reason to keep reading, a prompt. The prompts connect the next scene and serve as a lead-in. Avoid ending the scene with the character walking away from the room. Provide a reason to read-on. A cliffhanger will suffice. Some writers go a step further and do a reveal to end the chapter. A knock at the door reveals the character's worst enemy. What happens next? Turn the page to find out. In effect, the prompt provides the setup for the next hook and creates a new cycle.

Howard Taylor, of *Writing Excuses* fame, refers to this same technique as "Late In – Early Out." He avoids the setup and puts the reader into the middle of the action. Then, before anything happens from the prompt, he leaves the scene.

Consider using cinematic viewpoint when leaving the scene. If the scene's ending is reflective and provides some distance, you could zoom out the perspective of the scene. If an ending is intense or emotional, then you would zoom into the scene. Keeping the reader at the right distance conveys the proper tone and drives their emotions to where you wish them to be for the next scene.

Something must change in every scene. Perhaps the character learns new information. Perhaps their status changes by losing a job. Perhaps they are captured. Many options exist for the potential appearance of this change. The change must occur, whether the impact be internal or external. If your scene cannot do this, and your character remains in the same spot, assess whether that scene requires rewriting or discarding.

One potential trap when writing sequels is known as deepening. Use deepening sparingly to provide greater understanding of the character or setting within the scene, and its overall meaning to the larger story. One trap many writers fall into is putting too much deepening into the reactions. This extra introspective time (aka navel gazing) slows down the story. It should be done only to make an enormous impact. If it seems to be filler, eliminate the scene.

Another technique to help you understand if there is narrative balance in your scene. Use colors to mark dialogue, action, and description sections to identify any imbalance concerns.

As mentioned earlier, each scene is a microcosm of the larger story. Every scene shares similar elements with the main plot and structure. Address every element in your scene when writing.

- Elapsed Time – Do not lose focus on the duration of time that occurs in a scene. If a scene involves making cookies, make sure there is a ten-minute time gap and finish the cookies.
- Motion in the Scene – Most scenes have some sort of motion or action in them. Few are static and successful. The THAD (talking heads action device) incorporates character activities.
- Narrative Balance – Unless a scene is dedicated to dialogue or action, there should be a balance between the various narrative modes of writing (dialogue, action, description, emotion). Braiding these elements of your writing will provide a complete picture to the reader. Focus on a specific element may modify pacing to fulfill a specific purpose within the scene.
- Genre Requirements – A scene may be a designated scene for a specific genre of a story. Guidelines may be disregarded in those scenes to meet requirements. The objective is to avoid clichés and offer a fresh approach.
- Thematic Details – Provide something that keeps the theme running through the story. Setting, dialogue, and memorability are key. This may also include symbolism through imagery and words.

Scene Structure Comparison			
Scene/Sequel		5 Commandments	Explanation
Scene	Goal		Expressing scene Goals early identifies the purpose and character motivations.
	Conflict	Inciting Incident	Once the Goal is known, the conflict kicks off with an Inciting Incident. Conflict starts with the Inciting Incident.
		Dramatic Turn	The Dramatic Turn then occurs as part of the Conflict. It involves the obstacle not being easily overcome and forces the character to change directions.
	Disaster	Crisis	Our character then comes to a juncture where a Disaster will occur. This is the first part of the Crisis moment in the scene.
Sequel	Reaction		The character's Reaction to potential failure in the Crisis moment leads to a change in plans.
	Dilemma	Climax	The Dilemma initiates the Climax in the scene.
	Decision		The Decision plays a role in the Climax, and the character's following action brings it to a culmination.
	Action	Resolution	The Resolution follows the character's Action, whether they achieve or cannot attain the goal.

MOTIVATION REACTION UNITS (MRUs)

Many scenes revolve around two distinct ideas: action and reaction. Chords evoke thoughts and emotions, working in concert to build story flow. If a writer were to break down their scenes, they would appear to be many minor components known as motivation reaction units (MRUs). These are scene units functioning off cause-and-effect relationships. The primary catalyst for this entire chain is a motivation. The motivation is the stimulus. An example would be lightning hitting a house. This stimulus then creates a reaction.

Reaction is when you reveal how the stimulus has impacted the character. It should not prolong the beat. The beat should be a short section of text, if possible. Avoid disrupting the story's flow. In the lightning's case, the character may run from their house to see what happened. Following will be emotions and thoughts. They might act fearful or demonstrate some other emotion. Thoughts follow this. These thoughts could involve future plans or potential issues. This leads to action, ranging from roof climbing to passing out. Finally, they can talk with someone and discuss the event. We will go into more detail on the reactive process in a later chapter.

The MRU contains the elements required to keep the reader's attention. It can't be a series of steps. Immersing the reader requires conveying emotions, moods, and scenery. Feel the beat, portray emotions, find the takeaway, and exit. This will end the beat with a solid transition to the next. These units comprise the multiple pieces of your scenes. You can have several MRUs within the same scene.

TRANSITIONS

You have a clear vision for your scenes, but there's an awkward gap between them. Jack Bickham discussed the use of these breaks and termed them transitions. Since Bickham authored his book, commercial fiction has become faster paced and transitions have grown in importance. Bridging between scenes in modern commercial fiction has become an art form in the fast-paced thriller where the writer moves from one intense scene to another.

Transitions range from a few sentences to entire passages. Transitions allow the linear plot to flow but eliminate the unnecessary details and help convey the passage of time in as few lines as possible. All forms of transition share one purpose: progressing the reader to the next scene and keeping the story's flow. At times, they also provide additional information or emotional development of a character. Be aware that transitions should be inconspicuous when carrying out their task. Below are the principal ways transitions are used to connect the main story.

1. Bridge between scenes
2. Move readers through time
3. Denote a change in setting, mood, or viewpoint
4. Introducing new elements
5. Reflection on the prior scene.
6. Summarization of events

Passage of time is one of the most used transitions in writing. Each event doesn't immediately follow the previous one. These characters eat, sleep, and go to the bathroom. Seeing them all the time is unnecessary. Due to this, gaps appear in the story. We must assure the reader that we considered that time and not give the impression of losing the last eight hours, six weeks, or ten years. Simple lines like the the following excerpt from Marie Brennan's *A Natural History of Dragons* accounts for the passage of time.

"....Just as some girl-children of that age go mad for horses and equestrian pursuits, so did I become dragon-mad. That phrase described me well, for it led not only to the premier focus of my adult life (which has included more than a few actions here and there that might be deemed deranged), but more directly to the action I engaged in shortly after my fourteenth birthday."

This passage not only transports us to Lady Trent's fourteenth birthday, but the passage foreshadows events occurring later in the story. It provides insight into her motivations for her character. Using the terms mad and deranged foreshadow that she might go to illogical ends for her peculiar fascination.

The next three transition types deal with moving from one environment to another. Whether it be the setting, the mood, or the viewpoint. In a fast story, the key is to convey this change to the reader. Once you anchor the reader in the next scene, they will ride along with the story. If you cannot anchor the reader, they will be confused and pushed out of the story. The best approach for transitions is to place them at a scene's end or the next one's start.

The next item is adding new elements, like a character or information. Characters need a story connection. Communicate this connection to the reader, or they will believe we are providing characters to serve as plot devices. The character's presence should not appear coincidental or convenient to the reader. Reflective character moments are used to transition often, as exemplified by an excerpt from *A Natural History of Dragons* following the prior scene.

"But I was not lacking in common sense as to believe defiance would result in happiness, for me or anyone else. The world simply did not work that way.
Or so it seemed to me, at the wise old age of fourteen.
I therefore pressed my lips together, gathering my strength. Under the bandages that swathed it, my shoulder twinged.
"Yes, Papa," I said. "I understand.""

Lady Trent, against her own judgment, joined the men on a dragon hunt despite being warned not to. Her reflection in this moment reveals her realization of the danger, after her innocent frolic in the pasture and subsequent injury by the dragon. A lesson she would carry with her throughout the series.

Summarization is often done to give the reader a break. It keeps the reader aware of fast-paced story happenings. Another use is to demonstrate the impact of the resulting actions from the prior scene.

Another type of transition is the crosscut. Popular in visual media and with many appearances in modern fiction. The writer abruptly shifts scenes, leaving the first character in suspense to be revisited later. This often happens when multiple plot lines converge or tension filled activity occurs at the same time. This technique creates tension, but also shows the reader/viewer that both plot lines are of equal value.

In *Oathbringer*, the third book in *The Stormlight Archive* by Brandon Sanderson, the climactic chapter is 45 pages in length, but moves back and forth between several characters as they take part in a battle to save Thaylen City. Each time Sanderson moves to another character, he leaves the prior in a precarious situation.

Transitions are often considered an afterthought in writing. Without skillful handling, these text pieces may disrupt scene transitions. The story will fall apart, and the reader will be confused or disinterested. Neither is something a writer desires.

SCENE SEQUENCING AND CHAPTERS

One of the toughest aspects of writing a story is placing these scenes in the most effective order. The simplest and most often used method is to put them in chronological sequence. The one difficulty this presents is threading in the backstory. Determining the right placement for a preferred flashback scene is difficult.

Many stories contain parallel plot lines with sub-plots occurring at the same time as the main plot line. One method of showing these scenes is interspersing them amongst the major plot line in an alternating fashion. Scene 1 of the sub-plot follows scene 1 of the main plot line. For better results, try using a sequence of scenes. Build up to the resolution, leave the main plot at a cliffhanger, and repeat the process with the sub-plot. Then you resolve the main plot sequence and shift back to the sub-plot to resolve that sequence.

In *Argent's Menagerie*, the sub-plots are nested. The writer began the sequence by leaving the primary plot line at a cliffhanger. Then shifted to the sub-plots and wrote them to an elevated point of suspense. The author returned to the main plot and progressed through the midpoint sequence, leading to another high-tension moment. The sub-plots were then resolved before moving back to the climax sequence for the main story.

V. E. Schwab used a varied timeline to sequence the chapters in her book *Vicious* in a non-linear fashion. She created impactful moments for the characters in the main timeline, then jumped to another time to focus on character development, revealing the seeds of change. Schwab labeled each chapter to indicate its temporal relation to the main story.

Throughout a novel, there are many scenes. Many writers keep related scenes within a single chapter. There must be something that connects them. Perhaps they occur on the same day, perhaps they involve the same characters, or perhaps they revolve around the same plot point.

Or insert a chapter break after each scene. There are no actual rules around chapters as long as you break them up to create the best pacing for your story.

Perhaps the toughest part is deleting a scene that you love. No one wishes to kill one of their darlings, as the saying goes. Make sure your scene doesn't disrupt the story's flow or stray off into senseless tangents. Don't be afraid to cut a scene you think is extraordinary, but adds nothing to your story.

Remember, you should make each scene extraordinary and unforgettable. Can you do that in one scene? Yes. Then, continue doing this for all subsequent scenes. Mastering the construction of scenes is one of the greatest skills for any writer.

SCENE TRACKERS AND OTHER TOOLS

Many writers use tools known as scene trackers throughout their writing process. This tool tracks the elements of the scene and ensures the writer achieves their desired impact. These scene trackers can be individualized based on the project, writer preferences, or specific functions of the scene. There are two different versions for you to consider in your writing process.

Martha Alderson's *Writing Blockbuster Plots,* explains the use of a detailed scene tracker. One of these uses a graphical tool called the Intensity Scale. The graph moves horizontally, with each X-axis point representing a scene component. The Y-axis is a scale of 1 to 10. As the beats occur in a scene, graph the intensity of the beat. As you go through the scene, create an uptick in the intensity.

Alderson also demonstrates the use of a grid, or a spreadsheet, with the elements of the scene as headers of various columns. Each row's left-hand column identifies the scene. The scenes are then shown row by row as they appear in your work. The Super Story Tracker is included in your Vibrant Prose Toolbox and will accomplish the goals of Alderson's tool and more.

Another tool to help with the analysis of your scenes is the Vibrant Prose Scene Analysis tool. This identifies any missing components necessary to a successful scene. It allows you to evaluate your scene using either the 5 Commandments or the Scene/Sequel approach to determine if your scene contains all the required elements.

All these tools help you diagnose if your scenes need more work. The number of tools available emphasizes the importance of quality scene construction for your story's success.

EXERCISES

1. Identify specific scenes that your story will need to have because of the genre.
2. Examine a scene from your work-in-progress and identify its various components. Identify necessary changes in your scene to incorporate missing components.
3. Find transitions between scenes in your first ten work-in-progress scenes.
4. Rearrange the scene structure of the first ten scenes to suit your story. Rearrange the scenes in this order and update the transitional text.

REFERENCE MATERIALS

Scene & Structure by Jack Bickham
Make a Scene by Jordan Rosenfeld
The Anatomy of Story: 22 Steps to Becoming a Master Storyteller, Chapter 10 by John Truby
Techniques of the Selling Writer, Chapter 6 by Dwight V. Swain
Writing Blockbuster Plots: A Step-by-Step Guide to Mastering Plot, Structure, and Scene by Martha Alderson
Fiction Writing Made Easy Podcast by Savannah Gilbo

We covered the works by Truby, Gilbo, and Swain. Bickham's work, the standard thesis on scene development, still holds significant weight. Gilbo's podcast does an excellent job discussing the modern movement in scene development. Alderson's tome does a wonderful job in introducing tools that any writer can use in their process. Rosenfeld's tome on scene construction is also a practical guide useful to every writer.

12 – SETTING

When considering a novel's story, the setting is crucial. Plot, character, and maybe theme have equal importance. Setting provides the reader with a sense of immersion. It resonates because the reader experiences the location through the characters surrounded by a living world that interacts with them throughout the story. Without setting, everything could happen on a soundstage in California.

What is setting? Setting is not just where and when. Setting impacts the character, the action, the conflict, and plot components. It carries heavy weight in the way your characters interact in the story and will have consequences for how you write scenes. Most authors split setting into four distinct elements: time, place, mood, and context. Every element contributes to explaining character motivation and behavior in the story. But setting also includes a sense of wonder to pull the reader further into the story and highlight the magic of well-written fiction.

- Place – Perhaps the most important aspect is the physical location of the story. Can you use actual locations? Yes, but reflect them in an accurate manner for the locale and research them extensively. That goes double for period-specific locations. Most people associate intense settings to the genres of speculative fiction where world-building determines the success or failure of your story. Other genres writers take note of those practices and implement some of them in their writing. At a minimum, make sure the location feels real and consistent with our known world while incorporating the story's established rules.
- Time – The time is not just when the story occurs. It signifies the changing seasons and the transition from day to night. The period of time for historical fiction is key. This may determine what the social morays were at that point. Or what elements even existed. It would be suicide to write a story with King Kong climbing the Empire State Building in 1929. Time can also be used for dramatic

effect. Perhaps something happens after the sun sets in your story. Perhaps you have a time constraint. A bomb may explode when the countdown ends. These are all impacts of time.

- Atmosphere – This includes the weather, but also the tone and mood of the location. Readers perceive danger, altering their scene interpretation and your location description. Use different words to convey the tone you want to reflect. The point of view character drives how the reader sees the story. They convey the tone through their observations, emotions, and words to elicit the reader's mood while reading the story.
- Context – Cultural and social context have a direct impact on how a character responds in a particular setting. Context matters to how characters react. For example, if verbally attacked, a person will react differently in their home versus a social or cultural setting. These contextual elements can impact economic, social, political, or anything else within the underlying setting.
- Wonder - In Speculative Fiction, the immersive setting must captivate and surpass the reader's imagination. Don't settle for mundane, make the story world wondrous and expansive. Making an immersive setting in a non-speculative genre might be what differentiates you from the other writers. Help create a full experience for the reader by instilling a sense of wonder in your story.

SENSE OF PLACE

Your location contains geography, landmarks, and locations typical of a physical setting. These must be places that are integral to the scenes you write. Cinema and television rely on technology to fill in the openness, fiction cannot. We must pull in a setting that holds the interest of the reader.

Your story world should be able to contain your story. You, as the writer, need to manage the setting like you do your characters, plot, and everything else in the story. Choose the tale and acquire knowledge about this setting's importance. Your story happens in this location for a reason.

Here are a few things to consider regarding your setting. When we refer to direction and navigation, we must be consistent. Are the compass points your guide for navigating the city? Will your characters be in the city center or on the outskirts? This may vary by character and would be part of their voice. One character that uses the actual directional markers, another uses terms like uptown and downtown. Indianapolis residents, particularly older ones, call the Northside the area around 38th Street. People who live in Hamilton County, the northern suburbs, refer to the Northside as anything north of 75th Street. Ensure clear identification of locations and direction.

As a tip, create a map of your setting. This isn't something you include in the final product. What it will do is give a perspective on the various locations within your story. Use the map to estimate travel time by car, foot, and mass transit.

Also, if you set your story in an actual location, develop a strategy around the use of common corporate names. You can refer to the gas station or call it the Speedway. Is the restaurant a steakhouse, or is it Morton's? Utilizing proper names delivers a specific picture to the reader. These names evoke connotations and imagery in the reader's mind.

Last, let's discuss a concept called the Cauldron. All stories resolve conflicts at the Cauldron. If your story includes such a location, use it early in the plot. This does two things: it allows the writer to describe this setting in detail early in the story and saves them from adding unnecessary description that distracts the reader when the climax arrives. This concept also provides an opportunity to foreshadow the ultimate battle and build a sense of anticipation and symmetry into the story.

Make sure your hero knows this terrain to take full advantage of it. Have them visit it another time in the story. In *The Avengers*, it is no mistake that Captain America and Iron Man are giving orders involving specific streets. Their familiarity with the New York City terrain surpassed the other characters. They have a home-field advantage. Master the terrain of the Cauldron to incorporate its elements in the battle.

SENSE OF TIME

The temporal location of your story is perhaps even more crucial than the physical. Let's say you set your story in Atlanta, Georgia. Well, 1950s Atlanta is a lot different from Atlanta during Sherman's raid in the Civil War, or Atlanta of 2020. A single day changes everything. Or Dallas on November 21, 1963, versus the following day? The meaning of time surpasses the story's date. Depicting this location with the correct authenticity of the period is paramount to creating an immersive setting. It's what your readers will expect of you.

Another concern is the passage of time. Some stories unfold in moments, while others evolve over time. As the writer, you must convey the passage of time to the reader. The sun's movement, field growth, and downtown development illustrates the passage of time. The reader needs to feel the progression of time through the story.

> *"Joseph left me in the spring for his tour in the war. The wheat was barely in the ground when he left. He would be back in time for the harvest, his favorite time of year. He could see the fields waving in golden glory as he arrived home before they were scythed and left as empty reminders of the growing season that had passed.*
> *The wheat wasn't the only thing that had grown while he was away."*

The imprecise passage of time in this example indicates a substantial duration since Joseph's last visit home, portrayed through the imagery of the crops. It informs the reader something happened. What has grown? Could the woman be pregnant? Perhaps her fondness for Joseph, or perhaps her fondness for another person. Perhaps she had a tumor that she refused to tell Joseph and now her cancer has expanded its reach. Many possibilities arise from that text.

Time provides a source of conflict in the story. We have all seen the shows with the bomb's timer counting down or portraying the impending arrival of a feared person with doom. A constraint on time provides an immediate source of tension. As time slips, the reader senses the character's longing for dramatic choices. Instead of doing things logically, they will make rash decisions that perhaps make the situation worse and ramp up the tension even further.

Time isn't static. It moves through the story and performs an active role in the plot. Make it part of characterizing your setting.

SENSE OF ATMOSPHERE AND CONTEXT

Atmosphere and context often work together to provide depth and communicate the feeling of a place. Are the people welcoming? Is the weather palatable? Are community norms a little odd? These factors, including time and place, form a complete setting. These elements play a significant role in conveying the story's tone. The setting of Dante's *Inferno* is memorable due to its atmosphere. Smoke, ash, heat, walls, and dim light created an enveloping, uncomfortable atmosphere as Virgil descended through Hell.

A chief part of your story occurs outside. In that case, the weather will play a role in the story. Things happen differently if the sun shines or if rain is pelting the character in a thirty-knot wind. People talk louder when agitated; they are less patient. That one difference is driven by the weather. Storms destroying a city changes the tone in an instant. Tornadoes racing through Kansas plains override everything else. Perhaps your character's wife is giving birth in the hospital across the bridge that just got wiped out by flood waters. How does your character respond?

If the story happens inside, that doesn't exclude it from weather related impacts. The air conditioning may not be working during peak summer heat. In winter, the house may have no heat. Get the point? Weather is an equalizer. It makes us all look weak at times.

"*The little snot ran away on the snow-covered sidewalk, my wallet in his hand.*
He was faster, but I knew what was underneath the white carpet. I pursued him patiently.
He rounded the corner, and I heard a squeal and a thump. The ice under the snow got him like a hidden trapdoor and revealed his inexperience on these streets.
I knew the shopkeepers hadn't salted yet and the frozen sheet hadn't melted.
I caught up and saw the boy nursing sore ribs from plowing into the side of a Buick. He hit it hard. The dent was evidence of his impact.
I picked up my wallet from the snowbank as I chastised him. "Learn your lesson kid. Probably should get that looked at."
I walked away as the snow crunched beneath my solid mindful steps."

In this example, the viewpoint character knows something the child doesn't. He knows the weather's behavior and the outcome. Possibly, he did something similar during his childhood. Knowing he wasn't that different from the kid; the man gives him advice instead of turning him into the authorities. Again, we open potential avenues for tension and foreshadowing a later event.

Another major component of atmosphere are the societal pressures in a community. Do you live in a small Indiana town that outlaws dancing? Do you live in a town where a businessman runs an extortion racket on every business except the bar you work at? Are you living in a small Alabama town where assumptions of guilt persist for Black men, regardless of innocence, but fighting for freedom is imperative? Your setting may not resemble *Footloose*, *Roadhouse*, or *To Kill a Mockingbird*, but it possesses societal issues that shape the overall atmosphere of the town's streets and sidewalks.

Your job as a writer is to project those thoughts. Either do it directly or through subtext. When you do this successfully, you characterize the setting and make it an equal player in the story with plot, character, and theme.

SENSE OF WONDER

The story world you attempt to establish needs to be a world of possibility. It needs to capture the imagination of the reader and immerse them. It needs to provide a sense of wonder. This idea is associated with speculative stories and seldom thought of as a necessary element of romances, mysteries, or literary fiction. Every story should strive to create a sense of wonder around their setting.

In a sports fiction story, we want to build the arena into a cathedral of sport. In historical fiction, we want the reader to feel like they were transported to Victorian England. We want them to experience the authentic atmosphere of this venue. We want them to be awed. Avoid dwelling on the limitations in your world. Emphasize possibilities, integrating them into your story's plot and character development.

Fonda Lee's *Green Bone Saga* is centered around the city of Janloon. Throughout her trilogy we experience the city from its thug infested streets to the pageantry of their historical celebrations to the surrounding world impacted by the use of mystical jade found on the island of Kekon. Lee captivates us with dramatic gangster world details, hinting at our own reality, and then astounds us with the jade warriors' abilities. Imagine the potential if that existed in our world. Even without a mysterious island or mystical jade, your setting possesses the ability to captivate the audience with a sense of wonder.

THE WRITER'S JOB

Writers often begin the story in a setting to generate one thing, resonance with the reader. The setting must be immersive and pull the reader into the story, so they continue reading. Anchoring the reader in the scene is essential for the writer. Anchoring communicates to the reader where and when the story takes place. Time and place may be provided as chapter headings in certain works. This avoids weaving this information into the story, allowing the writer to focus on the important aspects of the setting. The writer must inform the reader when the story moves to a different setting. Keeping the reader anchored to the setting is fundamental.

After anchoring the reader, the writer emphasizes the significance of the location. When in a store, focus less on the setting if the characters' interactions are crucial and the store won't reappear. Slow the story to make a point. Doing this signifies importance to the reader.

One thing to note, make sure you maintain a level of continuity and believability in how your characters move between locations. They cannot jump from one location to another in a haphazard manner. These transitions need to flow. You need to be mindful of location hopping for no reason.

Review the locations of your scenes to assure yourself the movement makes sense. Identify the locations on a map to make sure things work in an orderly manner. Take note of travel times. In Seattle, it's impossible to leave the airport and reach the University of Washington in fifteen minutes. Ensure you reflect this passage of time in your details. This will help create an authentic feel to your story world.

You want your characters to interact with the setting through motion, conflict, or other actions. This provides emotional resonance for the reader and reveals details about the character. Does a character's backstory reveal itself when they see the theater marquee? Perhaps they recall when they kissed their future partner in the back row? Perhaps they sat in the back row with a guy to provoke jealousy? These things might hint at backstory or foreshadow later occurrences.

Through the setting, the character observes theme-related elements. Steam rising from the ground as the sun heats the morning dew conveys images of spirits leaving this realm and provides an imagery of death. Hide these subtle items among other components of the setting.

Different setting elements have different connotations. Dark alleys and lighted sidewalks give different vibes to the reader. One suggests danger, the other safety. Storm clouds and clear skies, tall foreboding apartment buildings compared to two-story bungalows, a dive bar with an entrance below street level versus a local public house in a strip mall. All these examples carry preconceived notions. As the writer, use these elements to convey the setting's tone and atmosphere.

Juxtapose these items by giving the reader a false sense of security. Architecture is a wonderful element to use for this purpose. How many buildings appear to be elegant masterpieces to only reveal secrets with more intense scrutiny? Someone looking at a building from the street misses gargoyles and other mysterious elements. Even in rural settings, this occurs. Have you ever seen barns with an extra wooden arm running out at the same level as the second story? In the day, they uses that for many jobs. Some not so savory.

Last, the writer needs to make sure the details of setting perform multiple duties within their writing. They should not only set the scene, but they should create tone, draw out emotion, and provide the tension with every element introduced.

Now let's shift gears and approach setting from the character's perspective. Ready yourself to inhabit the POV character's mind. The reader must understand and experience the characters' emotional ties to the setting elements and how they shape the overall story.

WORLDVIEW VS STORYVIEW

The difference between the character's world and the story's world is often overlooked by writers. Each character's world is a part of the story's world. If we apply our real world as a base reference, perhaps this image comes through much clearer.

The world has over 7 billion people. That world includes animals, plants, ecology, minerals, and anything else on Earth or in its realm. It includes the Moon, other planets, and the sun. It is expansive. Within that, every person on this plane has their own story world. How they experience life in their world. If we look at each person's bubble, their story world, and overlay this with every other person's bubble, we create a massive Venn diagram that would encompass the entire real world we inhabit. Yet, it still lacks completeness, as our understanding of this planet remains incomplete.

This is an attempt to show the problems within a story. The narrator of your story, unless they are an all-knowing omniscient storyteller, will not know everything about their world. They might know nothing about the story world, just their own bubble. Your character's view will take on one of three perspectives: native, tourist, or conqueror.

The characters native to the world will only understand their own part. Although they possess insights into some universal truths, their knowledge of other cultures, locations, or people groups in their world remains limited. The native knows and appreciates their own world's truths and relaying the emotional importance is the primary way to draw in the reader.

The characters alien to the word aim to understand the customs of this new world. The character shares their thoughts with the reader while experiencing everything anew. This often becomes immersive to the reader and enjoyable. However, this lack of knowledge hinders the character. Fish out of water stories are quite common. *Ted Lasso* exemplifies this story type.

Those with a conqueror attitude disregard established traditions and cultures. Their cultural norms will override and absorb this society as the old-world inhabitants assimilate into new norms. In some stories, the character may falsely claim knowledge of other cultures, which become appropriation and minimize that culture. R. F. Kuang does a fine job of exhibiting this type of world in *Babel*.

Once you have established this attitude in your main viewpoint character, you will have the same issue with any other viewpoint characters within the story. Each character has their own viewpoint. More characters create more viewpoints. Shared experiences yield different emotional connections for distinct characters. While these viewpoints share familiarity, their experiences vary. Who doesn't know of two people watching the same sporting event having different accounts based on their perspective, which is influenced by the color of jersey they wear?

Often, your characters with shared viewpoints, experiences, and histories will become allies in your stories. Those that have contrasting viewpoints, experiences, and histories will become adversaries. These varied viewpoints, experiences, and histories could be the source of conflict and mutual differences between the protagonist and antagonist. They share an understanding, but not of the entire world in the story.

SETTING AND CHARACTER

Every character perceives and interprets the world uniquely. Their voice conveys the world to the reader. If your character is a blacksmith, they may observe metal elements in a room or weapons on display. OCD individuals fixate on misplaced, off-center, and anxiety-inducing clutter. They both enter the room, but their perspectives vary. Their personal mood might trigger different responses. When calm, individuals notice more than when anxious.

We need to discuss how setting impacts the internal battles of the characters. The characters fight their internal battles based on how their emotions develop with the world, including the setting. The key is displaying this battle through emotion. Imagery can be a primary driver of displaying that battle, as the character interprets various outside details. As the character goes through their battle, reflect their impressions of the world differently to account for the character's change.

For Paul Altreides, this internal battle is fighting everything he learned as a youth within a privileged house and accepting another path. He must deal with his lack of belief in his mother's religion while also weighing his duty as the son of a duke. He accepts his destiny with the story of *Dune* and transforms into the Messiah of the Fremen and embraces his role as the Maud'Dib, knowing he will never be able to relinquish that position. As Paul changes, so does the world around him.

Setting must connect on an emotional level to the characters. Mary Buckham authored an excellent book titled *A Writer's Guide to Active Setting*. Her book's essence lies in crafting a setting as vital to the plot as the characters, almost a character in its own right. There are three fundamental ways that setting serves as a character.

One method is assigning the role of the antagonist to the setting. In this role, the story world is the chief obstacle for the main character. There are man vs. nature stories throughout literature. The world around our characters always presents emotional and meaningful conflict. Imagine a tale similar to *The Perfect Storm*. The core of this story is man's quest for livelihood amidst the unpredictable forces of nature.

You can use the setting as a refuge. In *Argent's Menagerie*, the author created a spaceship that became the one thing the pilot trusted in his life. A line of dialogue refers to this: "In Menagerie we trust." The message is emphasized on the back of the book. Argent, the main character, has varied levels of trust in the people surrounding him, but he knows his ship will never fail him. He relies on the ship to save his bacon every single time. That trust impedes his other relationships, and he will rely on that ship to his death. In this case, the trust in his ship juxtaposes against those other relationships and creates tension and thematic heft to the story.

DC Comics in recent years has used a planet known as Mogo as an actual Green Lantern. For decades, this character existed, but in the last twenty years, Mogo has emerged as a pivotal figure in Green Lantern Corps' storylines, evolving from a mere planet with a power ring into a fleshed out character. As time passes, the planet gains sentience and assumes a vital role in tales.

Another effective way to use setting is to make it symbolize or embody the conflict, the Cauldron Principle. A notable example is the Colosseum used in *Gladiator* starring Russell Crowe and Joaquin Phoenix as Maximus and Commodus, respectively. The fighting pit is the obvious location of physical conflict throughout the story, but the smaller fights lead up to the decisive battle between the two main characters. The smaller fights occur in smaller venues. With the growing importance of the fight, the venue and crowd also expand.

The final battle occurs in the Colosseum, which is why Ridley Scott takes us there multiple times. We become familiar with the platform, so with the world-building completed early and becomes unnecessary by the time we reach the main event. If you're going to have a central conflict resolved in a key setting, refer to it earlier in the story. Describe it in detail to the reader so they are familiar when you circle back to that location later. You get the exposition out of the way and let the story flow through to the climax.

Using your setting as a thematic symbol is a wonderful technique. The parties and mansions in *The Great Gatsby* represent superficial excess and empty characters. They drink all their liquor, eat all their cakes, only to be empty when they puke it back up again multiple times. While some argue Fitzgerald's story aged poorly, it remains a thematic masterpiece of the early 20th century.

CONVEYING SCENE

How does the writer convey the setting to the reader? There are several ways to provide information on your setting. These techniques vary in the depth of information they provide to the reader and in the skill level to perform them. The following paragraphs present these options, beginning with the basic level.

The easiest way to give out information on your setting is through exposition. Let your reader know what is necessary. Occasionally, this is more efficient, but only use it as a last resort. Excessive use of this tactic pushes readers away from the story by creating an infodump. This technique is often dry and void of any other meaning. We want to communicate information to a reader that has context and provides additional emotional impact. The proper use of exposition will be covered in a later chapter.

Sensory level description is often communicated to the reader to immerse them in the setting. It slows the story, but it can be effective. Everyone loves a great description, right? Here is one from *Great Expectations*.

"It was a grimy morning, and very damp. I had seen the damp lying on the outside of my little window ... Now, I saw the damp lying on the bare hedges and spare grass ... On every rail and gate, wet lay clammy; and the marsh-mist was so thick, that the wooden finger on the post directing people to our village — a direction which they never accepted, for they never came there — was invisible to me until I was quite close under it."

Dialogue is another way to deliver information. Many times, it delivers multiple messages to the reader. The thing to avoid is "As you know" or "Maid and Butler" dialogue, terms for communicating information known by the characters to the audience. If they know, why discuss it? Here's a bit of dialogue that offers a different approach to the "As you know" concept.

Harry drove like his life depended on it. Jack held onto the door thinking his did.
Harry asked, "What's the quickest way to catch them?"
"Going down Main. You know that."
"There's construction."
Jack asked, "On Main?" He then slammed against the door as Harry made a quick turn.
"Yeah, so that won't work."
"Then I guess we have to hit the bypass. Everything else will be backed up."
"Hold on and put the light on top of the car."

This police pursuit involves beating the criminal to a different location. Both know Main Street is the fastest, but Jack doesn't know about construction closure. That's why Harry asks the original question. All this happens while Harry drives erratically. Erratic driving and uncertainty escalate tension in the scene. This also foreshadows that something occurs on Main Street later in the story.

A third technique is expressing emotional importance through the vantage point of the POV character. This technique provides a view through their filter and carries with it the impacts of backstory and emotional development. It also conveys the importance of the location to the reader. Maybe it's where they got engaged, or where their mom was shot. It holds weight with the character and evokes a reaction.

In the final sequence of the movie *Titanic*, they revisit the site of the sunken ship. Rose drops the necklace to the bottom of the ocean. For how many years did she bear the burden of that moment? Then, with one action, she released years of love, regret, guilt, and shame.

A fourth technique is through conflict and tension. What if the story pertains to a serial killer who uses a circus fun house to attract his victims? You combine an enticing setting with the antagonist's motives, resulting in a lethal space. Perhaps, the killer uses the fun house to identify his victims and then stalks them. The fun house still fulfills its duty to the victim, but has a second purpose to the killer. If the reader is aware of the situation, their anxiety ramps up as another potential victim walks through the attraction, knowing the whole time the madman watches his potential prey. You can also include foreshadowing and hint at an upcoming murder attempt.

The last technique involves imagery to tie the story world to the theme through the setting. Repeatedly referencing specific world facets could accomplish this. Below, Emily Bronte uses this passage to tie to the gothic theme of her writing in *Wuthering Heights* while also alluding to the constant presence of the north wind.

"One may guess the power of the north wind, blowing over the edge, by the excessive slant of a few stunted firs at the end of the house; and by a range of gaunt thorns all stretching their limbs one way, as if craving alms of the sun."

An important aspect of developing your setting is making it something that enhances the story. Make it more than just four walls. Provide depth and detail through descriptive language and add emotional resonance through the perspective of the viewpoint character. Make the story immersive through sensory details that the readers relate to.

EVOLVING YOUR STORY WORLD

Layering in your world-building elements and creating settings that impact a character are just two aspects of developing your world. Elevating your setting to an evolved world involves expanding it over the length of your story, much like your characters undergoing their changes. What does that even mean? We'll use examples from well-known storylines to show you how this happens.

Most stories start in a regular world. This world reflects the status quo of the main character. Writers use the normal world early in the story to establish the main characters, setting, themes, and tone of the story. Through the character's eyes, we experience their normal status quo.

In *Star Wars*, we meet Luke living his comfortable life of a moisture farmer and accepting that his desire to travel the cosmos is secondary and he will deny his true calling because it is safe. In *Jaws*, Chief Brody tries to maintain his normal world, his status quo, by pushing off what he knows is happening around him. Introduce this world in the book's early chapters before the character embarks on their adventure.

Once the character answers their calling, often begrudgingly, they enter a new world. In this new adventure world, the main character pursues both external and internal goals. For Luke, he is pursuing the Princess while also seeking his true calling and traveling aboard the Millenium Falcon. For Chief Brody, it is trying to catch a shark and dealing with his fears while going out to sea with Hooper and Quint. Both examples involve a character stepping out of their comfort zone and into a world of potential doom.

Setting shifts are necessary in every story. The setting must change, even if you remain in the city. Perhaps the main character moves to a new location, and the tone becomes heavier. Character development parallels setting evolution.

The next evolution point heads towards what some refer to as the underworld, or dark world. Here, the character faces their crisis and transitions towards the climax and resolution. Some mythological stories move through the underworld, or some sort of mystical realm. In some ways, Luke does this as he explores his Jedi training, but the Death Star, a true representation of death, exhibits more aspects of the dark world. The character learns crucial lessons in this crisis world to resolve the story.

This world, or milieu, is the home of the story's thematic truth. The character picks up a skill, knowledge, ability, or something else that they take with them to achieve their goal. This creates the movement within them to push forward and attempt the impossible. For Luke, this truth involves trusting in the force as he destroys the Death Star.

In *Jaws*, the ship's sinking forces Chief Brody to confront the shark and his fears head-on, transforming his world. His ship is half-sunken, and Brody fears the water and the shark. This dark world provides a chance at rebirth for the character and allows them to accept the truth they have fought hard to avoid throughout the story.

The new world is our last stop. The character's new status quo is reflected in this world. This world should resemble the character's original world, but with changes influenced by their story. Luke is now part of the rebellion and accepts his role as a Jedi. Chief Brody dealt with his fears and came home to a joyful beach, while swimming in the water alongside Richard Dreyfuss.

For a writer, a changed world, world-building, and setting development are essential. Plotters plan early, pantsers wait until revision to tie it together. Regardless of when you do it, pulling this off sets your story apart from others in your genre.

In The Goblet of Fire the story world evolves through the four stages.

The Normal World: Harry lives with the Dursleys.

The Adventure World: Harry goes to Hogwarts and experiences the Tri-Wizard Tournament.

The Dark World: Harry and Cedric are pulled into a graveyard by the portkey and face Death Eaters and Voldemort.

The New World: Harry escapes with Cedric's body and returns to Hogwarts with the knowledge that Voldemort has returned

Figure 12-1 The Evolution of the Story World

As a final review, the following is a list of possible dos and don'ts for using setting within your story.

- Anchor your reader and story in a setting that enhances the emotional journey of the characters.
- Display the setting through the perspective of the characters with emotional responses.
- Don't overwrite the details to the degree they overwhelm the story, i.e., infodump.
- Every setting should be complex. If simple, you are wasting the time of the character, reader, and yourself.

EXERCISES

1. Create a setting profile listing the setting details of a scene you have read.
2. Write an essay about the important aspects of your story's setting.
3. Look at your story and focus on what you believe will be your Cauldron. Write a brief scene introducing this location.
4. Draw a freehand map of your world and denote the distances that exist between various locations.

REFERENCE MATERIALS

A Writer's Guide to Active Setting: How to Enhance Your Fiction with More Descriptive, Dynamic Settings by Mary Buckham
Helping Writers Become Authors – K. M. Wieland podcasts.
Wonderbook: The Illustrated Guide to Creating Imaginative Fiction by Jeff VanderMeer

Buckham's book is by far the best in exploring the character aspects of setting in your story. It covers implementing setting in a three-dimensional manner, considering time, location, and contextual impacts on character development and story progression. Wieland and VanderMeer's resources can prove crucial for developing the story world and character arcs.

13 – WORLD-BUILDING

When you hear the term world-building in the writing arena, everyone conjures up images of guys hiding away in the basement with their D&D (Dungeons & Dragons for the uninitiated) role playing guides wishing they were dungeon masters. Fiction writers can learn from these world-builders and apply their principles, regardless of genre.

The setting of the book enhances the story beyond character and plot. The setting immerses the reader and places them amid the action instead of just observing. The details of a high-fantasy novel should set the standard for how everyone pursues the setting of every piece of fiction. From Mordor's moors to New York City's subway, your work becomes a transporting tale and submerges readers in those worlds. World-building is as vital as plotting and character biographies.

Developing any world requires two ingredients: research and creativity. Whether writing about a racehorse in Kentucky or a steampunk librarian in turn-of-the-century London, it doesn't matter. There is much to research and creativity comes into play in using the information to construct your world and applying it within the story.

Research takes various forms. If you set your book in an actual location or a location modeled after a real-world setting, the easiest way to reflect those sites is to visit them, immerse yourself in the setting, and understand what to include in your writing. If possible, visit the location at various times of the day or year, unless all your action takes place during lunch in San Diego at that one soup place with the great chicken velvet every single day. Research how the location may change when the leaves turn or how the locals deal with the winter snows. Interview the residents and pick up on peculiarities in their speech, how they turn certain phrases, and soak in some local slang. Analyze the area's geography for story potential with landmarks and water features. If your base of operations has a harbor, use it. Know your surroundings.

Develop your idea for a world beyond the ordinary using your creativity. Have you determined what makes your world special? Your cool idea, the magic bullet, the shiny jewel is going to be used as a plot device to drive setting details in the story along with plot, conflict, and character development.

Your concept impacts the society of your world in a certain way. You need to ask questions about how it impacts the world your characters inhabit. Does this idea drive economic activity? Does it impact both the rich and the poor? Who does this item hurt? Who does it benefit? These aspects drive conflict and enhance character development.

M. L. Wang uses the rules of her world's magic to affect her society in *Blood Over Bright Haven*. In that world, magic leaves clear victims. The revelation of the secret exposes the true location of power in that society. Having that secret exposed identifies much greater consequences than you can imagine.

Perception is also a key factor. Your story will focus on a core group of characters and present a new world through their perspective. Capture both the negative and positive aspects of your world with a diverse cast. Sharing additional world aspects immerses readers in the special place you've crafted. It's best to consider multiple viewpoints, if possible.

This isn't just a character discussion. Look at ways your new world presents opportunities to drive scenes and plot points. If your world has a region named "The Forbidden Forest," it must play a significant role in the plot. What's the point of creating this world if you don't show it off? No one wants to see your characters sit in their version of studio apartments, cubicles, and court rooms. Give the reader an adventure. Here are some suggestions to experience how these writers shaped the story through world-building.

- *The Lost World* by Sir Arthur Conan Doyle
- *The Journey to the Center of the Earth* by Jules Verne
- *The Land That Time Forgot* by Edgar Rice Burroughs

THE SETTING SPECTRUM

Before writing, envision the world for your story. What is the ratio of research to creativity in that particular domain? World-building requires a balance between truth and fantasy. The Setting Spectrum contains broad categories defining various levels of creativity and research for fiction based on the level of world building. This includes understanding the impact of time, place, mood, and context. The following paragraphs provide a better explanation around the mix of research versus creativity required to develop various worlds.

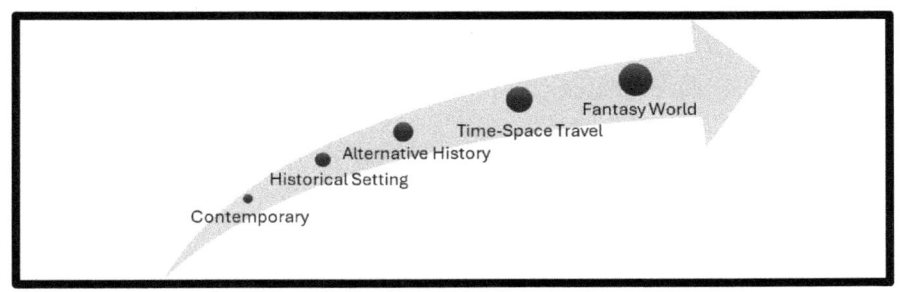

Figure 13-1 The Setting Spectrum

(Spectrum from lowest to highest: Contemporary, Historical Setting, Alternative History, Time-Space Travel, Fantasy World)

Contemporary Fiction itself doesn't have any steadfast rules around creating your story world. Many times, the writer creates a facsimile of an actual city as the fictional setting in their book. This allows creativity to take hold. Suppose the story needs a river, yet the real city lacks one. Using a facsimile allows for inserting a river without people becoming angry because you just put a make-believe waterway in their hometown. And yes, that happens.

You can still use creativity when using an actual location. You are just faced with limitations to the terrain based on the actual aspects of the location you use. Thoroughly research the location for exploitable story details. Research only gets you so far. Personal experience in the city is preferred.

For *Legends in Addington*, the author researched Addington for a non-fiction project and found it perfect for his first fiction story. The author researched the area for weeks online, including spending several evenings scrolling through Google Earth images to become intimate with the area's geography. The author could portray Addington without fearing backlash for misrepresenting any minor details. The author made setting an active part of the story as a result.

In *As the City Burns*, a great deal of research involved determining how to use one of the key features of the downtown Indianapolis landscape, the White River Canal. This included determining how water entered the canal. The author used this knowledge to depict the setting honestly and provided a way for the main character to show their acumen in the story to build a connection and confidence with the reader.

"Plane turned and immediately got on his phone.

Gus pulled me aside. "He is just doing his job. Don't be a jerk about it."

"Really Gus. I don't think so. He's just here for damage control. IMPD doesn't want anything to do with what will come from this. Look at the evidence. Somebody dumped this body in the canal to send a message."

Gus laughed. "Why do you think that?"

"Someone went to a lot of trouble to exhume that body from a coffin. Then they dropped it in the canal somewhere between here and the basin at Eleventh Street."

Gus hesitated as he thought. "Wait, could they have dumped it in the river, and it just found its way into the canal?"

He should know the answer to that question. I wasn't on the force, but I knew.

"It doesn't work that way, Gus. The underwater flow is controlled."

Plane joined us and they both had a glazed look over their eyes. Neither knew this information.

I explained, "The water runs through a pipe the size of your thigh, then through the dam at the north end of the basin, and then under the footbridge. No way that body makes it through all that in one piece."

"So, why was the body still in the canal?" asked Plane.

"Look at the lack of current. It is hardly moving on top. Whoever dropped this body knew it would be visible in the morning."

Plane smiled. "Well, then we should be able to find out who did it."

"I doubt it. My guess is they dropped it from one of the street bridges between here and the basin. None of those bridges have cameras to catch any footage. Maybe forensics will find something, but I doubt it. We have one question left that might give us a clue as to who did this."

"What's that?" asked Gus.

"Is there anything in Venice Lake's coffin now?""

Historical Fiction creates its own can of worms. Anytime you portray a specific time frame in history, you open yourself up to criticism. Research in this genre is paramount or you could alienate a core group of your potential readers.

In the US, numerous individuals are passionate about the Civil War, possessing vast knowledge of events, battles, and people. If you are writing about the Civil War, you need to know the weapons used in the field of battle, the medicine they used, what they did with their dead soldiers. One error upsets and alienates readers, jeopardizing your book's success. These individuals form a vital segment of your audience. Don't make them angry.

The Regency era in the United Kingdom is another popular example. Mary Robinette Kowal provides an excellent portrayal of this period in her *Glamourist Histories* series. The series focuses on small-scale fantastical elements combined with the societal normalities of the time. It is an ode to Jane Austen's writing, with a bit of magic sprinkled in for good measure. Awareness of these issues will improve your precision in using historical details.

Alternate History is perhaps the perfect balance of research and creativity. The writer needs to study the moment that changes history, understand its consequences, and anticipate the future. *The Man in the High Castle* by Phillip K. Dick is a prime example of this story type. Dick portrays a world where FDR was assassinated in 1934. The story assumes the United States then falters in World War II and falls under combined occupation by Germany and Japan. Ironically, the dominant story is a framing story for another alternative history within. Within the story, Dick presents a banned book that imagines what if FDR had lived but served as President until 1940.

Dystopian Future is a type of alternative setting that assumes a catastrophic event occurs which changes life from how we live it today. This story type relies on creativity, but excellent research into the potential change agent is required. A popular example from the past is *Nineteen Eighty-Four*. This style of book regained popularity in recent years within the Young Adult genre and books like *The Hunger Games*. In the case of *The Hunger Games,* the nation suffers an apocalyptic event that centralizes the power into a central Capitol with the other regions suffering in poverty. A consistent theme of this story type is the growth of centralized government to dominate life after the dramatic event occurs. Variations exist where the world is decimated, requiring people to fend for themselves. Perhaps the most famous attempt at this is Stephen King's *The Stand.*

Fantasy & Science Fiction are the main genres associated with this level of world-building. In these genres, creativity is paramount, but grounded in our understanding of life's basic rules. The same things still motivate everyone. *The Lord of the Rings* is an often-cited example of great world-building. Unfortunately, this style of world has become almost cliché and derivative forms of medieval Western European culture have proliferated the genre.

Frank Herbert's *Dune* was published in 1965 and has become considered a masterpiece of Science-Fiction and Fantasy literature. *Dune*'s setting, the planet Arrakis, is considered the best in modern fiction by many writers. The setting influences the lives of the people residing on the wretched planet and the off-worlders present solely for mining the mineral spice. The setting drives the theme of the book. Arrakis is the story's central character.

Where your story sits on the Setting Spectrum will impact how you build the setting, but how your characters interact with it, and how your reader understands the way the world functions. How much suspension of disbelief are we asking of the reader? These are considerations for every writer, not just the Fantasy or Sci-Fi novelist.

ICEBERG PRINCIPLE & WORLD BUILDERS DISEASE

Research is a great tool to identify situations to enhance your setting. For *Argent's Menagerie*, a book set in a far-flung solar system, the author attempted to include some crazy stuff. But the laws of physics don't change. The author spent significant time researching theoretical uses of fusion energy, which led to introducing such items as fusion reactors, cold bombs, force fields, and space flight. To write effectively, the author gathered abundant information on the subject. Two issues emerged: determining the amount to include in the story and knowing when to cease researching.

All writers come across items they need to research. If you are writing a historical novel, you want to research details germane to the time period or location. Research is your friend. What does research buy you? It gives you credibility with the reader. Get the basics right for reader's leeway with the fantastical elements.

But be forewarned, you don't want to write everything you learned into the story. Know when to use restraint. This speaks to the Iceberg Principle, an aspect of writing attributed to that great Fantasy writer Ernest Hemingway. All kidding aside, Hemingway's quote says that you provide enough detail to show 10% of the information and let the reader believe you comprehend the other 90%. You see only 10% and assume 90% exists behind the curtain.

"If a writer of prose knows enough of what he is writing about he may omit things that he knows and the reader, if the writer is writing truly enough, will have a feeling of those things as strongly as though the writer had stated them. The dignity of movement of an iceberg is due to

only one-eighth of it being above water. A writer who omits things because he does not know them only makes hollow places in his writing." — Ernest Hemingway

One of the problems world-builders face is called world-builder's disease. The writer gets consumed with developing their world and never gets to the actual writing. Yes, Tolkien built an amazing world over his lifetime and kept tinkering with it until his death, but he put pen to paper and began his story. You must decide when to stop world-building. To make it easier, establish a time limit for world-building prior to writing. If you write and find unaddressed needs, revise to catch any impacts. Don't get stuck in that hole.

"But I've done all of this work! I want to show them how great this world is." We hear you and have an answer for you. It is called an appendix. Again, the example of Tolkien becomes useful. His tales were dense, but he recognized when to cease with the backstory and details. He compiled remarkable data and placed it in the back of the book. Or perhaps the publisher forced his hand. Either way, it was the correct choice. If you have the desire, create a separate document to record everything in your world for later use. Get it out of your system and store it for another day. Preserve its essence but separate it from the narrative. Perhaps you can include it in an exclusive edition down the road. Or offer it as material for your readers who subscribe to your newsletter.

The other problem many world-builders fall into is the dreaded information dump. They aim to explore their world's details at the book's outset. There are few instances where that works. It is much better to weave in the details as they complement the story and show the reader the majesty of your world, instead of telling them until their eyes drift shut. To quote H. C. Harrington, "World-building is an attempt to create a sense of reality for the reader to sink into, not to bog them down with an overload of uniqueness. The best world-building blends with the other elements of the story."

The amount of world-building information provided to the reader induces a learning curve. The more information we provide early, the steeper the learning curve for our world. Avoid overwhelming readers by subtly introducing information. This approach builds trust with the reader for later developments. Also, if you are dealing with a reader that consumes sci-fi or fantasy novels, they are more willing to let the author take them places. Just be careful with that freedom.

WORLD-BUILDING ON THE FLY

Pantsers often approach world-building from a perspective of "I'll tackle it as I need to" when they write their story. The setting may be part of the initial kernel of their story idea, but more than likely just that, an unpopped kernel. We now need to turn that kernel into a fully blossomed world. Most likely, descriptive language and guiding the character through the story world accomplish this.

Then, there are plotters, people that outline their story somewhat before writing. These are not necessarily world-builders. Typically, the plotter defers the complex world-building to a later stage, like the discovery writer. Plotters and discovery writers can avoid distractions while plowing through the first draft with these helpful techniques.

World-building heavily relies on all the facets of story location, including the element of time. The setting encompasses time and its passage. Making the time feel true to the situation in each scene is important to keep the reader in tune with the story. An example might clarify the concept.

Let's say your character is fixing a nice dinner. Your character won't be able to throw that together in five minutes after coming home from work. Your story needs to account for the realistic passage of time. This occurs with everyday things like laundry, or getting a haircut, or fixing meals. Accomplishing all those items takes time. Use a calendar or planner to schedule your character's activities in the story or scene to avoid timing conflicts.

Also, make sure your reader understands that time is passing. Rather than pointing it out, seek an alternative method to portray the passage of time. In the first Marco Flynn story, *As the City Burns*, the start of each chapter identifies the date. It signified the reader's awareness of time passing and the character's movement between days. The reader will get the inference that your character slept overnight, took a shower, or whatever else before they started their day. You get the benefit of glossing over the boring parts while telling the reader you have moved forward in time.

Making notes while writing might enhance your story during revisions. If you lack time to research, mark world-building elements with a specific notifier (XX or KT) in the text. Later, you can find that spot during revisions.

The last tool to discuss is a reference file. Not an encyclopedia, but a quick reference for story details you'll frequently use. This could include character descriptions, setting descriptions, and other details in order to use a single reference. For example, your main character's girlfriend can't have blue eyes in one part of the story and brown in another. Or your character can't live at 1124 Drury Lane and then later live at 1124 Bakery Boulevard unless they move during the story. Having these details documented for quick reference can save you time on editing and revisions later.

A STRUCTURED APPROACH

Contrary to what many discovery writers believe, creating a fantasy world is a free form activity. You don't want to impede any creative juices, but using some guardrails will help keep everything inside the big bowl you are creating. World-builders often categorize their elements and consider the interplay of various aspects. The structured approach allows for full development of the world's scope, enabling characters to explore and exploit their story world.

1. Rules of Extraordinary Physics – If you are building a world, there are basic aspects that you will need to take into consideration. The most important ones are the rules of your world. Like the laws of physics, your world needs its own set of ground rules if it is speculative in the least. For your world, rules still govern spaceflight, time travel, magic, and technology. If these rules don't exist, the reader will believe the writer is conveniently changing things as they go along to avoid worrying about causality and continuity.
2. Natural Factors – Every Fantasy writer loves a good map. A map serves as the foundation for the world's physical attributes. Geography shapes many aspects of your world. Other major geographic, ecological, and geologic features will be key to the way your story unfolds. Climate also plays a significant role in the story. It's a powerful tool for evoking tone and mood in the story. Water, vital for life and present in all societies, underscores the importance of ecological understanding. Account for water in your story if humanoid life is present.
3. Technology and Magic – Every society has technology. Ponder the driving forces and future trajectory of your story. Include weapons in this category. Nothing speaks more about the technology of a world than their weapons. Most fantasy stories involve some magic system. It is best to develop the mechanics

of that early in the process, so you have consistent treatment of its use throughout the story.
4. People – Define the basic lifeforms that dominate your world. This will help determine the characteristics of the various races: their biases, their interactions, their status, etc. You can build the most fantastical elements in literature, but if you don't know how your elves, your dwarves, and other made-up beings interact, it could create a jumbled mess in the middle of the second act that sinks your story. Also, pay attention to anatomical concerns. Your humanoids should function like regular people with perhaps one unique quirk.
5. Cultural Norms – All the elements above will impact the development of any cultural norms. This will consist of the trade systems, holidays, government structures, clothing, and food. Upsetting these social norms will create grand theater and often drive conflict between the hero and their own society. Language and architecture are two other items to build into your story. Language peculiarities and housing methods signify cultural importance.
6. Ruling structures – What type of government, noble, or religious structure oversees the land? The gods the locals worship and how their government runs are key factors in every society. Ignoring them will be a sizeable gap in your world-building. They can also be a great option for conflict within your story.
7. Flora and fauna – Every world will have plant and animal lifeforms. You may have magical creatures, like unicorns and dragons or deadly plants or something else. But exploration of the food chain in your world is an encouraged activity.

These large buckets capture obvious items for building a fictional world. While writing your story, other ideas and lessons for approaching the setting will appear, but you should always ask yourself a set of questions. How is the current culture of the city impacting your protagonist? Do they have concerns with the direction technology is impacting their world? What natural obstacle does the world face? These questions exist beyond speculative fiction. They exist in genre stories across the spectrum.

If you are struggling with beginning, find one of several world-building templates on-line. Many are free and serve as excellent springboards to ignite your creativity. One such tool exists in the Vibrant Prose Toolbox included with this textbook.

As with anything else of significance in your story, document your world-building components. You will refer to the details for consistency as you reuse settings and characters and other elements of the story within the manuscript. You will also be able to identify trends in the setting that provide a realistic feel and drive themes.

WORLD-BUILDING TOOLS

The world-builder likely has a complete and detailed world building process. Pantsers, and many plotters, have no clue most of the time. This section provides tools that may help you in that process. Use these tools in the revision passes, but you can also experiment as you work through the rough draft.

One word: maps. You might be rolling your eyes as it has been mentioned before in this text. Countless books include maps. It's almost a requirement in the Fantasy genre. Many books don't require a map in the story. Sometimes, a story with a map is helpful, but it's rare. While including a map in your book may not be mandatory, a map can prove valuable for every writer.

Regardless of the story, a map is a great tool to track your characters as they move through the setting. If you have a real-life setting, just print one out or do a screen capture of it on your computer from Google Maps. A map proved vital in the development of all three Marco Flynn books. For the second book, *The Young & the Wicked*, the author tracked the characters' positions because they lacked familiarity with the Emerald City. This allowed the author to ensure reasonable transportation times from one spot to another, whether it was by car, train, or walking. Focusing on these details will assist your reader in following the story.

A second application is ensuring the characters' placement makes sense. For example, in *The Young & the Wicked*, Marco Flynn and his ex-wife get into an argument, and she kicks him out of the house. He needed a place to stay. The guy couldn't crash in a random Marriott near the university when he was much further south in the city's geography. This world created an issue with the character bouncing between two distinct locations miles apart from each other in consecutive chapters. Using the map to track the whereabouts of your character can help maintain the illusion for the reader and keeps the character from crisscrossing the city.

For *Argent's Menagerie*, the author developed a map to determine the distance and the reasonable amount of time it took to travel between various planets and created consistency across the story.

There are online resources as well. World Anvil and Campfire are online writing/world-building tools for creatives to develop their story worlds. Though they can be expensive, they also support various writing tools to accompany the world-building aspects of their products.

World-building relies on conveying information to readers. Although it often takes a backseat to characterization, plot, and tension, it is not something to be shirked. To fully experience a novel, one must immerse themselves in the story through a character's eyes. A realized world includes people, places, events, and details. Getting those to the reader is a key function of the character's narrative.

EXERCISES

1. Create a map of your favorite story, identifying the important locations for that story.
2. Find a historical event and identify five setting details you would need to use to portray it well.

REFERENCE MATERIALS

Worldbuilding For Fantasy Fans and Authors by M. D. Presley
Worldbuilding for Novices by Jon R. Osborne
World-building for Writers: The Complete Handbook: From Constructed Languages to Mythical Realms by H. C. Harrington

These three world-building guides are geared towards the different points of the plotter/pantser spectrum. Presley's book is a deep dive into the theoretical aspects of world-building and understanding why we make the decisions we do about settings in a fantasy or science-fiction story. Harrington's book helps pantsers integrate world-building into their drafts without the usual effort and research put in by world-builders. Osborne's book is for those who want to world-build before starting their story without the commitment of Presley's effort.

14 – CONFLICT

Now that we have discussed our plot, theme, setting, and the main characters, conflict is our next topic. In this chapter, we will dive into the sources and types of conflict. Then we will discuss establishing the objective and identifying the motivations of the character. Then we will walk through ways the character copes with or resolves the conflict. We will finish with how you implement the conflict into your writing process. Let's establish what conflict is and what it isn't.

- Conflict is not fighting or violence in your story. Fighting or violence are often an effect that is caused by the conflict within the story. For example, in a war story, a battalion needs to cross an expanse of land to defeat an enemy. The enemy has set traps across the expanse in the form of land mines. Violence arises as the battalion advances and stems from the conflict.
- Conflict is not tension or suspense. These are narrative qualities that you build into your story. The following chapter will cover these topics in more depth.
- Obstacles don't solely cause conflict. The obstacle is a component of the conflict process.

So, what exactly is conflict? Conflict encapsulates the objectives (goal and motivation) of the protagonist meeting an obstacle, the protagonist's struggle to clear the obstacle to either achieve or not achieve their desired outcome, and the impacts (cost, consequences, and stakes) of that resolution. After reviewing this chapter, you should be able to document the entire conflict cycle in your story by defining these elements.

What problems arise from conflict? Without powerful motivation and real stakes, why should the audience care? Without any struggle, an obstacle lacks genuine conflict, leaving the audience indifferent. If the outcomes and impacts are shallow, then the conflict seems inconsequential. Every element matters and must resonate with the reader. If you are missing one or more of these parts of the cycle, the entire process appears weak, and the reader doesn't want to read your story. A clear red flag.

Let's talk about the conflict we want to depict in our story. Early in your story, you will need to ask a question of the character and define their objective. You have two options: they desire something, or they wish to prevent someone from taking something. The details of what they specifically desire grow from those possible options.

Sci-Fi books explore reaching new planets. In a Romance, it's about how they find true love. Defining desire implies a contract, promising a resolution by story's end. Immediately, this provides tension in the story. Can you fulfill your part of the agreement? That tension must build through the story to keep the reader interested. Your story needs a strong core conflict to succeed and to drive your main story.

SOURCES OF CONFLICT

The various types of conflict could be internal, external, or interpersonal. Moral dilemmas arise from internal conflict, leading characters to unexpected decisions. External Conflict is the most action oriented and requires a physical sacrifice by the lead character. Interpersonal deals with the relationships amongst characters in the story. Conflict in different forms creates a complex narrative plot. This conflict arises from various sources to set up a battle for supremacy, a test of man versus...

VS. MAN

This is the simplest and most common source of conflict, hero vs villain. It often takes the form of physical confrontation and is the most personal between the combatants, interpersonal. Connections usually stem from shared backstories. Perhaps they are brothers, perhaps they were on the opposite side of an event in their past, or some other connection that creates angst between them. These often require a deep connection for us to believe that one man wants to battle someone so intently.

VS. NATURE/TIME

Conflict can involve battling nature or a wild beast, always physically. Often, nature presents a secondary conflict within the story. Perhaps, the objective becomes harder as the rainy season complicates travel.

Survival is often the primary goal of the protagonist in this battle. Time can present certain obstacles and conflict for the protagonist.

VS. SELF

These conflicts often center around a character making choices against their set of beliefs or values. These are almost exclusively internal battles. Batman has a code that prohibits him from killing anyone based on what happened to his parents. In *Batman Begins* he repeatedly upholds this value. By contrast, in *Man of Steel*, Superman kills his opponent to prevent him from hurting innocent people. Viewer disappointment with the film may be due to this out-of-character element. The character's fear and flaw determine their actions in defending their core. How much can the character endure before reaching their breaking point?

VS. SOCIETY/STATE

The character becomes a champion of a cause. Be it Civil Rights, freedom, unification of a people, or some other noble effort. The character must confront society, government, or a formidable foe in an unwinnable fight. They pay the greatest price through sacrifice. This conflict encompasses all three conflict forms. The battle that Rin faces in *The Poppy War* falls into this category.

VS. SCIENCE/MAGIC/TECHNOLOGY

The character is now battling something beyond them and often this type of foe accompanies one of the others listed above. In *Jurassic Park*, it is a combination of science and nature. Surviving the island is the primary aim, but understanding the larger question of scientific cloning is the recurring thematic conflict. The character needs assistance to overcome this formidable challenge. Tech and magic symbolize society and nature and often encompass indirect conflicts.

Conflict sources can be varied or combined in a story. They also drive internal, external, or interpersonal conflict. When the sources and types are combined, it gives a large variety of options in developing meaningful conflict. As you become more experienced as a writer, you will develop more layered approaches around conflict and create multi-faceted stories that strike upon multiple themes throughout your work.

OBJECTIVES

The first step in creating conflict is knowing what the character desires. This creates a simple and concrete objectives. This is where knowing your protagonist in intimate detail drives the story. Their motivations will provide the information on how to resolve the story while also creating as much conflict as possible. The antagonist, or other characters, conflict with these motivations. Some basic examples are given below:

- Fears and Phobias – Fear becomes a great motivating factor. We all have fears. They drive us toward or away from something. Demonstrating concern and a desire to retain or regain their possessions. In *The Poppy War* by R.F. Kuang, Rin fears being stuck in her tiny town for the rest of her life and assured death, prostitution, or slavery.
- Relationships – We want to protect those we care about. We will do anything to prevent them from being harmed, even doing something illegal. Love for someone or something inspires action.
- Values and Beliefs – Perhaps our characters have an unstoppable sense of justice. Harry Potter stood up to Voldemort because he opposed evil. There is a sense of higher purpose among these characters.
- Status – The character may not be able to handle losing their position of power. Status also motivates the antagonist. They refuse to relinquish their possession.
- Revenge – Did the character lose someone close to them? Did they lose something valuable? Pursuing that revenge leads to a significant moment of conflict resolution. Do they follow through or prove stronger at the end? Do they exact revenge and strike down the evil dictator and free their nation?
- Motivating Incident – Did something occur that encouraged the deviant behavior of the antagonist? Or were they broken by the lack of a parent's love? Did the protagonist see their father lose to the same evil they fight today and have that as his motivation? A single event motivates many characters.

Many other motivating forces could exist in the character's life. The key is to identify those early on in your story so the reader latches onto them and understands the character. They empathize with the protagonist and comprehend their plight. The character then must become proactive and push the story forward by pursuing the objective. Once the objectives are clear, four character questions remain. The answers give us a glimpse into the protagonist's perspective.

- What is their motivation for achieving that goal?
- What are they willing to do to achieve it? This will reveal their intention.
- What is the limit they will not cross to achieve it? This will reveal their internal limitation.
- What happens if they succeed or fail? This will reveal the stakes.

Authors must remember their promises to readers. The protagonist's objective must align with our reader's expectations. A corpse appearing in the first scene with no priority on identifying the murderer is an issue. We need an alignment of our promises to our protagonist's objective. The character may have additional objectives, but the story must fulfill the main promise.

Once these elements are defined, they must be communicated to the reader. At some point, we need the protagonist to express their motivation and desire to the reader. We must show their determination and the consequences of not achieving their goal. Consequences must compel the reader and the pursuit will be worthwhile. These stakes should be tied to the fear and flaw of the protagonist. Acknowledging these early and building them into the potential impact will help relate the struggle to the reader and up the ante for the lead character.

Our goal is to heighten the stakes, creating a precarious situation for our protagonist. Heightening stakes adds tension and holds reader interest in the plot.

CONFLICT AVOIDANCE

Now, our protagonist has gazed into the enemy's eye and decided to escape, conceal, and avoid conflict at any price. For some reason, our character lacks courage, or that necessary element of moral fiber. Perhaps the sheer size of the task overwhelms them, or they lack the financial means to succeed, or they do not know how to proceed. What will they do? Here are the ways our characters avoid conflict but still progress the plot forward.

- They recruit others to their cause. This could assist with the task's size or provide the needed financial support for the activity.
- They join the opponent's cause for lack of an alternative, but still hold their motivations close and act on them if given a chance. You will need to show them still openly plotting to act if the opportunity arises. This is a tricky option, and it needs to be believable.
- They hide, especially if they need to recover and heal. We've all seen the movie where the wounded hero hides to avoid death and then later comes back to get revenge for his fallen comrades.

The character should only avoid conflict as a last resort. Remember, the protagonist drives the storyline's action. If this happens, we need to get the ship righted because without someone pursuing a resolution, the story stops. The character should consider other motivations. Perhaps they discover an old friend/flame will leave the enemy if they convince them to switch sides. The payoff is crucial if this approach is chosen.

THE ANTAGONIST

We need to understand the antagonist, and their motivations. This especially applies to characters that betray others in the story. All characters in the story can obstruct the protagonist and should be treated equally. Their motivations fall into four categories in a variation of the MICE acronym.

- Money – This can be financial, but also status. Greed, revenge, envy, survival are all underlying reasons for this type of motivation.
- Ideology – Vindication, Fear, Esteem. Their belief remains steadfast, regardless of the path's appearance.
- Coercion – Using strong-arm tactics like isolation to force others to act negatively toward the protagonist.
- Ego – Narcissistic characteristics drive the antagonist.

It is important to know each character believes they are in their own story. They believe they are right, and this is their story as much as the protagonist's. Having said that, this also allows them to proactively pursue their own path. Choosing a path that doesn't provide an obstacle to the protagonist fails to create engaging narratives.

OBSTACLES

In this section, we will discuss how to use obstacles to build conflict, tension, and suspense into your story. In your story, you will have multiple obstacles. If tension stems solely from a schoolyard brawl, you have a problem. More obstacles are needed for the main character, beyond just a shop class thug.

In an earlier chapter on building characters, you learned how to identify two aspects of your main character: their greatest fear and their greatest flaw. These complications create something referred to as "The Knot." The character's self-made obstacle generates conflict in their story. There are five general categories of internal obstacles listed below. This section discusses how to use these in your story to build conflict.

- Fear – Using the greatest fear of the character is a simple obstacle to incorporate. Perhaps it is a fear of losing the love of their life. The character must face and conquer their fear. Consider this a small triumph.
- Flaw – The character has a serious internal flaw. Perhaps it is a personality disorder, or an addiction to drugs. Whatever it is, we need to see them struggle with this and have it stand between them and their objective. Perhaps it drives a wedge between them and someone close to them.
- Intention – This is perhaps the easiest to address and would be the first obstacle you would put in front of the lead. You can't allow them to go in a straight line from point A to point B. What would hinder them from completing their stated intention to achieve the goal? Use this to block that from happening.
- Limitation – This is a higher-level obstacle. Define what it would take for your character to cross the line. Do they refuse to kill someone? Prompt them to confront a moral dilemma and decide. Delay this obstacle, making it the ultimate or penultimate hurdle. You need a compelling reason to cross this line. In *The Poppy* War, outside pressures deprived Rin of the opportunity to study for the academy test. She resorted to some extreme techniques to learn the material.
- Decisions – Have the decisions of the character create additional complications and conflict. Perhaps they must decide whether to help their love interest or another person. After they decide, have the love interest think negative thoughts about that choice to set

up a later conflict. Also, have the character make incorrect decisions and suffer consequences.

As with internalized obstacles, external obstacles take numerous forms, but these are directly tied to the sources of conflict. These obstacles impact motivation, intention, and objective simultaneously. They also create multiple instances of conflict within the story.

- Nature – The simplest and least predictable obstacle could be something that occurs through nature. A storm, an earthquake, or volcano eruption are things that change the entire landscape. To use any of these tactics, you must first foreshadow them in the story. It's a great way to incorporate the setting into the story.
- The State/Society – Perhaps you are taking a stand against some injustice and there is a reaction from the state. It could be legal problems, job loss, or another obstacle. But the result could impact everything around the character.
- System Limitations – This type of obstacle is something you want to set up when you define your world's magic or technology environment. There might be a limitation in your magic system, requiring a substantial sacrifice to overcome. Or perhaps the technology has limitations that the protagonist must override. The hero uses his capabilities to overcome these obstacles. These issues become part of the final resolution.
- Other Characters/Sub-Plots – Your hero and the other characters on their side don't see eye-to-eye on every issue. These side characters may go on their own and their actions create obstacles for your main character.
- Antagonist – The most direct obstacle is the antagonist and any possible henchmen they have on the payroll. This is the simplest source, but it could also be the hardest to overcome. As discussed in an earlier chapter, it would be best if you analyzed the motivations and objectives of the antagonist, so you and the reader understand their driving ambitions in the story. In most stories, defeating the antagonist ends the story.
- Change Motivations or Objectives – What if something happens that changes the motivations or objectives of the lead? The girlfriend has been taken hostage. A bomb destroys the building that stored your character's tools. A death in the family prohibits restoring a relationship. Any of these could happen. Upon this occurrence, it is crucial to redefine objectives, motivations, and

commence the new pursuit. In *The Poppy War*, Rin's motivations shift when she must prepare for an unexpected attack on the academy. Because of that, the stakes increase dramatically for her.

Having identified these various options, you need to decide what obstacles you are going to use on your character. We need to punish the character and make them earn any chance of success. We don't want a weak victory. The character must also emerge changed from the gauntlet. **All conflict in the story must elicit a response, either physical or emotional.**

The next part of the problem is getting past the obstacle, the struggle. To quote Saruman from the movie version of *The Fellowship of the Ring*, "…you have elected the way of pain." We need to demonstrate this pain for the main character. Things we can't do are make things easy, convenient, lucky, or contrived. The hero must fight, bleed, sweat, and cry through this ordeal. This will impact your narrative. This struggle will be shown through various writing mechanisms.

- Try-Fail Cycles – This technique invokes a series of attempts by the protagonist to achieve their objective, but each is met with failure. Each attempt presents a unique format. Perhaps the first interaction is a polite conversation, the second is a legal battle, and the third is a direct confrontation. Their struggles cannot be identical. Also, each attempt rewards the protagonist with something to help them achieve their goal. A clue, information, or another element can lead to a confrontation.
- Yes-But-No-And – This is a bit more complex approach. If the character succeeds in their attempt, a second complication presents itself. Yes, you won the court case, but you alienated your girlfriend. Or perhaps the character fails and something else happens. You lose the court case and alienate your girlfriend. The idea is to compound the complication by adding additional sources of conflict through the story and raising the stakes.
- Murphy's Law – This is the worst-case scenario and is a staple of tension driven fiction. Whatever happens at the end of the scene, you ask yourself, "What could make this worse?" It's possible that the girlfriend goes with the other man. This tactic is often used to set up the crisis moment within the story.
- Direct Conflict – The simplest but also the hardest to determine the right time to implement. The protagonist and antagonist duke

it out in the streets for everyone to see. A possible ending or the beginning of troubles for the protagonist.

- Raising the Stakes – This happens when motivations or objectives change. Raise the stakes to worsen the potential outcome. The original objective of a happy life with their girlfriend is interrupted when she is held hostage. Now, the focus is on bringing her back unharmed.

OUTCOMES

Once you have completed the process of pain on the protagonist, we must present the outcome of their struggle. It includes the protagonist's decision to risk everything, "The Moment of Truth," sacrifice, and character transformation. The "Moment of Truth" is where the character makes their fateful decision. This leads directly to the climax of the story. The character, on their last leg, faces one last hope as tension peaks. Both the character and reader must understand the significance of this decision.

There are multiple components to this outcome. The main character must make a final heroic choice. Perhaps, up to this point, they decided based on selfish desires, but now they must make the heroic decision to resolve the conflict. They must rise from their lowest point, the crisis, and make their stand.

At this point, the hero faces their dilemma. They must make a choice between equal options, either two bad or two good. Whatever they choose involves a sacrifice of some part, a cost for them. It can be physical, emotional, or both. However, they must decide despite overwhelming odds. Most times, this will resolve both the external conflict and their moral dilemma they dealt with the entire story.

Then, the hero must act. They must have that heroic moment when they jump into the climactic battle. They've acquired the required knowledge, and it's their moment to shine. They have gained the necessary skill or tool to battle the enemy and win. Then they give everything they have to defeat the enemy. Sometimes it is more than they can bear.

After the climax, we are left with the results. Yes, victory or defeat matters. What matters more are the consequences. Perhaps the character wins and achieves their goal, but it is always at a cost. If the hero escapes unscathed and nothing changes, then what was the point? Their challenge was overblown and a waste of the reader's time. Perhaps the hero falters, but his defeat unifies the characters, and they save the day. Even in tragedy, there must be a valuable impact that resolves the core conflict. And sometimes that resolution is negative. Sometimes, the bad guy wins and the impact we feared comes to fruition. If we proceed through the process, this may be the outcome.

The finish of *The Lord of the Rings* is a classic example. It reveals the intricate conflicts and underlying components, not only the high note ending. Yes, destroying the ring resolves the core conflict, but leading up to that, Frodo makes his choice and acts by running into Mount Doom. The twist then occurs when his personal demons become too much for him. Then, we witness Gollum's actions as his story reaches fruition. Gollum regains the ring, and we realize Frodo's story is not over. He makes the fateful decision to regain the ring, falling victim to his compromised desires. Even though he has already had to sacrifice bodily harm, he will go further by pushing Gollum into the lava. This act completes the core conflict of the entire series, the destruction of the greatest evil of the age. Tolkien then throws us a bone as he saves Frodo through some clever writing because he knows we can't handle the death of the halfling. But resolving the conflict exacted a price, and the impacts are measurable. To quote Théoden, "So much death!"

Consequences follow the climax, whether good, bad, or in between. Something must result from the hero's choice. Once the consequences surface, the character must then carry the accountability for their choice. These consequences must linger to impact the character or someone else after the story. It's part of the change we need. Without it, the decision carries no weight, or the conflict required feels unneeded. The reader will feel like it was for nothing. Consequences manifest as physical or emotional sacrifices, possibly leading to death in certain situations. Frodo lost a finger and suffered a nasty wound that haunted him for years after.

Many outcomes are possible, but the ultimate climax determines if the objective is met or not. The conflict's stakes must matter to the reader. The main character must face costs and consequences. If nothing changes through the outcome, then it doesn't matter.

As your story moves on and your characters try and fail multiple times, eventually you must have a resolution. Present the resolution as a choice: stop the gorilla or face the consequences. But the greatest stories often have a multi-faceted approach to the resolution.

- **Double-Attraction Conflicts** present a resolution that offers two positive options. Romance stories often present these options, usually love or career. Neither option is negative, but each has unique effects on the character's life.
- **Double-Avoidance Conflicts** present a resolution offered through two negative options. The character must decide between two options and face the consequences. The classic example of having to make the choice between a loved one or other innocents.
- **Attraction-Avoidance Conflicts** are complex. They involve a choice that avoids, or masks, pain now but leads to further pain down the road. Or short-term pain for the potential of long-term gain.
- **Heroic resolutions** often come at a cost, such as losing a loved one or one's own life. This can be seen psychologically as they're forced to make an abhorrent but necessary decision to resolve the problem. Understanding character motivations requires gaining knowledge of their driving factors in these instances.

If you know your story but lack the fulfilling ending, consider outlining or writing potential outcomes. Once you have accomplished this, select the outcome that is the most surprising yet inevitable.

That inevitable conclusion then needs to reflect a change in the character. They must have experienced a profound emotional realization, like the saying "Rebellions are built on hope." Change manifests as a physical alteration, a shift in status, or acquiring new abilities or knowledge. Something must change about the character. No change, no meaning, no value to the story.

Fulfilling promises to readers is another concern. If we haven't discovered the killer of the initial victim, we must find that answer. Early alignment of objectives prevents this issue from occurring. It's crucial to address reader promises with our outcomes.

Whatever you do for a resolution, you must resolve the outstanding questions in the story and leave no open storylines. The only exception is when you develop a series, and the unanswered question becomes part of the next book's storyline. You will want to stagger these resolutions as you reach your conclusion. It may be overwhelming to answer all questions and fulfill promises simultaneously in the story's last scene.

Some tools help document the conflict process. To determine whether your conflict has the components, and they flow together, you can fill out a conflict flowchart. A conflict flowchart shows the elements of that conflict on one sheet. This allows you to explore options in three categories: objectives, obstacles, and outcomes. A copy of a conflict flowchart is provided in the Vibrant Prose Toolbox.

If you are looking for more complex conflict tools, you could refer to the elements identified in your exercises with the GMC identification process earlier in this curriculum. The combined character web and conflict/theme square could identify other options for developing additional conflict between characters other than the two dominant forces.

You now have a full understanding of the various aspects of conflict and how to implement it in your writing. If you build your conflict correctly, you will have enough fuel to make your characters seem real, your tension to continue rising, and your plot to feel explosive through the end of the story.

EXERCISES

1. Create an alternate ending for your favorite book.
2. Use the conflict flowchart. Define the various elements of the core conflict and put those into the conflict flowchart to determine if you have significant elements necessary.
3. Identify the source of external, internal, and interpersonal conflict in a story.

REFERENCE MATERIALS

Mastering Plot Twists: How to Use Suspense, Targeted Storytelling Strategies, and Structure to Captivate Your Readers by Jane Cleland
Understanding Conflict: And What It Really Means by Janice Hardy
Story Trumps Structure: How to Write Unforgettable Fiction by Breaking the Rules by Stephan James

Cleland's and Hardy's books are the best in defining conflict and other various tension elements of fiction. Hardy focuses on conflict itself and helps define the aspects of a core element of writing. Cleland is perhaps the best tome on the entire gambit of tension in the writing guide realm. A dedicated tome is needed to cover this overlooked aspect of writing. James' excellent book covers a plethora of writing topics, but dives into the concept of tension-driven fiction as the centerpiece of modern genre fiction.

15 – DRAMATIC TENSION

Tension is that element of your writing that keeps the reader glued to the page. They anticipate what will occur on the next page, next paragraph, or next chapter. Tension grabs your reader at an emotional level. You can do everything you want to your characters to keep the reader intellectually involved, but tension grabs them in the feels. Once the reader takes an interest in your characters and they follow them through the escapades of the plot, the emotional hook takes hold and they become interested in the stakes and consequences that face the character.

Many people solely associate tension with conflict. Conflict is just one of many tension elements available to use in your writing. Most Eastern based fiction relies much more on other tension elements such as suspense, intrigue, mystery, and irony.

In this chapter, we will break down the discussion of tension. We will then discuss techniques that create tension and pull the reader deeper into the story. There will also be a section that goes into detail about how tension feeds its close relatives, pacing and momentum.

Each of us has read character or plot driven popular fiction. J. D. Salinger's classic *The Catcher in the Rye* is a notable example of the character-driven novel. A modern novel filled with teenage angst, *Ready Player One* by Ernest Cline, is an example of a plot driven novel. Consider a third option that combines character development with an exciting plot. Have you heard of something known as tension-driven fiction?

TENSION-DRIVEN FICTION

Tension-driven fiction is a fairly new concept, but aspects of the idea date back to Gothic literature popularized by the writings of Edgar Allan Poe, Mary Shelley, and Bram Stoker. Stephen James describes tension-driven fiction as follows in his book, *Story Trumps Structure*:

"To uncover the plot of your story, don't ask what should happen, but what should go wrong. To uncover the meaning of your story, don't ask what the theme is, but rather, what is discovered. Characters making choices to resolve tension – that's your plot. If your protagonist has no goal, makes no choices, has no struggle to overcome, you have no plot."

Conflict, tension, and struggle lie at the core of these stories. Predefined plots are tossed aside, cute character attributes are pushed off the board, deep thematic significance is out of mind, and literary devices are relieved of duties. All taking a back seat to that constant tension. Much like the traditional character arc, the tension-driven story has its own cycle. This cycle consists of five components that repeat throughout the story as each new conflict arises. These markers appear on the image depicting the cycle.

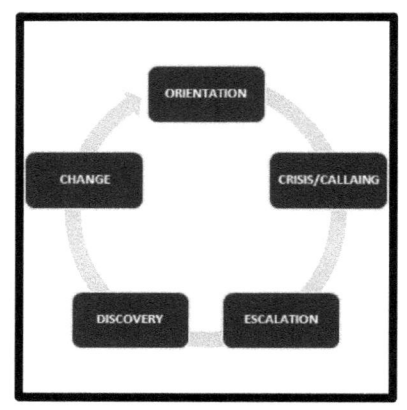

Figure 15-1 - The Tension Cycle

Throughout this cycle, similarities to character arcs and plotting techniques become evident. We also notice the distinctions in this approach compared to the others. The tension-driven model emphasizes fulfilling promises in every story.

The cycle begins with the orientation phase. Orientation is where the writer introduces the principal components to the reader. You must convey key aspects of your story to readers early in the novel.

- Orient your readers to the setting. It encompasses the setting's time, place, and tone. The reader must know the significance of the story's location from the beginning. The tone reinforces this aspect of the setting.
- Communicate the genre. Genres carry with them certain expectations. You need to communicate to the reader that you will provide the classic elements they crave from their favorite

genre. Start from the front cover, back blurb, and first scene. Then carry it forward.
- Introduce your narrative voice. Establish the narrative voice of this story. It needs to be consistent for the reader and pull them in.
- Introduce the main characters and force the reader to either care about them or despise them.
- End the orientation with a surprising and satisfying conclusion to snag the reader's attention.

The orientation is like a hook that we discussed in the structure chapter. It contrasts against the introduction of the character arc as it focuses much more on the entire story instead of the interior characterization of the lead. As we transition from one part of the cycle to the next, there are certain questions to ask yourself.

- How would the reader react in this scenario? The reader must find it believable, and the actions must connect to the story.
- How can I make things worse? This will "raise the stakes." Utilize the Yes-But-No-And technique, as discussed in the previous chapter.
- How can I end the suspense and story unexpectedly and inevitably? The surprise should be integral and organic to the story, even if unexpected.

If you ask these questions as you build your scenes, you will build a better story. Consider the reader's thoughts at this point in the story. Where do they believe the narrative is headed? Address those questions for a captivating story.

The crisis, or calling, is like an inciting incident within plot and character driven stories. In each, the lead either accepts or rejects the calling. They may not accept the calling initially, but they will. If not, you have no story. In a tension-driven story, the crisis or calling is demonstrated in three possible ways.

- Give the protagonist what they desire and then take it away. The plot centers around the character attempting to regain his desire. Broken marriage stories are fitting examples.
- Dangle the desire in front of the protagonist but do not give it away. Romance stories where people chase the person of their dreams are a big winner in this group.

- Force the greatest fear on the lead and see them struggle. *The Shawshank Redemption* delves into the struggle of those wrongly imprisoned and their relentless pursuit of freedom.

The struggles come in the form of three distinct types: internal, external, and interpersonal. Your character may face some of each type throughout the story and, at times, the struggles may overlap. A common occurrence is the internal struggle being the foremost for the character, with a series of external struggles spread throughout the story. Adding a couple interpersonal (relationship) struggles is a great technique. But first, the calling gets the lead moving toward their resolution and on the path to tackling these conflicts.

Next comes the escalation. The escalation relates to rising tension throughout the bulk of your story, much like the middle of the three-act structure. The tension is never released in a tension-driven story, whereas in an action-driven story it could be alleviated through successes. Each scene has the job of raising the tension and not letting it go. This is where we continue to "raise the stakes" and continue the struggle and punish the lead character with worse and worse situations. After every scene, question yourself, "How can I make this situation worse?" and include that in the story.

You want the reader to feel the tension rising. That anxiety and anticipation keep them invested in the story. You want them to wonder what happens on the following page. You want them to fear for the character. And you want them to enjoy it. The reader wants the lead character to earn their resolution.

There are things you want to avoid when you escalate the tension. First, vary the conflicts, character reactions, and dialogues to avoid repetition. Second, don't de-escalate the tension. If the lead defeats a character, the reader's tension fades unless other story elements alter that impression. For example, once the lead character has sex with his girlfriend, the relational tension is lost and cannot be recovered. Once tension is lost, trickery is needed to regain it, and readers become less accommodating.

The discovery stage is like the climax of a plot or the epiphany of a character. At this stage, the lead decides to resolve their struggles and move forward. Struggles can be resolved at different times, not always together, but the main struggle should be resolved last. Here are guidelines for the climax.

- The resolution needs to be believable.
- The conclusion should be unexpected, inevitable, and satisfying.
- The ending must also culminate all the tension.

Without holding the tension, the writer wastes his efforts, and the ending disappoints the reader. Also, don't leave the ending up to chance or coincidence. Avoid using a *Deus ex machina* to resolve the conflicts in the story. The reader wants the lead to resolve the story within their own abilities.

Change concludes the cycle. You need to determine if the changed status is internal or external to your character. This determines their makeup and susceptibility to change. As stated earlier, characters like James Bond or Superman change extraordinarily little. Characters like Holden Caulfield in *The Catcher in the Rye* change significantly. The protagonist's viewpoint discloses the new normal at the end. How does this alteration look to the character?

- Circumstances – the city is safe
- Outlook – the lead is open to a new status quo
- Skills – newfound abilities to help later stories
- Revelation – overcoming fearful circumstances
- Relationships – new or renewed relationships

Other key aspects of the tension-driven story are the promises the writer makes to the reader. The writer proposes a contract, starting with the book title, cover art, and first page. You must fulfill these promises to the reader, or they will be unsatisfied with your book. Keep track of the promises you put in your story and fulfill them in your manuscript.

INFORMATIONAL TENSION

Hopefully, by now, you have a solid understanding of tension. Tension appears in various forms. There are three categories of informational tension: suspense, intrigue, and mystery. Perhaps we need to provide an example of each to make the difference clearer. The fundamental distinction lies in who possesses the knowledge that causes tension in the story.

- Suspense – The reader knows something is going to happen. The suspense builds the longer the story progresses until the character gains the same knowledge that the reader holds. A city harbors a roaming monster, a room conceals a bomb.
- Intrigue – A character holds some key information but withholds it from the reader. The tension increases until the reader gains the piece of information. A spy reveals a secret that has driven the mission. The character is holding onto a secret that they wish to keep concealed from everyone.
- Mystery - The writer poses an unanswered question, engaging both the character and reader in solving it. Who killed a character? Why did the event happen?

The reader must be emotionally hooked into the story and concerned about the character's goals and motivations. The reader carries a sense of anticipation until the information drops, which creates a positive or negative outcome for the character. This reaction varies based on the reader's attachment to the character involved.

Suspense generates fear in readers as they anticipate the unknown: the beast, the monster, or the ax murderer. These create short-term suspense in the story and create additional tension over the long haul. It has become a hallmark of horror fiction.

Some books thrive on having minor sources of suspense in them, with one overarching suspense element that drives the main part of the story. A book relying on this source of tension falls into the Thriller genre. The intention is for the reader to always be engaged. *The Girl with the Dragon Tattoo* exemplifies a suspense story.

Intrigue is a hallmark of political and spy novels. There is a secret that one character holds. Someone wants to gain this secret, and someone wants to keep it. Tom Clancy's early novels exemplify this type of story. *The Cardinal in the Kremlin* revolves around a single secret: the identity of the spy Jack Ryan aims to rescue from the KGB. Espionage sucks us in because we believe that one little secret could cause empires to fall. Without that belief, would James Bond still be alive?

Perhaps the category most people understand in this group is the mystery. Again, this is about gaining information. Information and not knowing it creates a conflict, which drives tension. Finding something you think is a clue and then gaining frustration when it leads you down a wrong path has been a time-tested story since the novel was born. We all have our favorite mystery, right?

Writers should aim to include all three elements of informational tension in the story. The key is balancing them and keeping the tension of the story rising. Another tactic of the skilled writer is knowing when the game is up and revealing that hidden information to whoever needs it.

Next, exchanging tension from one of these types to another within a scene is a great way to resolve some questions within the story without letting the tension drop. For example, the character seeks a secret known by only one person. The character catches the person who holds the information, and, in their last breath, they reveal the answer. A bomb is set to detonate. But they don't tell them where it is located. In one swift move, we switch the tension in the story to be from a source of intrigue to suspense.

This revelatory moment must be accompanied by one thing: RAISING THE STAKES! You must make the new potential outcome even worse. Consider doing this only once or twice, perhaps at the Midpoint or the Crisis. Overusing this tool during the story will ruin the believability of the story and kick the reader out.

Information control is crucial in various genres. Fiction writers control information to provide a variety of suspenseful, intriguing, and mysterious components of their stories. The best prose weaves elements of each to enhance the story, characters, and themes.

IRONY

Irony and juxtaposition are two other ways to build tension within your stories. The concept revolves around the contrast between actuality and appearance for the reader. This irony falls into four distinct categories: comic, verbal, dramatic, or situational. The following paragraphs will walk through what irony looks like.

Satire and sarcasm often go together with comic and verbal irony. This irony often involves humor or absurdity. A book from author Pres Maxson called *Bastards of the Revolution* involves someone tracking down the lost diaries of a woman who was involved in sexual relations with many of the Founding Fathers of America. The comedic irony is that one woman gathers all the gossip about a group of men by providing one thing to them all: companionship.

Dramatic irony is one of the best-known instances of this tension. Typically, the audience has more knowledge than the story's character. In many stories, the action of the characters result in at least one death to create a tragic irony. The classic example involves *Romeo and Juliet*.

Use situational irony in instances to portray one image that amplifies an undercurrent that exists in another portion of the story. Visual media gives movies an advantage over fiction in this regard. In Peter Jackson's film version of *The Lord of the Rings*, the scene where the riders charge on Osgiliath accentuates the contrast by flashing back to Denethor savagely eating his meal and the dirge sung by Pippen amplifies the tone. To contrast the different emotional notes of impending doom on Faramir and the despair and madness exhibited by Denethor, the parallel images display two characters in opposing situations, heightening the irony.

OTHER TENSION TECHNIQUES

As a writer you have other tools at your disposal to help create tension through passive methods. These tools present tension, but not necessarily from an external source.

- Uncertainty is the act of not allowing the reader to predict the story. Predictability kills a story. Stay ahead of the reader and use distraction, misdirection, and red herrings to keep them guessing. Uncertainty builds tension with the character through their internal anxieties and fears.
- Relationships carry multiple forms of tension depending on the specific character and their status compared to the protagonist. This type of tension functions off the shifting of status and hierarchy between the various characters and their roles in the story. Chapter 6 provides a more detailed discussion of this.
- Withholding and isolating acts something from readers or characters. It could be in the form of information, love, or objects. This creates frustration, fear, and longing and force a character to make a decision that goes against their grain.
- Micro-tensions are those incidents that we take for granted that occur in everyday life to distract us from our actual purpose. Before saving the world from a bomb, make sure to drop off little Jenny at daycare. Or their wife took the car with the tools the protagonist needs to defuse the bomb. They exist at various levels, either alongside or related to the scene's main tension.

- THADs – This acronym stands for the Talking Heads Avoidance Device as coined by Melissa George. This is when characters' tasks symbolize the greater problem. The cliché involves characters arguing while cooking, but the argument has a different underlying subtext. Employ this tool to symbolically guide characters and propel the plot forward.

FORESHADOWING

Foreshadowing uses narrative to suggest a potential event that may happen later in the story. Foreshadowing lays the groundwork for the most dramatic scenes, character transformations, and secrets that will impact the storyline. The Marvel Cinematic Universe does an excellent job of using the Infinity Stones as MacGuffins to foreshadow future events and movies. The stones are used to provide insight into what may occur if Thanos captures them. All the foreshadowing through umpteen movies lays out the story that comes to fruition in the set piece *Avenger* films to complete the saga.

But this tool doesn't setup the complete story arc of the individual movies. Foreshadowing of character change in the movie *Thor* occurs when Odin banishes his son to Midgard and speaks the oath into the hammer, Mjolnir. First, Thor proves his worthiness by providing a physical sacrifice in the small New Mexico town. Then, Thor shows he has learned his lesson concerning the Frost Giants of Jotunheim and destroys the Bifrost Bridge, providing an emotional sacrifice. He completed his personal transformation from being a spoiled boy to a worthy successor of the king.

As for foreshadowing secrets, *The Forsaken Protector* used this technique to allude to the origin of Ankara Bellitis while also hiding this information from the other characters. Foreshadowing provided an opportunity to elevate the character and demonstrate how she was more worthy of the crown than her uncle, the Imperator.

Foreshadowing in your writing can be accomplished through multiple tools. Mood and setting aid foreshadowing of some hidden danger waiting around the corner. Symbols and motifs project specific meaning and evoke certain thoughts on what may occur down the road. Another popular tool is the use of secondary characters and subplots that later dovetail into the main plot and portend future events.

You want to foreshadow at key points of the story, while also attempting to conceal the eventual payoff. Clear foreshadowing leads to early conclusions, depriving readers of the awe and wonder they experience when your talents become apparent with clever reveals. You need a deft hand to employ this technique in every story you write.

TWISTS, REVERSALS, DANGER, (TRDs) AND CLIFFHANGERS

Once you create tension, the secret to success is to continually stretch that tension and make it greater over the length of the story. You do this through linking scene after scene to amplify this tension. One scene can be a very physical scene, another a dialogue scene, another an internal reflection (keep these short), followed by another physical scene. To do this, there are specific tools writers use to link scenes, build suspense, and stretch tension.

Writer's essential tools include the TRDs: twists, reveals, and danger. These tactics are also considered "prompts" used to prompt the reader into turning the page and reading the next chapter. The list could include two additional types of prompts: cliffhanger and reveal.

Plot twists are the things people crave. They keep the readers on their toes because they rely on the psychological aspect of your reader more than anything else. If you introduce a twist in the middle of the story that your reader doesn't anticipate, they become hesitant or doubt their judgement. Then, if you continue and pull off a solid twist at the end, you blow their mind. But readers are not stupid. Effectively executing a plot twist is among the toughest tasks in fiction.

- Twists cannot be obvious. When you reflect on the story, they become surprising yet inevitable. Imagine the perfect ending, then work backwards to ensure success. But you cannot leave noticeable tracks, or the reader will see the twist coming.
- You must use redirection. Mysteries do this all the time. Bury your clues in plain sight without making them obvious. Use red herrings and dead ends to make the reader think they know what is happening and dash their hopes. Make them believe they have no clue, figuratively speaking.
- Write twists into the ending. Make the reader certain they know the answer and then reveal they were wrong. Create uncertainty in their minds over the ending. The protagonist triumphs by using a previously hinted item, making the ending seem impossible. What is the reaction you want? Determine that and write the reader in that direction.

- The rule of three. Many writers will employ a strategy of using three twists in the story. One at the midpoint to create doubt in the reader. One before the climax to give them a false sense of security. One at the end to provide the unexpected but inevitable finish.

One of the great plot twists occurs in *Rebecca* by Daphne Du Maurier. Spoiler warnings if you have not read it. Throughout the story, we are told of the love between Maxim de Winter and his dead wife Rebecca as Mrs. Danvers (the housemaid) torments Maxim's new wife. We find out toward the end that Maxim and his first wife were not happy, and Rebecca had several lovers. Maxim believes he killed her. We then see Maxim's world unravel as we discover Rebecca not only lived, but ultimately committed suicide. Then when Maxim and his new wife return home from London, their home has burned to the ground and Mrs. Danvers is gone.

Plot reversals are events in the story that create additional obstacles for the character. Reversals can be man-made or natural. For instance, a character betraying the protagonist is man made. A natural reversal would be an earthquake opening a chasm and the protagonist must clear the chasm to reach their goal. There are specific guidelines for reversals.

- The intensity must be greater the later in the story it occurs. Late in the story, the betrayal of a trusted sidekick inflicts profound emotional damage.
- Information reversals work best if teamed with action reversals. Betrayal by your sidekick is bad. Getting shot by them is worse.
- Reversals demand a reaction. If it doesn't matter to the hero, it won't matter to the reader.
- All reversals should increase the stakes. The reversal may hinder the hero or halt their progress. These will require the lead to change their plan to achieve the new, short-term objective.

Danger is the element of risk for the character. The character may face physical danger, risking their life. Danger also takes the form of emotional danger where they wage an internal war over their beliefs. A common method of increasing the tension through heightened danger is through physical or emotional harm. Tying to the results of the conflict, the risk of death for a character raises the story's danger level.

Death is seen as a simple exit in certain narratives. Some stories give the option of damnation, loss of honor, or death of a child.

A Cliffhanger is a tool that abruptly ends a scene and leaves the conclusion in doubt. Those who watch soap operas are familiar with their workings. These can either be a dangerous situation or the revealing of shocking information. To create suspense, end a scene with a cliffhanger and delay the character's reaction until the next scene or chapter. The writer faces peril when using a cliffhanger. If they cannot provide an adequate payoff, they could lose the reader. The best cliffhangers are foreshadowed ahead of time, so the reader is not shocked. The reveal on the other side should be surprising.

Another useful tool for writers is the reveal. No, we're not talking about the ultimate reveal, but smaller versions sprinkled through the story. When tension is overwhelming, writers offer readers a glimmer of hope through character triumphs. This gives the reader a taste of success for the character and lets them breathe. Rarely do you desire to captivate your reader and guide them through the story without pause. It takes a sadistic or brilliant writer to do that. Your contract with the reader involves fulfilling occasional promises throughout the story.

In *As the City Burns*, the main character finds a dead body in a canal to start the story. Within a few paragraphs, the sleuth identifies the body. The author builds the reader's confidence in the ability of the writer and the character to answer their questions through the story. Fulfilling promises and answering questions through small reveals in the story also avoids bloated endings.

Pulling off a mind-blowing final twist is the ultimate achievement for writers. One that they tell all their friends about. We're talking about Vader revealing he is Luke's father level of satisfaction. How does one go about doing that? Per Jane Cleland and her book *Mastering Plot Twists*, there are three notable ways to do this.

- Seamless Integration – This relies on the main plot intertwining with the sub-plots and having those sub-plots impact the ending with a seamless integration. In *Argent's Menagerie*, various sub-plots through the story provide pieces of information that impact the conclusion of the story. This is the most common approach from Cleland's list.
- Unreliable Narrator – Agatha Christie's *The Murder of Roger Ackroyd* is the quintessential version of this. Once we know the narrator has been lying to us or hiding information, the ruse

becomes clear, and we feel like schmucks because we didn't see it coming. With increasing reader sophistication, executing this technique becomes more difficult.
- Wider Lens – This relies on the reader believing their perception of the story is the full picture. Once the veil lifts and the lens broadens, the reader comprehends the world within the microcosm. In the final scene of *Men In Black*, Earth appears as a small marble in an alien teenager's locker.

Characters in fiction experience high-stress situations as intense, pressure-filled moments that push them to their limits—whether emotionally, physically, or mentally. Here's a short list summarizing how the authors crank up tension and conflict:

- Add Unpredictability: Stressed characters act unpredictably, keeping things exciting.
- Boost Internal Conflict: Stress digs into characters' fears and doubts.
- Create Snap Decisions: Quick, messy choices lead to bigger problems.
- Escalate Tension: Stress makes everything become urgent, keeping readers on edge.
- Force Confrontation: No more avoiding conflict—stress brings issues to the surface.
- Reveal True Character: Under pressure, characters' real selves shine or crumble.
- Raise the Stakes: Stress turns failure into catastrophe, upping the drama.
- Strain Relationships: Stress cracks even the strongest bonds, fueling conflict.

Lastly, let's cover the TRDC Tracker tool. This tool notes the location and type of TRDCs used. The basic version of the tool monitors page, event type, and page count since the last event in the story. The tool serves two main purposes: ensuring event variety in the story and maintaining a steady pace by avoiding long gaps. The TRDC Tracker is an effective tool to monitor the pacing of your story and as a diagnostic tool during revisions to determine why the story feels too fast or slow for the reader. A version of the TRDC Tracker exists in the Vibrant Prose Toolbox.

Chapter	Scene	Page #	Explanation of Tension Element	Type	Pages since last element
1	1	1	Casemiro reads the ad	Intrigue	0
1	1	1	Boy asks about the extravaganza	Mystery	0
1	2	2	Forrest appears	Danger	1
1	2	3	Casemiro takes the chain	Intrigue	1
2	1	4	Forrest stops at the flower shop	Mystery	1
2	2	5	Casemiro leaves his sword	Danger	1
2	3	6	Casemiro feels uneasy about the Prince	Irony	1
2	3	7	Laural appears	Suspense	1
2	3	8	Casemiro says he's had enough	Cliffhanger	1
3	1	9	Answer questions	Reveal	1
3	2	11	What is Laural's job for Casemiro	Mystery, Irony	2
3	3	12	Laural explains	Suspense, Reveal	1
4	1	13	Casemiro is withholding info from us	Intrigue	1
4	2	14	What is the platform for?	Mystery	1
4	3	15	Atheron explains the Extravaganza	Twist	1
4	3	16	Dragon is foreshadowed	Foreshadowing	1
4	3	16	Atheron explains the missing money	Reveal	0
4	3	17	Geoffrey dies from poison	Cliffhanger	1

Figure 15-1 TRDC Tracker

PACING AND MOMENTUM

Pacing is the unsung tool of great writers and is used to control the reader and hack their brain. Pacing accomplishes two things: regulating the reader's perception of story progression and managing tension levels. Let's discuss the tension and how writers manipulate it in the story.

Imagine a graph that shows the tension of the story. The graph rises throughout the story until the climax. Thriller writers desire an unceasing ascent that maintains a relentless pace, propelling you towards the climax. This style of book applies pressure on the writer. If you take the reader on that ride, it better be worth it. You do not want an anti-climactic ending.

Many stories escalate tension while providing relief along the way. Most non-Thriller genres operate in this manner. The trick in using this method is providing the release within the scene and then escalating the tension again as you leave it. Putting this break at a different point in the scene will yield different results. Good writers

VIBRANT PROSE

vary when they apply this tactic during the scene to provide specific effects.

Placing the release at the end of the scene provides the greatest relief to the reader and creates a natural breaking point in the story. For a long story, consider including natural breaks to give the reader a chance to rest. For a novel under 300 pages, avoid these until the story's end. You want a reader to remain captivated.

Releasing in the scene's middle creates a beat for reflection, but tension must ramp up immediately for the next scene. The Yes/But/No/And technique works well in this scenario. The lead may overcome a physical danger like a man-eating monster, but with that victory he now must face the beast's master. The hero moves from one disaster to another within the same scene. The writer must find a natural break for chapters, mastering tension and story speed.

Beginning a scene with a release is a hallmark of cliffhanger writers. They depart the previous scene, risking the hero's life by jumping off a cliff. Then they move to the next chapter and reveal they landed on a ledge and are fine, a literal cliffhanger. Cliffhangers prompt readers to continue into the next chapter. Beware of too many false cliffhangers, as they frustrate readers without adequate payoff.

Pacing also involves controlling the speed of the story for the reader. You have control over various techniques that make this happen in your story. Keep in mind, this is an illusion. The story is still 300 pages, it just appears to the reader that they experience a quicker read. Here are items that control the speed of the story.

- Action moves faster than non-action. You do more showing and less telling. Detailed exposition and reflection do the opposite.
- Brief dialogue bursts that occur in arguments and confrontations are faster and provide white space on the page. Deep discussion and pondering slows you down.
- Short sentences, scenes, paragraphs, and chapters progress through the plot and book quicker.
- Successes move the story forward faster. Failures push us back, but these ramp up tension. It is a balancing act.
- Scene cuts that move the lead forward in time, with simple summarization explaining the time lapse. Flashbacks and flashforwards do the opposite.

- Movies often use montage scenes to reflect intensive training that would take months. If you have seen a *Rocky* movie, you know what this looks like.
- Scenes with exposition and description are momentum killers. Front load your story with these elements for unhindered progress in later portions of the story.
- Long, complex paragraphs slow down the reader.
- Many short sentences in sequence slow down the reader. The brain slows us down because of the punctuation. Run-on sentences produce the opposite effect.
- Pulling the reader out of the main flow of the story is a killer. Doing something like this requires pivotal information.

The other major consideration under the category of pacing is momentum. This concept deals with the sense of progress and passage of time within your scenes. Achieving scene objectives brings a sense of progress. Each scene should have a goal that helps move the dominant story along that plot-path. It is your responsibility, as the writer, to define and achieve the goal in the scene.

Joe Abercrombie, a successful writer, doesn't always follow this advice. After deciding how the character will resolve the problem, Abercrombie often breaks the scene and later continues the story with the character having already taken the action they decided on earlier. However, this only occurs when the character easily accomplishes the act, and we later catch up with them to see the summarized results. At times, this creates a problem for readers in feeling the plot doesn't progress as desired.

The passage of time accompanies progressing the plot. Our task is proving time's non-stagnancy in the story. Whether you have a ticking time bomb or a countdown, it does not matter. These tools are useful for accomplishing this. Another technique is using a style of story called a travelogue. Time passes as characters travel. Tolkien did this in his stories to show off his world to the reader, thus revealing his world while progressing the story forward.

This momentum must continue through the story. If you have a diversion with a flashback or flashforward, you must ensure that you have advanced the plot before moving to the next scene. Tension and its companion, pacing, are critical tools in writing. The mark of a skilled writer is using techniques and tools to create reader tension.

EXERCISES

1. Put in a plot twist in your work.
2. Identify a moment of success for the main character and transform it into failure to heighten tension in your narrative.
3. Rather than fully disclosing everything in a chapter, incorporate a cliffhanger to conclude it.

REFERENCE MATERIALS

Mastering Plot Twists: How to Use Suspense, Targeted Storytelling Strategies, and Structure to Captivate Your Readers by Jane Cleland
Story Trumps Structure: How to Write Unforgettable Fiction by Breaking the Rules by Stephan James

Cleland is perhaps the best tome on the entire gambit of tension in the writing guide realm. A neglected aspect of writing, desperately calling for a dedicated resource. James' excellent book covers a plethora of writing topics, but dives into the concept of tension-driven fiction as the centerpiece of modern genre fiction.

16 – VOICE & PROSE

Analyzing voice in writing is complex. Everyone wants their own voice, mostly because the publishing industry says we need to have a distinct one. Agents say you need to find it. We look to other authors to help define it. Readers want yours to speak to them. What exactly is the "Author's Voice?"

Defining it is much easier than explaining how to develop voice. Do not mistake voice for style. Voice refers to the distinctive features of your written work. That's something we need to clarify that distinction. We will discuss style later in this chapter. Let's examine the three categories of voice and explore methods to enhance your authorial voice.

- Author's Voice – The authorial voice is not filtered through the viewpoint of the character. It controls the entire story and aspects of how the story is told. The author essentially provides the script for the narrator. This is your voice.
- Narrative Voice – The voice through which the story is told. First person narratives express the viewpoint character's voice. In omniscient or third person narratives, the voice may belong to the author or a character.
- Character Voice – The voice through which a character speaks, whether it be through dialogue, monologue, or narrative.

The only limitations of an author are their imagination and vocabulary. Voice is where the limitations become most apparent. The Author's Voice presents the story and controls how everything comes across to the reader; the words chosen, the viewpoint expressed, the use of descriptions or metaphors or similes. Your voice develops over time as you assimilate life experiences into your writing. Can it be trained? Yes.

TRAINING YOUR VOICE

From the start, writers have a voice. Your life experiences, your mood, your emotional state, and everything that makes you who you are shape your writing voice. When you hear that adage, write what you know. This is where that comes into play. You can only write the words you have in you. So, how do we create a voice that publishers and readers crave? There are four ways to improve your voice.

The first is practice. How do you get to Carnegie Hall? Practice, practice, practice. Writing more develops your voice. You will pick up new words, new techniques, and new tricks. Your voice gets better with practice. Ultimately, you want your voice to be your reflection presented to the reader. This advice might sound trite, but you want your voice to be natural. If you attempt to create a false voice the reader will know. Relax and let the storyteller inside you come forward. Finding your eventual voice may take time.

The second item is emulation. Almost every writer starts out thinking they want to sound like Tolkien, Austen, or Hemingway. You won't. One approach to doing this is studying the way these authors write and simulate it. Often, this takes the form of freewriting and copying their passages to mimic things like rhythm and sentence structure and where they apply stress and get this built into your mind, akin to muscle memory. Mary Robinette Kowal talks about doing this exact technique before writing her Austen inspired works. It establishes a frame of mind to emulate the voice of the chosen master.

The third item is adaptation. Writers need to adapt their voice to different writing situations. Perhaps your genre has a convention you want to follow, but your regular voice needs to change. Perhaps the tone of the work requires you to alter your writing style. You will almost invariably do this through specific word choices, rhythms, and imagery, but you will also change your voice. Doing this flexes those muscles and strengthens them. You will become a more rounded writer. Do not be afraid to occasionally do this.

The fourth item is evolution. Over time, your voice will naturally change. You will flower your writing with those new experiences, new thoughts, and new ideas. Do you think Hemingway started out with the voice he mastered later in his career? No, that voice developed over time. Read this excerpt from Hemingway's *The Old Man and the Sea* to experience his distinctive style.

"The old man's head was clear and good now and he was full of resolution, but he had little hope. It was too good to last, he thought. He took one look at the great fish as he watched the shark close in. It might as well have been a dream, he thought. I cannot keep him from hitting me but maybe I can get him. Dentuso, he thought. Bad luck to your mother.

The shark closed fast astern and when he hit the fish the old man saw his mouth open and his strange eyes and the clicking chop of the teeth as he drove forward in the meat just above the tail. The shark's head was out of the water and his back was coming out and the old man could hear the noise of skin and flesh ripping on the big fish when he rammed the harpoon down onto the shark's head at a spot where the line between his eyes intersected with the line that ran straight back from his nose. There were no such lines. There was only the heavy sharp blue head and the big eyes and the clicking, thrusting all-swallowing jaws. But that was the location of the brain and the old man hit it. He hit it with his blood-mushed hands driving a good harpoon with all his strength. He hit it without hope but with resolution and complete malignancy.

The shark swung over and the old man saw his eye was not alive and then he swung over once again, wrapping himself in two loops of the rope. The old man knew that he was dead but the shark would not accept it. Then, on his back, with his tail lashing and his jaws clicking, the shark plowed over the water as a speed-boat does. The water was white where his tail beat it and three-quarters of his body was clear above the water when the rope came taut, shivered, and then snapped. The shark lay quietly for a little while on the surface and the old man watched him. Then he went down very slowly."

If you struggle with finding your personal voice, undertake an exercise to define it better. Ask yourself questions about your motivators, desires, and the other factors that influence you as a person and a writer. Dig and discover a lever to amplify your voice. Perhaps you have a particular incident that created a comedic bone (aka the humerus!), or an event that created a sarcastic side of you.

NARRATIVE VOICE

In the event you use omniscient narration, you are using the narrative voice and the reflective viewpoint of your authorial voice. Shaping the narrative voice involves some basic techniques.

- Be consistent in how you use your narrative voice on various characters. If you have snark with one, have it with all of them.
- Be formal or informal and don't swerve. This is tied to being consistent with your word choice and grammar. Whatever avenue you choose, stick with it.
- Be concise and use direct, active language. Narration itself slows down the story. Don't add to the problem by overwriting and using passive or indirect language that prolongs the slow pacing.
- Use tone effectively. Your voice shapes the story's mood along with action, imagery, and dialogue. Evoke emotion through your tone.

In writing with a primary first-person or third-person limited viewpoint, a character voice is employed. This voice may vary from your authorial voice. Multiple factors influence the character voice.

- Their own personal education/background. Each character's vocabulary and worldview inevitably shape their communication style.
- Their geographic origin. The character will say certain words or phrases that make sense for that region. Ensure the voice distinguishes the characters without being overshadowed.
- Their attitude. How do they talk to people? Do they try to intimidate them? Are they introverted? Does their communication differ from their internal thoughts? This may be a great tool to drive conflict in the story.

Writing guides and teachers often talk about voice in this nebulous way that makes it a challenge to understand as an element of your writing. There are no hard and fast rules around it. It depends on the reader's interpretation and response.

Your voice is the medium for interacting with readers as a storyteller. Refine and elevate it to the highest level it can achieve. With introspection, effort, and a dash of luck, you can discover a voice that pleases readers.

AUTHOR'S INTENT

Whenever an author begins a project, they establish an intent they wish to fulfill, their vision for the title. It includes everything in the book -

the tone, structure, plot, and more. Painters do this with their work. Golf course designers have an intent with every course they build. Poets have an intent with their process. Like other artists, novelists hold a specific intent for each project.

The writer's intent remains a private aspect of the project. We won't know their intentions unless they express them. Due to this, intent is difficult to assess. The book may not meet the reader's expectations, despite the author's intentions. It's something you, as the writer, must accept. You cannot please everyone all the time. Develop the perfect story for the project and modify as required.

In standalone works, the intent is much easier to accomplish in practice. Everything is self-contained. Maintaining the intent across a series is tough, as things may change from book to book. The reader and author want everything in a series to appear cohesive and each component to carry its own weight. Sometimes, that just doesn't happen.

The Horse and His Boy by C.S. Lewis, a part of the *Chronicles of Narnia* series, comes to mind. The book is set in Narnia but outside the main plot line from *The Magician's Nephew* to *The Last Battle*. The story feels like a standalone or side story within in Lewis' magical world and series. Many people love the story of *The Horse and His Boy*, but we may forever wonder at the intent of Lewis for that book.

In your writing, determine some project intent at the outset. Define what you want to accomplish with each project, a mission statement. Perhaps you wish to attempt something new to enhance your skill or write about a central tenet that drives the overall project. The *Marco Flynn Mysteries* focused on a very clear intent. The author wanted to hearken back to the mysteries of Raymond Chandler and Dashiell Hammett, with a modern spin, and write a group of shorter novels while offering a complete arc in a straight-line plot structure.

You won't see any great texts that refer to design intent. Use intent to guide your project, your mission statement, and don't waver throughout the entire project. If your mission creeps, you are starting something new, which isn't bad; it's just a different story. You, as the writer, need to ensure that your project stays true to that intent. If not, reconsider your intent or switch to a new story. Once you decide on your intent, it informs the voice of your story.

TONE

Tone is an overarching topic that has several sub-components. The initial step is to define the essence of tone. Then, we will discuss reader expectations and how to work with them. A large factor in the story's tone is the mood, the companion to tone. The tone of a story is also influenced by the dramatic question. Lastly, we'll explore the impact of tone on other key aspects of storytelling.

What is tone? Tone is the attitude of the author rising through the story. Tone establishes a feeling and helps to pull the reader into the story. If they love the tone, then the audience will forgive a lot of your sins as a writer. What else explains the popularity of some dreadful movies that become cult classics? The answer is tone. Readers, like movie-goers, are geared to similar stories. Judith Roof explains tone in her book, *Tone: Writing and the Sound of Feeling* in the following manner:

"Tone is the quality you imagine you hear when you read. Tone both produces and seems to emanate from an imaginary voice recounting a printed text. The text's diction, syntax, contexts, and connotations merge to produce tone as a complex, imaginary audial phenomenon."

The writer's tone reflects the attitude portrayed in the story. That tone can be humorous, sarcastic, or dark. This tone takes on either a formal or informal persona. Properly applying tone within your story will differentiate it from other works in the genre and evoke emotions from the reader.

Tone is often confused with voice. Voice is the personality of the author; tone is the attitude. The author's voice varies with words, viewpoint, and grammar style. The voice, tone, and style blend to convey ennui to the reader.

Expectations from readers include tone. One of the implied aspects of your tone comes from your decision to write in a specific genre. If the story is Romance, Mystery, or Fantasy, you are telling your reader what to expect within your story. It encompasses all tropes, conventions, and associated elements of this story type.

Establishing the tone warns the reader about the story type. It implies a promise to the reader. Darker tones evoke more intense thriller style novels. Lighter tones could transform the book into a cozy mystery or romance. Telling the reader it was a cold day expresses the tone, but that's uninteresting. You want to show them through words that evoke the thoughts and images of that tone. One of the easiest to recognize is a noir tone that displays a darker and grittier story. Below is an example from Michael Morelli.

"I was on my second cup of mud the next morning. I told the waitress I took it black, but she gave me two sugars by accident. I don't do sweets and I don't do cigarettes. I must be the only cop in New York who didn't have coffin nails as part of his daily diet. I also didn't gamble, didn't drink, and didn't go out late looking for broads. All I really wanted to do with my life was to be a cop. Pretty boring, huh? Jack finished with his food, and we hit the road. He was a little more talkative now. Probably just accepting the fact that we were partners and that talking to me was better than not. I didn't care. I was there to solve crimes, not to meet the best man for my wedding."

A brief word on formality. Formality is determined by how the writer uses standard language and punctuation. Typical indicators of formal writing include avoiding contractions, clichés, and slang. Using the passive voice is another indicator. Informal writing is much more in line with normal conversation and relaxed grammatical rules. A formal tone is often found in non-fiction, academic writing, and some literary fiction.

Much of your story hinges on one overarching dramatic question. That question, when answered, will resolve the story. It impacts and shapes the tone while evoking particular feelings in the story. How the question is asked affects the tone. Is it a sense of suspense? Perhaps mystery or horror? This intended tone provides the frame within which the story operates.

The character is central to your story; they impact the tone experienced by the reader. This is the best way to connect from the page. This will feed through the conflict, plot, and character arc of the story. Use larger story elements to communicate the tone to readers, instead of solely relying on prose. It ensures the reader understands your intended emotion.

MOOD

Mood involves reader connection. How do we establish that connection? Understanding your promises as a writer and anticipating reader questions are crucial. You need to constantly ask yourself, "What is the reader thinking at this point?" This is the part where the term "hacking the reader's brain" becomes important. This is where we make that connection; tone and mood form a symbiotic relationship.

What differentiates mood from tone? Mood is the emotional reaction your writing elicits from the reader. Can the writer's projected mood match your readers' responding tone? Sometimes, it should. It would seem odd to have a noir tone but have humor as the predominant mood. The mood changes in every scene as you progress through the story. Your reader's emotions reflect that change as well. The more you connect with the reader's emotions, the more powerful and lasting your story will be. Within your story, there are four ways to drive an effective mood. To establish the mood in each scene, include at least three, if not all four, of these.

- The setting not only includes the physical location but also establishes the mood. Rain indicates sadness; a dark room drives fear. The setting drives feelings within the reader based on how they interpret the location.
- Theme is the primary driver of mood. If your theme is about trust, you will create tense situations where the trust between characters is tested. If your theme is about death, numerous scenes could be somber, sad, or melancholy. Another component of theme is the imagery and symbolism used. These tools reinforce theme, mood, and tone.
- Diction covers the words you choose to put into the story. Maybe generate a word list that reflects the intended mood and tone of the story. Use those words in your descriptions, in your character's actions, in the dialogue to evoke the emotions of the reader.
- Tone. How do you use tone to drive mood if mood is related to the tone? Mood is driven by your viewpoint character and their emotional connection with the reader. Control the tone of your story to solicit the desired mood from your reader.

STYLE

Alongside voice and tone, comes the topic of style. These three elements of writing combine to make the comprehensive style of a story. Style, in this context, refers to the technical way the writer builds their narrative on a line by line, sentence by sentence basis.

Despite our dislike for them, rules govern English usage, which we incorporate in our story. Perhaps the best-known book on the topic is *The Elements of Style*. Three key components in this little book serve as a writing guide.

- Rules of Usage - The expected grammatical usage regarding sentence structure, punctuation, use of possessive, agreement of singular and plural, and the usage of pronouns. Using proper grammar is never a poor decision. Fortunately, most word processing programs come with suitable grammar check applications, or these can be purchased online. Keep these principles in mind.
    - Form the possessive singular of nouns by adding 's.
    - In a series of three or more items, use a comma after each item except the final one.
    - Enclose parenthetic expressions between commas.
    - Place a comma before a conjunction introducing an independent clause. Don't join independent clauses with a comma.
    - Use a colon after a clause to introduce a list of details.
    - The number of the subject determines the number of the verb (singular and plural agreement).
- Principles of Composition – These guidelines are a little more open to interpretation but are standards to be followed unless you have a suitable reason to divert from the norm. These deal with using an economy of words, avoiding loose sentences, and using standard design for your composition.
    - Retain a suitable style throughout the work.
    - Use the active voice.
    - Use definite and concrete language.
    - Keep to one tense whenever possible.
    - Omit needless words.
    - Put statements in positive form.
    - Pay attention to proper composition of sentences and paragraphs.
- Approach to Style – This group of advisories are even more open-ended. A careful examination will indicate the expected standard, unless there is a justifiable reason for deviation.
    - Stay in the background.
    - Use subtlety, do not overwrite or overstate.
    - Avoid the use of qualifiers (adverbs)
    - Use orthodox spelling.
    - Don't use awkward adverbs or fancy words.

- o   Make it clear who is speaking to the reader.
- o   Do not affect a breezy manner.
- Professionalism – Taking the above words at heart and implementing them will show that the writer is professional and able to meet certain minimum standards. Though not mentioned in Strunk & White's book, the industry holds all writers to this standard.

The main lesson is that a strong narrative is created by selecting precise words to convey the desired meaning. Then, taking those words and creating powerful sentences that lead to poignant paragraphs. Mastering stylistic techniques enhances a writer's skill with basic structures.

THE JOB OF PROSE

When we refer to prose, what are we talking about? Prose consists of the words you put on paper to tell your story. These words are told through a perspective and form scenes that portray the plot, characters, setting, and theme through dialogue or other narrative language to communicate your story. The words you choose and how you use them.

In the prior chapters, we discussed the planning stage of writing and preparing for the large building blocks of your story. Your prose fleshes out these ideas and communicates each aspect to the reader. Prose addresses one or more of its four primary jobs in each line. In a perfect world, each line would address multiple jobs from the following list.

- Progress the plot and develop scenes that create momentum through the story.
- Provide characterization that reveals the thoughts of the character and builds a connection to the reader.
- Increase and/or sustain tension using conflict or other techniques.
- Provide necessary information or world-building to develop the entire story for the reader.

Seeing that list may put a lot of pressure on the prose you use. And rightly so. Can your prose hold up to that scrutiny? All writers ask this question. Your job is to write your best story with what you have.

The story you want to tell influences the workings of your prose. If you are telling a story that winds between various plots and timelines, keeping tension is going to be harder. When telling a thematic story about a single character, pay attention to plot progression. If you attempt to portray a specific tone, like humor or horror, then ensure you don't sacrifice the characterization aspects of the story. Perhaps you want to subvert the usual tropes and typical things that happen in writing. It is your story, and you can do what you want with it, but your narrative still has the same four jobs it needs to accomplish.

One last thing to consider in putting your narrative to the page is the entertainment factor. Bored people won't stay. Entertainment is one of the main reasons people read fiction. Be engaging, have fun.

You, as a writer, control the ultimate tool to develop prose. That tool is known as revision. Although it may seem like a cop-out, we have the ability to revise our writing and correct any errors. As a writer matures, the process becomes easier and requires less adjustment.

Every writer wishes for beautiful prose. They want their story to be perfect with stunning dialogue, brilliant description, gripping action, and thoughtful narration. Yeah, we want it all. We want our narrative skills to be masterful and our prose above reproach. Unfortunately, perfection escapes all of us. Even the masters have their weaker points. To achieve a higher level of proficiency, we should gain a better understanding of the heights we are striving to reach. In this section, we will introduce the narrative forms we may use.

FICTION-WRITING MODES

Narrative, in its simplest form, is the act of telling a story. It appears in many forms of presentation. Obviously, we are concerned with the written variety in our study. That writing takes the form of poetry, song, screenwriting, or prose. Prose is the form of writing that uses full sentences and paragraphs. Poetry and song include rhythm, rhymes, and formulaic structure. Screenwriting is often presented in the form of simple dialogue, action, and narration. Let's begin our study of the various forms that narrative prose takes.

Fiction-writing modes (or just modes) are the various forms of narrative prose. They often have specific functions within the structure of our story and have specific rules we follow when using them. These modes will express everything from thoughts and emotions to dialogue and action. Based on reviewing various sources, the most complete coverage of these modes is in Mike Klaassen's tome titled *Fiction-Writing Modes*.

The modes fall into four major categories depending on their purpose: interiority, activity, conversation, and exteriority. Klaassen identifies four specific modes under the grouping of interiority. These are the modes of writing that reflect what happens internally to the character. They include emotion, sensation, introspection, and recollection. For activity, we have two modes: action and summarization. Conversation includes only one mode, external dialogue. The last group in Klaassen's system is exteriority, and this deals with items that exist outside of the character. It includes narration, description, exposition, and transition. Below is a list providing a brief definition of each mode per Klaassen.

- Narration is how the narrator communicates directly to the reader.
- Description is the fiction-writing mode for transmitting a mental image of the details of a story.
- Exposition is used to convey information.
- Summarization condenses events to convey what happens within a story.
- Introspection is the fiction-writing mode used to convey the thoughts of a character, allowing the expression of normally unexpressed thoughts.
- Recollection is the fiction-writing mode whereby a character remembers a detail or event.
- Sensation is used to portray a character's perceptions.
- Emotion conveys the feelings of the character and is a vital component of creative writing.
- Action is demonstrating events as they are happening in a story.
- Transitions in fiction are used to signal various changes in a story, including changes in time, location, point-of-view character, mood, tone, emotion, and pace.
- Dialogue represents a character's speech.

One other aspect of using these various narrative modes is combining them with each other. An enormous block of dialogue might be nice to help speed things along, but without showing emotion or thoughts alongside it, the impact gets lost. Action without emotional reaction is meaningless. Exposition without context is wasted. Description without tying it to the plot, character, conflict, or scene means little to the reader. We portray a complete picture by alternating modes. We move from action to thought to dialogue to description to emotion. They interweave into a braid of narrative. Braiding your narratives modes creates complexity, and makes your writing more appealing, and resonates with the reader at a much greater level.

Other writers take a different tactic toward these modes. If you watch any of Brandon Sanderson's series of lectures on YouTube, you will see he defines four categories: dialogue, description, beats (which includes action), and emotion/thoughts. Others will add a fifth category for exposition on top of those. The following chapters will provide detailed discussions of each mode.

STYLE OF PROSE

When discussing style and voice, writers must be cautious not to let prose overshadow the story. Avoid the overuse of melodramatic and fanciful descriptions or phrases that draw attention to themselves and away from the actual story. Using these flourishes is often referred to as "Purple Prose." But the extent the writer controls their prose depends on their own personal preference.

Over time, categories of style arose and are used today to provide analysis and comparison of stories. These styles vary from the celebrated minimalistic approach of a Hemingway to the other extreme of stream-of-consciousness writing favored by William Faulkner. And there are several valid choices in between. Don't be too strict when applying these categories to writers, as their style often varies between projects. Following is a summary of the five main categories, along with an excerpt to experience each style.

- Minimalist – Use of minimal details. Simple sentences and straightforward plots. Rare descriptions in the writing. Relies on subtext and subtlety more than other styles. Critics find it boring and unrefined. Hemingway and Raymond Carver are examples.

"So early it's still almost dark out. I'm near the window with coffee, and the usual early morning stuff that passes for thought. When I see the boy and his friend walking up the road to deliver the newspaper. They wear caps and sweaters, and one boy has a bag over his shoulder. They are so happy they aren't saying anything, these boys. I think if they could, they would take each other's arm. It's early in the morning, and they are doing this thing together. They come on, slowly. The sky

is taking on light, though the moon still hangs pale over the water. such beauty that for a minute death and ambition, even love, doesn't enter into this. Happiness. It comes on unexpectedly. And goes beyond, really, any early morning talk about it." – Raymond Carver, *All of Us*

- Invisible Prose – Most common in genre fiction. Relies on scene/sequel balance and sensory detail to immerse the reader in sensory details. Approaches prose as if it presents the story through a clear window. Daphne DuMaurier and Kurt Vonnegut are examples.

"I went back there with an old war buddy, Bernard V. O'Hare, and we made friends with a cab driver, who took us to the slaughterhouse where we had been locked up at night as prisoners of war. His name was Gerhard Müller. He told us that he was a prisoner of the Americans for a while. We asked him how it was to live under Communism, and he said that it was terrible at first, because everybody had to work so hard, and because there wasn't much shelter or food or clothing. But things were much better now. He had a pleasant little apartment, and his daughter was getting an excellent education. His mother was incinerated in the Dresden fire-storm. So it goes." – Kurt Vonnegut, *Slaughterhouse-Five*

- Muscular Prose – Regaining popularity. More complex sentence structures and use of varied POV and scene structures. Uses metaphors more often. Encapsulates the characteristics we most prize in solid prose. Ursula LeGuin and Joyce Carol Oates are examples.

"His voice made no echo off the rock walls. Silence snuffed it out utterly. There was no sound but the faint trickle of the spring, and my breathing, and his. It was absolutely dark. My eyes fooled me again and again, making faint lights flash, and colors blur and vanish in the black in front of me, that sometimes seemed to be right up against my eyes like a blindfold, and then deep and far as a starless sky, so that I feared to fall as if standing on a cliff's edge. Once I thought I saw a glimmer taking form, the shape of a letter, but it went out suddenly, utterly, as a spark goes out. We stood a long time, long enough that I began to feel the rock pressing through my thin shoe soles and the ache in my back from not moving. I was dizzy because there was nothing in the world, no thing at all, only blackness and the sound of water and the pressure *of the rock under my feet. No air moved. It was cold. It was still."* – Ursula K. LeGuin, *Voices*

- Ornate – Purple prose with extended use of metaphors and long sentences. Hyperbole and exaggerations of prose elements exist. Opulent, detailed, and full of sensory descriptions. Salman Rushdie and K. J. Bishop are examples.

"And there are so many stories to tell, too many, such an excess of intertwined lives events miracles places rumors, so dense a commingling of the improbable and the mundane! I have been a swallower of lives; and to know me, just the one of me, you'll have to swallow the lot as well. Consumed multitudes are jostling and shoving inside me; and guided only by the memory of a large white bedsheet with a roughly circular hole some seven inches in diameter cut into the center, clutching at the dream of that holey, mutilated square of linen, which is my talisman, my open-sesame, I must commence the business of remaking my life from the point at which it really began, some thirty-two years before anything as obvious, as present, as my clock-ridden, crime-stained birth." – Salman Rushdie, *Midnight's Children*

- Stream of Consciousness – Free flowing. Punctuation may not exist, and grammar is an afterthought. Usually lacks editing and falls within the realm of literary writing. William Faulkner and James Joyce are examples.

"Through the fence, between the curling flower spaces, I could see them hitting. They were coming toward where the flag was and I went along the fence. Luster was hunting in the grass by the flower tree. They took the flag out, and they were hitting. Then they put the flag back and they went to the table, and he hit and the other hit. Then they went on, and I went along the fence. Luster came away from the flower tree and we went along the fence and they stopped and we stopped and I looked through the fence while Luster was hunting in the grass." – William Faulkner, *The Sound and the Fury*

George Orwell offered his perspective on presenting prose. "Good prose should be transparent, like a windowpane." Brandon Sanderson is a popular speculative fiction writer that adheres to this same philosophy. He uses the windowpane analogy in most of his lectures about writing. Orwell and Sanderson, along with many others, believe your prose is a vehicle to present the story and be invisible to the reader.

Others believe your prose should be as beautiful as your story. If your story is excellent, but the prose is transparent, some argue you have failed to reach the highest form of art, a masterpiece. William Faulkner, Ursula LeGuin, and Toni Morrison are examples where their prose is eloquent and is part of the experience of the read. The allure of reading their works lies in their ability to craft phrases and present ideas through words. Enhancing the prose is fine, as long as it doesn't take away from the story.

As writers, we want our words to be impactful. There's always the occasional desire to use elaborate language or add a flourish. Regardless, it must be the right word, or flourish, to achieve the exact effect desired. Otherwise, you risk pushing your prose into something no one desires.

SUBTLETY, SUBTEXT, AND MELODRAMA

One aspect of narrative that we still need to address is the use of subtlety, subtext, and melodrama. Subtlety is the act of alluding to something with minimal suggestion. Subtext omits and allows readers to infer meaning from context. Melodrama involves excessive additions to convey your point. Each narrative mode benefits from these three elements at times.

When we talk of subtlety, we wish to not draw attention to something unless it is necessary. This falls in line with the invisible prose theory espoused by Orwell. Using subtlety requires the writer to trust that the reader will derive the meaning after receiving the slightest hint, such as a foreshadow or an allusion.

Subtlety in style relies on showing much more than telling. Avoid excessive modifiers to maintain subtlety. Other things to avoid are clichés, melodramatic displays of emotions, elaborate words or phrases, and flowery language. Concealing a clue in a mystery often requires setting subtlety aside. Prominently display specific imagery you wish the reader to focus on. Drawing attention to the image creates a perfect opportunity to subtly insert something else the reader might notice at the edges of the scene.

Subtext is a much tougher nut to crack. Sometimes characters, or people, cannot express what they wish, for many reasons. Perhaps they find their true thoughts uncomfortable (hatred of a man they should like), perhaps they wish their feelings were opposite (love for the wrong person), or perhaps they don't want someone to know their internal thoughts and emotions (love for the other person). We must determine how to interpret the piece of the puzzle that is missing. We're left with a hole in the jigsaw puzzle. Understanding the context and characters allows us to provide the evidence for the writer. Subtext works in every narrative mode, but it works the best within dialogue. So, we will cover it in more depth in that chapter.

Melodrama stands in stark contrast to subtlety. Melodrama is the act of creating an overdramatic piece with exaggerated characters and events that appeal to the reader's emotions. Melodrama is recognized by frequent use of plot devices like cliffhangers or revealing secrets. In dialogue, melodrama is apparent in the form of using slang, accents, or dialects to the point that they become cliché and detract from the overall story and scene. It borders on the line of stereotyping and can become offensive.

Skilled writers may use melodrama for specific impacts and to draw attention to a specific character as comic relief. Shakespeare repeatedly did this in his tragedies by creating villains that were over the top in their depictions. This was not limited to role players. The character of MacBeth could belong here, or the deaths within *Romeo and Juliet* were melodramatic due to their exaggerated manner. Shakespeare also did this to equal effect in his comedic efforts such as *The Merchant of Venice*'s character Shylock and *The Taming of the Shrew*'s female leads of Katherina and Bianca.

Defining the voice in writing is challenging and multifaceted. Developing your voice and mastering the inherent elements of tone, mood, and style will make your writing technically correct and will capture the reader. Whether your intent is to write with the flourish of Faulkner or the normalcy of Orwell, you as a writer should strive to write the best narrative possible. Let your voice be heard.

EXERCISES

1. Pick one of your favorite authors and retype a scene from one of their stories. Identify two specific items you notice during this exercise that may be unique to their writing style.
2. Identify one aspect of your story that is a predetermined intent for you going into the writing process.
3. Identify one aspect of your story that you will use to enhance the tone or mood.

REFERENCE MATERIALS

The Elements of Style by William Strunk, Jr., and E. B. White
Writing Voice: The Complete Guide to Creating a Presence on the Page and Engaging Readers by the Writer's Digest Editors
Tone: Writing and the Sound of Feeling by Judith Roof
Politics and the English Language by George Orwell

More writers use Strunk & White's tiny book than any other. It's always been seen as the industry's go-to for style and grammar guidance. Some newer editions of this book, along with others, purport to achieve the identical objective. A reference along these lines is necessary for every writer. **W***riting Voice* is a collaboration on this central topic and is a valuable resource in a challenging area while covering several aspects of the topic from various writers. It is also an example of the high-quality writing craft books produced every year by Writer's Digest. Roof and Orwell wrote two resources that are nice frames to help present aspects of the voice discussion.

17 – SHOWING & TELLING

Now we address the notorious writing axiom "show, don't tell." It doesn't matter if you are reading a book, perusing an article, or listening to a podcast on writing that the topic isn't mentioned. In the following paragraphs, we will review this concept in detail. There have been entire books written on this topic, the poster child of modern writing advice. Can we address the subject in a few pages? Maybe.

From where did show, not tell, originate? The phrase is often credited to Anton Chekhov, a Russian playwright who famously said, "Don't tell me the moon is shining; show me the glint of light on broken glass." The concept became industry parlance after WWII due to the rise in creative writing programs in the United States and has since become a mantra ingrained in every writer's mind.

Fairly, some dislike "show, don't tell." Many anti-showers will declare, "It's show and tell, you will do both." One YouTube host declared, "Show, not tell, is a scam!" There are some writers that view the idea to be an insidious plot to propagate specific political beliefs. Yeah, no kidding!

Why do we continue to bother with the turmoil of trying to show? Because we keep hearing this from literary elites like Anne Lamott, Donald Maass, and their ilk. Also, when most people, especially editors, lack the ability to express what they view as flawed about your writing they find uncomfortable, they blanketly reply with, "Show more, tell less." The phrase has become a crutch and makes you wonder how people like Cervantes, Austen, and Dickens wrote anything without that advice being bellowed at them 24/7.

"Show, don't tell" is now a cliché and lacks originality. The phrase should be show AND tell. Neither versus, nor or, and definitely not, not. Showing and telling, that's what we do as writers. The best stories achieve both, not one. Is show preferable? In certain circumstances. Is telling a terrible thing? Not always. There is a balance. What fits the story and elicits emotional response matters. Everything we do as writers comes back to those factors.

There are specific benefits to using this adage. Showing delivers the story with significant and specific detail to portray emotional imagery that, in turn, creates an emotional and connective journey for the reader. Showing captures a story's full context more effectively.

On the flip side, there are plenty of reasons we use telling in our writing. Telling conveys information quickly in the form of summarization. This happens often in a story when one character needs to relay information to another. Telling enables a writer to transition scenes seamlessly or indicate the passage of time with a concise sentence or two. Telling is also excellent at providing a quick sentence to ramp up the dramatic impact. Clever versions of telling make great first and last lines of chapters.

Is "show, not tell" a scam? No. Still, the excessive focus on convincing writers to show everything at all times is unwarranted. It's a false belief, and our projects would become as long as Brandon Sanderson novels (who tells a lot, by the way). Below is a list of the benefits for each to summarize the main points.

- Telling is generally quicker and more efficient.
- Telling avoids emotional detail and communicates information.
- Telling lacks characterization and is often communicated through the narrator's lens.
- Showing is generally slower, richer, and less efficient.
- Showing uses emotional detail and specificity to communicate dramatization.
- Showing uses characterization and is often communicated through the character's lens.

Writers should aim to show as much as possible, but there are instances where telling is better. The skill we develop as we practice and write more will guide us on mastering both and will assist us in knowing when to use either at the appropriate time.

USING TELL APPROPRIATELY

Don't be afraid to tell. Every writer tells, some conceal it better. Sometimes, they get by because of their reputation. When should you use "tell" in your writing? Let's go through four scenarios where telling is preferred and provide some examples.

The first scenario involves summarization. Summarization is a great mode to use for various elements of your writing. In a sentence or two, the writer communicates essential information to maintain the story's flow and resolve plot issues without unnecessary words. To summarize, use direct and layered language to encapsulate events, avoiding simple be verbs like is and was.

Displaying time and place on screen is a great storytelling technique in movies. This bit of telling saves the characters from telling us this information and allows them to continue the story without adding this burden that could upset the flow of the story.

Another fitting example of this is when summarization communicates information between characters already provided to the reader. This works well when a sub-plot is resolved, and the supporting character shares their discovery with the main character. The bigger your cast, as in an ensemble book, the more often this occurs. The line below illustrates this point.

"I let Jovis talk, absorbing his tale with both sympathy and horror." – *The Bond Shard War*, Andrea Stewart

Summarization compresses the time and moves to the next point in the story. Using summarization often provides the best results when transitioning between scenes. Whether it's moving through a house or getting out of the car from the grocery store. No need for tedious details that bore readers. According to Alfred Hitchcock, "Drama is life with the boring parts removed." If there is nothing exceptional about the tedium, don't include the dull.

Another skillful use for telling is providing a line for dramatic effect. The chapter's beginning or end is an ideal location for this element. One key factor of the dramatic line is they are often told with more narrative distance. Increasing tension sometimes requires the use of a narrative voice, not a character voice.

"She was going to have to go rescue Charlie herself." – *Tress of the Emerald Sea*, Brandon Sanderson

Every writer uses preferred methods of storytelling and relaying information. One of the cleverer approaches is used by John Scalzi. Scalzi infodumps in dialogue scenes to reveal backstory and world-building details. In *Kaiju Preservation Society*, there are many instances where information is necessary to move the reader to a state of suspended disbelief. Every few chapters, an explanation about the world is necessary. Understanding kaiju science is crucial for the novel's ending. Having a scientific character relay the necessary information to the non-scientific lead character helps make the telling much less obvious to the reader.

To clarify, infodumps are often used to present information pertaining to world-building. A character's backstory can be conveyed through an alternate infodump. The focus here is on developing characters. When doing this, it's crucial to hide the telling so that the reader accepts it as natural.

Other writers, like Brandon Sanderson, build these details in the story through training montages to provide the world-building to understand a magic system, or how the character grows into their powers, or how the larger world provides context for the magic system. Sanderson introduces these magic system rules early and utilizes these rules in resolving later conflicts.

Occasionally, writing the information dump in one scene works. In those circumstances, the writer must comprehend their audience's preferences. Certain readers desire clarity on the story world before immersing themselves in the story. Once they understand how the world works, they can focus on the characters and plot without any extra context slowing them down.

Beyond these specific examples, there are several other opportunities for telling. Description is nothing but telling with flair. Many books excessively describe character appearances, terrain scenes, and fight details. Some might argue the entire story is telling, but prosaically. Even though telling sometimes gets a bad rap, it is an essential part of the writing process. You need to tell effectively.

USING SHOW APPROPRIATELY

When we discuss showing, we should focus on dramatization that reveals emotions, sensations, and action. Dramatization requires depth in the writing, so the reader understands the entire process of emotion generating thoughts that lead to action and the subsequent reaction. The reader wants to see that processional movement from the character.

Much of how you show, or tell, depends on the viewpoint you are using. The perspective and narrative distance both play a part. Others may refer to viewpoint as the narrative filter. Embrace the character's voice without filters. Avoid discussing the character through a narrative filter.

If you use first person, showing the character's emotions up close becomes easier. Even third person limited works well with this. Omniscient and other distant viewpoints complicate narration by increasing the gap between narrator and story. To gauge the characters' distance, shift your viewpoint to a narrower focus and see how the story shifts. This is easier to do in third person narratives. The general rule of thumb is the shorter the narrative distance, the more show in your writing. The prevailing rule presents one potential problem.

As the City Burns centers around Marco Flynn, a former FBI agent. His personality is about process and procedure and all about telling. Despite the first-person perspective, Marco's viewpoint sometimes lacks necessary details. This plays into Marco's character and only works because of that fact. The difficulty falls in balancing the aspects of his character that "tells" the reader crucial facts while his emotions are processing the effects of the story's events. You should always show emotions and the resulting actions.

A second guideline of effective showing relies on relaying significant detail. When we show significant detail, writers want to make sure we communicate detail that connects with the reader. We want to show the experience of the character through their senses (sight, smell, sound, taste, and touch). How does the scent impact the character? Is it a warning they are being chased by a creature? Why does a pie on the table evoke memories of their grandmother's kitchen? We need to reflect the impact of the sensory experience at an emotional level. To do that requires details. We want to show the reader the details that matter and lead to revealing characterization, progression of the plot, or increasing the tension in the story. If not, then the information is unimportant. Let's be clear and avoid terms like some, about, or nearly. We want the numbers, locations, and impacts to be specific.

When relaying significant information, avoid character judgment unless necessary. Character bias is wonderful if we comprehend the motivation behind the bias. What does that mean? For example, one of the quirks in *As the City Burns* is that Marco Flynn uses last names in his head when referring to characters he dislikes. He passes judgement on those people and their actions, but he has a motivation to reinforce the judgement. Liking the character removes his edge, and he becomes less judgmental of the details surrounding the relevant character. Losing his edge means he is not a good detective.

Why are we so obsessed with detail? This relates to the phrase, "Hacking the Reader's Brain," and knowing how to create the image in their imagination that you want them to have. A concrete image grounds the reader in the story. Concrete words are straightforward and interpreted in a specific way.

There is an allegorical tool referred to as the Pyramid of Abstraction. The Pyramid is a popular tool used by Brandon Sanderson to explain how we use description. As you move up the pyramid, you become more abstract. The lower within the pyramid, the more concrete your language becomes. If you mention a dog in your story, the word conveys an ambiguous image. Each person will have unique mental images. Some may envision a poodle, retriever, shepherd, or some small breed. Writing about a white husky gives readers a specific animal to imagine. We are aware of the thoughts of both the reader and writer.

Part of what you aim for in your writing is driving the reader to understand information in a specific way. Making your descriptions more concrete will help. Employ this method to portray the world surrounding your characters and manipulate the reader's thoughts. Skilled writers understand their readers' thoughts throughout the story by guiding their thinking. The stronger your words, the more concrete and better the image is conveyed.

The third aspect of showing that we must understand is conveying the imagery of emotion. This means dramatizing action that pertains to specific emotional stimuli. In a perfect scenario, we show the response to the stimuli through the character's senses. That sensory information then drives emotional responses, thoughts, and then action from the character.

Our writing to show these emotions must be evidence based. We can't say our character was angry. We need to "show" why they are angry. What drives their emotion and how does this emotion manifest in the character? Accomplish this with minimal use of "thought" verbs. Another clue is to avoid reliance on body language. Give priority to the motive behind one's feelings. Use these moments to provide an immediacy to the reader and use big actions to demonstrate the impact of the stimulus. In cases that are dramatic, use visceral actions, such as fainting, vomiting, or other over-the-top reactions. But these should be used sparingly to prevent your character from appearing melodramatic.

Sometimes, we rely on body "beats" to demonstrate character actions. But how many comprehend the correct reaction for a flummoxed character? A useful tool in handling these small actions is *The Emotional Thesaurus*. Writers benefit from this type of source.

Another key is to describe the reaction without specifying the emotion. Let's say your character is nervous, and the emotion generates a visceral reaction of nausea. Opt for a paragraph instead of a simple statement to describe your character's nervousness.

"Helen laid her head on the deli counter; the pounding filled her ears. The ding of the bell signaled a new customer, and their familiar voice froze Helen. Without looking she imagined the face of the man that chased her through the graveyard. Her stomach grumbled and turned over, the reaction was immediate as she dashed to the restroom."

The last component of strong showing involves the use of active prose. Let's minimize passive prose in our writing, especially when using emotional imagery. You want your word choice to dictate how your readers interpret the scene with specific and impactful prose. These words can also control how quickly the reader gets through your scenes.

Writers can control pacing by using show and tell. At times, we wish to expedite the pace and summarize a series of events. In alternate scenarios, our goal is to captivate the reader and emphasize significant story details. So, we focus on descriptive details to draw out a scene. All these tools are used to draw specific emotions from the reader.

FINDING TOLD PROSE

Right about now you are probably saying, "Fine. How do I find these places where I am telling poorly?" There are a lot of red flag words and phrases. Janice Hardy's book *Understanding Show, Don't Tell* would be a worthy investment to get a complete list. In some instances, you may still want to "tell" but looking for these words will help you eliminate flat prose and use layered and direct prose. Our desire remains the same, regardless of your stance on the axiom. Below are the categories of tells, along with the "telltale" red flag words that mark the sentences as such.

- Motivational tells - These are "to" verbs (infinitives), because, decided, and when. If the motivation is clear, the key lies in the reader's perception. If not and you are using one of these words, revise the text.
- Emotional tells – "In (insert emotion)," "with (insert emotion)," or felt, try to make certain emotions physical when you can't really feel "in love". Felt emotions are not physically experienced. Also, watch for the character that is too self-aware and thinking thoughts that are specific or too inwardly focused.
- Mental tells – These are words that involve mental activity. Not all are telling, but if a character possesses undisclosed knowledge, depict the catalyst for their thoughts. Sometimes dialogue tags denote internal dialogue, which is always a tell.
- Directional tells – As, when, by, since… These are words that infer an order to a series of events. The term can be eliminated, and the sentence rewritten without it.
- Descriptive tells – Verbs for using senses and could/would/should (sense) verbs. Instead of seeing, state the observation.
- Passive tells – The dreaded was/is/be verbs. Most times, the simple solution is reversing the order of the sentence. What acted? First state one acting, then the action, followed by the recipient. Not "Bob was bitten by the dog," but "The dog bit Bob."

RED FLAG WORDLIST

about
after
as
because
before
caused
could
during
felt
had
heard
in
it
just
knew
like
made
noticed
observed
only
realized
saw
seems
should
slightly
smelled
that
to
to be
until
was
watched
were
when
while
with
wondered
would

- Adverbs – This part of speech slows down the story. They have a purpose, but most of your writing can be adverb free.
- Other Tells - Besides those mentioned, we also seek tells that clarify a character's emotions and actions. Summarization of scenes from a distance is another type of tell to identify and may often read like vague internalization. The last one would involve relaying information that the character would not share otherwise, like they are too self-aware.

All the previous examples are ways to identify told prose at the sentence level. Sometimes, told prose is difficult to detect at the sentence level, but permeates more through an entire scene. There are specific scenes that lend themselves to telling more than others. Pay attention to your prose in these scenes to avoid excessive telling.

The favorite reason for telling is the relaying of information necessary for the story to develop. Infodumps and heavy doses of backstory occur at the beginning of many scenes, along with introducing new characters and settings. This includes any recent history to bring the reader up to date on details. We don't need all that information relayed in a series of told sentences. The biggest problem with infodumps is they don't flow with the story. Communicate the information to the reader in a creative and gradual manner.

Description is another tricky topic where we try to avoid using telling prose. For example, details of a room should not be listed. We need to show them through the character's perspective as they experience them. The reader must perceive the room as the character does. We need to show them what the character sees. This also allows us to foreshadow. Perhaps amidst the room's various objects, there is one that impacts the story's future without drawing notice. Also, avoid simply seeing, hearing, smelling. We need to dramatize the complete sensory experience of the characters.

Introspection is the next thing we need to show, instead of tell. This involves the thoughts and internal emotions of the character. We need to show them to the reader. Our choice of verbs is crucial. Let's steer clear of passive words like "realized" and "thought." We desire the dramatization of these revelations in some way. You need to see the character's decision-making process instead of relaying the process step-by-step.

FIXING TOLD PROSE

While working on your story draft, we must find and correct our told prose. There are several ways to run through your manuscript and fix these issues.

The first option you may employ is using an editing tool like ProWritingAid. The software detects passive sentences, excessive filter words, and incorrect verb usage. A powerful editing tool can detect many of these stylistic mistakes.

The second option is looking at word choice. Are your verbs action-oriented and shown to the reader, or passive and told? Are your nouns implying a level of specificity beyond the general? Are the words you use direct and concrete or are they vague abstractions? Word choice is the number one way to fix almost any told prose.

Another option is relaying everything through the character's perspective. Character perspectives shown, not told, have more impact. Maintain the character's voice when infodumping. Also, only provide information that provides context or helps to achieve the scene's goals. Keeping these scenes short will also help the reader keep focus.

The "Search and Destroy" technique focuses on a section of text. Within the section, use your word processor program to highlight the words you wish to change. Employ a tactical approach to resolve these items and remove the Red Flag words identified in this chapter to reduce excessive and vague text.

One other piece of advice is you should learn to master the use of imagery in your storytelling. Telling is difficult while using imagery and figurative language. Conveying your story through metaphors, allusions, and similes allows your prose to appear much more shown.

Sometimes, sentence structure requires examination. Very often passive and told prose requires us switching the subject and direct object of the sentence. See the example below.

Told Sentence: The girl watched the waves move the bobber up and down while she waited for the fish to bite.

Shown Sentence: The waves moved the bobber up and down while the girl waited for the fish to bite.

Using this technique shifts the visualization in your reader's mind to the waves and seeing the image of them moving instead of fixating on the girl. Then the second half of the compound sentence pans out to a wider image of the girl waiting.

Mastering show and tell improves the readability of the prose. The reader will stay engaged in the story and enjoy it more. The art of effective communication is demanding. Either way, becoming proficient with this style of writing will make your stories come alive in the reader's mind, the true desire for our writing.

PROPER EXPOSITION

Exposition is the narrative mode designed to relay information, and is often associated with "telling" and viewed as a dreadful thing. Many experts denigrate exposition by lumping everything into the dreaded "infodump" and indiscriminately assaulting the reputation of one of the primary narrative modes available to writers. But don't fear exposition. Managing exposition is one of the most difficult skills to master. If you understand how to use exposition, you can leverage a great tool.

The foremost role of exposition is to get necessary information to the reader. When conveying context, writers often provide background information about the story and its world. A skilled writer considers what information the reader needs. In the Science-Fiction, Fantasy, and Mystery genres this is a key aspect of the writing. In Mystery, the sleuth uncovers the information and explains the relevance to the reader. In Science-Fiction and Fantasy, world information sets context and explains world operations.

Exposition is a flexible tool that can be used with other narrative modes. Characters relay information through thoughts and dialogue. Description conveys elements to the reader to provide context about the setting. Action conveys story details to readers. Until Hermione taught Ron to say "Wingardium Leviosa," how many realized the value of proper enunciation in the wizarding world?

A quick summarization provides information to another character in the story. A skillful use of summarization appears at the beginning of each of the *Star Wars* movies with the scrolling font. Movies allow for freer exposition compared to fiction due to time limits. Authors need a clever, inconspicuous method to include this. The following example from Genevieve Cogman's *The Invisible Library* is a skillful use of exposition to give the reader a summary of the situation in front of the main character.

"Two doors down along the corridor was Irene's destination: the House Trophy Room. It was full of silver cups, all engraved with variations on Turquine House, as well as trophy pieces of art and presentation manuscripts.

One of those manuscripts was her goal.

Irene had been sent by the Library to this alternate world to obtain *Midnight Requiems*, the famous necromancer Balan Pestifer's first published book. It was by all accounts a fascinating, deeply informative, and highly unread piece of writing. She'd spent a month looking for a copy of it, as the Library didn't actually require an original version of the text, just an accurate one. Unfortunately, not only had she been unable to track down a copy, but her enquiries had caught the interest of other people... She'd had to burn that cover identity and go on the run before they caught up with her."

Within three paragraphs, Cogman acquaints the reader with the backstory of the heist and the action is ready to begin. We know why she wants the book and why others want to stop her. That leads to our action and conflict.

Another role for exposition is to bring forward aspects of the story to build anticipation and suspense. *Othello* has a scene in the first act that informs the audience greatly as Roderigo and Iago lay their cards on the table. Iago reveals his true nature. His deceit is revealed, and the play's themes are conveyed through dialogue and innuendo.

Exposition is the mode used to convey information to the reader. That includes deciding what information to reveal and when. Whatever information you reveal or don't reveal should not only add clarity but introduce tension into the story. Selectively providing information may be more effective than revealing everything in one fell swoop. Offer enough to address the reader's immediate question while inviting further inquiry.

Don't tell the reader everything. Leave out a critical element to be used later in the story. Withholding information builds tension within the story. If readers sense a void, they anticipate the next development. If they don't sense the void, they will be surprised when the information surfaces. Ensure this doesn't come across as a contrived plot element. You need to leave breadcrumbs showing how that information relates to the story.

Exposition does not have to appear as narrative text within your story. There are several ways to provide information to your reader through elements of characterization. Dialogue is an effective way for characters to convey the necessary information. Avoid excessive explanations to prevent your characters from coming across as know-it-alls. A perfect example includes the television series *Dragnet*. To move the story along, the detective utters the famous line, "Just the facts, ma'am."

Direct thoughts and emotions provide character rich moments. Revealing a character's innermost thoughts about the world creates reader attachment. Make sure your viewpoint character tells the reader what they know, as this builds trust with the reader and helps create that connection between them. This is a common occurrence in first and third person narrations.

Character backstory is another version of exposition for us to use. Flashbacks, or dream sequences, are a terrific way to show a scene to convey information that is necessary. These methods also create questions in the reader's mind. Information doesn't have to consist solely of facts and figures about the story world.

Combine your exposition with description and imagery to provide a shocking visual impact to the reader. Use contrast of the uncommon against the common. Two concrete images that are complete opposites compared against one another is a technique called juxtaposition, which creates a tension within the scene. Dickens accomplished this with the opening line of *A Tale of Two Cities*.

"It was the best of times, it was the worst of times, it was the age of wisdom, it was the age of foolishness, it was the epoch of belief, it was the epoch of incredulity, it was the season of Light, it was the season of Darkness."

The terrible reputation of exposition is due to the carelessness of writers in the form of hidden infodumps. Sometimes the writer believe themselves clever and attaches an attribution and quotation marks to disguise the infodump as dialogue. How do we avoid that? Exposition, as with every element, requires a judicious hand.

Start with the exciting stuff. Tell us the juicy details if you are dealing with backstory. Give us the cool elements if you are relating cultural or setting information. Whatever you do, don't bore us. Avoid agonizing details unless necessary. Also, don't provide long stretches of exposition. You need to layer in description, action, and dialogue as well. If the information breaks the momentum of the story or doesn't provide the needed information, don't include it.

Exposition is often associated with older works where the economy of words lost its priority (*Moby Dick*, anyone?). The trend in today's literature often looks at exposition in the same light as narration, use only as necessary. Learn how to wield exposition, and it can be a secret weapon that separates your writing from someone else. Exposition serves a critical role in the fiction writer's world. Not using exposition, or using it poorly, will be a hindrance to your work and keep you from achieving everything you need to get out of your story.

EXERCISES

1. Identify a scene early in your story and first write it using tell. Then rewrite the scene using show throughout. Improve scene presentation by finding a middle ground through these two examples.
2. Go through a section of your story and use the red flag list of words to find and replace all the words mentioned to show that information instead of telling.
3. Edit a section of your story to identify weak verbs and non-specific nouns. Substitute these with verbs that have greater impact and nouns that create vivid imagery.

REFERENCE MATERIALS

Understanding Show, Don't Tell: And Really Getting It by Janice Hardy
The Emotion Thesaurus: A Writer's Guide to Character Expression by Angela Ackerman and Becca Puglisi

In her detailed tome, Hardy provides guidance on working with show, not tell, and correcting overtelling or overshowing in writing. Ackerman and Puglisi have put together one of the top writing resources for any writer working through their draft. This book is a perfect quick reference in how to depict certain emotions through a character.

18 – DIALOGUE

One of the major components of writing is dialogue. It is also one of the most difficult aspects of writing to pull off effectively. Which is counterintuitive, as almost every person communicates through dialogue in their daily life. Why is it difficult to depict an act we regularly engage in? We aim to generate conversations about seldom-discussed topics, rather than recreating informal chats in everyday settings like home, work, or on the bus. All the while, eliminate everything that does nothing to advance the story. Writing conversation isn't easy. Hopefully, the following paragraphs help you in that endeavor.

THE JOB OF DIALOGUE

Dialogue carries a heavy burden in your writing. Roughly 50% of most stories, on average, are represented through dialogue. No other narrative mode carries such a high percentage. Some stories rely on dialogue. This point shows why Shakespeare remains the greatest writer in history. His plays pulled off everything that any other story does, but only through dialogue. Characterization, plot progression, building tension, presenting themes, and world-building were done through the spoken lines of a few characters.

Dialogue is capable of handling all the jobs that we would expect of our prose. It provides information and answers many questions for the reader. It reveals characterization by showing off the aspects of a character's voice and demonstrating their true motivations. Dialogue helps with plot progression by presenting conflicts. It also builds tension by asking questions of the characters. Beyond these chores, dialogue is also viewed as a prime source of entertainment for the reader. Witty banter and clever conversations between characters are often cited as the favorite part of many novels and movies.

What if dialogue is only entertaining and cannot accomplish other tasks? While entertainment is acceptable, dialogue should serve the author's intent and connect with the character's purpose. Ultimately, if your dialogue isn't accomplishing that, then it is just wasted breath for the characters. Your dialogue should do at least one of the previously mentioned jobs, or it needs to be cut from the story. Much like information dumping, you can't just have characters blathering to fill space.

Dialogue seldom reflects the way people truly talk. Let's be honest, we don't want writers to replicate natural conversations. Filter out the flotsam, remove the incoherence, and reflect the conversation's soul to readers. Dialogue should evoke conversation, not copy it.

Beyond evoking conversation, dialogue should communicate a character's motivation. As mentioned earlier, only the POV character can communicate their thoughts, emotion, and motivations without speaking. Unless the other characters express these facets of themselves in the story, the reader remains clueless. Getting these character elements into the story opens us up to experiencing the pursuit of their desires and goals.

Once the motivations of multiple characters are clear, dialogue becomes a prime source of conflict in the story. Arguments abound when your protagonist runs into obstacles while the dialogue, and the associated beats, go a long way to showing conflict and tension.

CHARACTER VOICES

Characters' voices establish the primary communication with the reader. The POV character communicates to the reader through thoughts. Everyone else must do it through the spoken words of dialogue, or their related actions.

Character voices should vary from one character to another. If your characters sound alike, you have an issue with your dialogue or with your characters. If you write dialogue effectively, you should be able to tell the difference between each character without attributions. Specific aspects of dialogue differentiate characters.

- Diction – Certain characters use certain words. Some of those words may be vulgar, bold, off-color, or official sounding to you. Diction communicates backstory, emotional standing, status, and several other issues. This is the most effective tool for the writer to differentiate character voices.
- Tone – Characters often speak in specific tones. Some are more serious than others. Some are more sarcastic. Humor is attempted

in most situations. Tone is an effective tool to provide subtext while providing clarity around characters.
- Rhythm – Some characters use short blunt sentences, some longer sentences. Some speak with a certain rhythm. This could display the character's self-image. Characters with high opinions of themselves talk more. Caution is necessary with this approach. You don't want everyone to come off as a bunch of clichés.
- Dialect – Though it should be used sparingly, a character speaks with a certain dialect or accent. They could drop their g's at the end of gerunds. They use certain turns of phrase that are regional. Care should be used with this tool. Overuse creates offensive stereotypes and runs into the area of melodrama, something we want to avoid except in specific circumstances.
- Jargon – Characters use a specific jargon that relates to a job or specific fascinations. The situation becomes more apparent through a conversation between characters in the same industry. Otherwise, avoid jargon and slang. Use cursing and swearing only as needed.
- Along the lines of jargon is a phenomenon known as code-switching. This occurs when a character moves between two different communities and switches their conversational tone, diction, and other facets to conform to the varied audiences. A character talks different when at work than they do at home. Expect some of this, but occasionally, it may be extreme.

Developing a distinct voice for each character in your story is important to create realistic dialogue that doesn't sound like copies of the same person. Realism is key. Without it, the dialogue will sound "stilted," or wooden in nature. We want dialogue to sound as natural as possible. Also, keep the character's voice consistent.

People advise listening to conversations to capture realism. Eavesdropping may uncover their speech patterns, but duplicating their dialogue is unattainable. People use sentence fragments that only they and the other person understand. The conversation will contain "uhs" and "ahs" that you won't use. The act of listening offers a sense of exchange flow. Along with how a person responds to a question, how a person makes a declaration, and how their body moves while they talk.

SUBTEXT

In dialogue, we often beat around the bush. We avoid the thing we wish to directly discuss. Let's sneak up in case the unsaid topic becomes scared and runs away. In many ways, it is the opposite of "on the nose" dialogue. We prefer not to mention that one thing. We would rather it go unsaid, and we get an answer in kind. How can we identify the unspoken?

The context of the situation is the key to understanding these unsaid words. Reader comprehension relies on understanding character relationships and emotions. It makes no sense for a character to declare love for a man while content in another's embrace. We need to show the woman struggling with her thoughts, her guilt, her reluctance. Then she needs to push the other guy away. Despite her silence, we can infer from the story's events what is happening.

Let's analyze this subtext example. This is from the fourth Harry Potter novel, *The Goblet of Fire*. It is the scene where Harry, Ron, Hermione, and her date, Viktor Krum, are attending the Yule Ball of part of the Tri-Wizard Tournament's festivities.

"It's hot, isn't it?" said Hermione, fanning herself with her hand. "Viktor's just gone to get some drinks."
Ron gave her a withering look. "Viktor?" he said. "Hasn't he asked you to call him Vicky yet?"
Hermione looked at him in surprise. "What's up with you?" she said.
"If you don't know," said Ron scathingly, "I'm not going to tell you."
Hermione stared at him, then at Harry, who shrugged.
"Ron, what–?"
"He's from Durmstrang!" spat Ron. "He's competing against Harry! Against Hogwarts! You–you're–" Ron was obviously casting around for words strong enough to describe Hermione's crime, "fraternizing with the enemy, that's what you're doing!"

We understand what Ron is droning on about if we have consumed the movies or read the books, his obvious infatuation with Hermione. This affection would be reciprocated if they expressed their feelings. But two teenagers, unaware of love's complexities, fear mentioning it due to embarrassment and potential consequences.

To underscore, for subtext to work, the reader must understand the relationship dynamic between those involved. The reader needs to comprehend the topic and the characters' emotions. Remember, the character using subtext wants to get a reaction. As the writer, you must imply feelings through dialogue and character actions.

When it comes to subtext, the writer must choose what information to leave unsaid. Would revealing the information relieve the story's tension excessively? Is there a fear of the plot's unraveling if this information becomes known? If so, and you keep it unsaid, then you are trying to idiot-proof your story and the reader will not stand for it.

How do we go about implementing subtext in our dialogue? We have various approaches to consider. Below is a list of recommended tactics on getting subtext into your dialogue.

- Contradiction between words and body language. We've seen the rebuffed woman when she expects a kiss. It started with Scarlett O'Hara in *Gone With the Wind*. In order to preserve their image, they must deny any desire for a kiss.
- Flirting works all sorts of wonders. It's even better if the character acts innocent during the flirtation. The conversation covers anything except what they are talking about.
- Reaction to a smaller issue is really about a larger one. Who wants to call out their best friend or anyone else they like on a big issue? No one, so they veil it behind another problem they have.
- Sugarcoating works wonders if one of your characters is not that observant. Many women hate it when their man says, "I'm fine." They believe there's a hidden meaning, even if it's just as he said.
- Implied accusations happen all the time in media. Have you ever watched an interrogation on a crime drama? Mariska Hargitay's acting career lasted twenty-plus years because of this.
- Passive-aggressiveness bothers many people, but do you understand its prevalence? Because it works. Being passive-aggressive pushes people in the direction you want them to go, so they pick up on the clues you are giving them.
- Sarcasm never works… How important is sarcasm in our discourse? Message boards across the internet have defined fonts so that your sarcasm can be understood by others.
- Euphemisms and innuendo are time-tested ways to leave something unsaid. It isn't just about high schoolers referring to sex in every conversation.

- Misinterpretations occur when a character cannot grasp the subtext or perceive nonexistent elements. Such situations increase tension and conflict in the plot.
- Miscommunications occur when the character expresses something unknowingly that portrays their emotions or thoughts in a different light than reality, much like misinterpretations.

NON-VERBAL COMMUNICATION

Most of the communication in real life is through non-verbal means. Observe mannerisms and incorporate them into your dialogue scenes. Body language could indicate how your character feels beyond the words they say. These mannerisms ride alongside the dialogue sequence as "beats." Beats are the actions that happen as the conversation occurs to convey emotion and action to the reader.

Example: "I don't think so," said James as the gun shook in his hand.

In the above example, the words alone convey a message, but the character's action clues us into their emotional state of nervousness. They lack comfort with guns or have never faced a situation of threatening someone with a firearm. Something is wrong.

On a technical note, when we capture body beats with dialogue in the same sentence or paragraph, it is called blocking. This "block" of text contains everything pertinent to the same idea and provides a complete view of the emotions of the character by capturing this physical act and showing it with other elements that will provide the proper context to deliver the complete message.

Non-verbal communication is crucial for writers to convey messages to readers. You can reveal the true characterization of someone by showing their instinctual reaction to something instead of their measured response. This reaction may reveal a guilty criminal in a mystery or an unrequited lover in a romance. It shows context beyond what's apparent in dialogue. A character may roll their eyes because of a lack of disrespect toward a teacher when on the surface they act like they respect the person.

MONOLOGUE

Using monologue in fiction writing is the method of presenting the character's internal thoughts. The writer accomplishes this by having a specific character as the viewpoint character. While expressing one thing to others, the character secretly reveals another to the reader. It gives the reader inside knowledge of what that character is thinking. It develops trust with the reader and builds a connection.

The writer presents these unspoken thoughts in one of two ways. They can be represented as self-talk or set apart in the text, typically in italics. The former is referred to as indirect internal dialogue. This is often presented as a third-person narrator telling you what the character is thinking. The latter, direct internal dialogue, is presented as if the first-person character is addressing you. Note that the italicized direct internal dialogue in example two. This method is correct. You may also show direct internal dialogue just as you do external dialogue, as in example three.

Example one: Whatever I said to them on the outside, I knew how I really felt. I reassured myself, I hate vanilla pudding.

Example two: Whatever I said to them on the outside, I knew how I really felt. *I hate vanilla pudding.*

Example three: Whatever I said to them on the outside, I knew how I really felt. "I hate vanilla pudding," I thought.

Direct internal dialogue is a primary tool of conveying the third person deep viewpoint. Internal dialogue serves several purposes:

- Establishes trust with the reader by ensuring the narrator and author's honesty.
- Show differences between what the character thinks and speaks. This reveals an internal struggle within the character when their emotions and thoughts do not align.
- Reveal thoughts, opinions, plans, motivations, and objectives that the character wishes to remain their secret. Not every character may know this information. This creates suspense and intrigue.
- Set the story's tone by revealing the character's inner thoughts.

- Show reflection and character development. Having access to a character's thoughts will show how they are changing over the length of the story.
- Change the topic from what is happening outside the character.
- Describe what the character is seeing. Internal thoughts will color the story's presentation through your character's perspective.
- Internal thought affects pacing. Thoughts can be rapid fire for a quicker pace. The character chooses to reflect and pause the story to focus on plot-relevant details. Think of a detective examining a crime scene.

Another way to relay the character's thoughts is through a method known as free indirect speech. This method conveys the character's thoughts by expressing them in narration. Essentially, something written in a first person narrative but presented as third person. This method aligns with the deep third person viewpoint and eliminates the narrative distance of a limited viewpoint. It is believed Jane Austen popularized the method of blending the words and thoughts of the narrator and character. Below are examples demonstrating the usage of the technique.

Third Person Limited: *For six years, Anne had thought Harry dead. But there he was, alive and well. He lied all this time, Anne thought. But why? Because he's a lowlife, that's why. No, worse – he's a coward. She turned and left, without saying a word.*

First Person: *For six years, I had thought Harry dead. But there he was, alive and well. He had lied all this time. But why? Because he was a lowlife, that's why. No, worse – he was a coward. I turned and left, without saying a word.*

Free Indirect Speech: *For six years, Anne had thought Harry dead. But there he was, alive and well. He had lied all this time. But why? Because he was a lowlife, that's why. No, worse – he was a coward. Anne turned and left, without saying a word.*

The differences in the examples are subtle, but the last one has a slight shift in verb tense to past perfect. The other change referred to Anne in the last sentence, assigning thoughts to her rather than to the narrator. This technique allows the writer to dive into that character's interiority and expose it to the reader.

DOS AND DON'TS FOR DIALOGUE

Dialogue follows strict rules in almost every situation, with few exceptions. These are the rules of the road.

- Don't use intricate or constantly changing attributions that are overanalyzed or impossible to express while speaking (smiled, sneered, chortled). These varied forms of attributions are sometimes referred to as Tom Swifties. Stick with simple attributions (said, asked, answered) when possible.
- Avoid using adverbs along with your attributions. The character should say nothing glowingly.
- Avoid summation dialogue to catch up the reader. Old plays would have characters (the maid and butler) set a scene and provide background information for the audience. Also referred to as "As You Know" dialogue. Characters should not repeat things they already know.
- Steer clear of explicit dialogue. Don't show us a character is nervous and then have them tell us they are nervous. Emotions are better conveyed through actions.
- When only having two characters converse, avoid using attributions as much as possible.
- When dialogue begins a paragraph, put the dialogue before the attribution.
- Include punctuation within the quotation marks. Place a comma within the quotes when the attribution follows and end the sentence with a period. For questions and interrogatives, put the question mark and exclamation point inside the quotes and finish the sentence with a period after the attribution.
- When a character speaks in multiple paragraphs, keep the quotation marks open at the end of each paragraph and use a new set for the next paragraph.
- Avoid the exchanging of pleasantries as much as possible.
- Avoid rambling dialogue and keep it concise.
- Dialogue often contains incomplete grammatical sentences. They happen, but don't fear sentence fragments.
- Dialogue has sections where beats and speech are grouped together within the same paragraph. This is referred to as blocking. This condenses the writing by combining each line of dialogue and the

corresponding physical actions into its own paragraph. Together, this conveys the entire message a character is delivering.

Below is an example of dialogue from John Steinbeck's classic *Of Mice to Men*. The first example lacks attributions, the second example includes only attributions, and the third example is the final version with both attributions and beats.

"*I forgot. I tried not to forget. Honest to God I did, George.*"
"*O.K.—O.K. I'll tell ya again. I ain't got nothing to do. Might jus' as well spen' all my time tell'n you things and then you forget 'em, and I tell you again.*"
"*Tried and tried but it didn't do no good. I remember about the rabbits, George.*"
"*The hell with the rabbits. That's all you ever can remember is them rabbits. O.K.! Now you listen and this time you got to remember so we don't get in no trouble. You remember settin' in that gutter on Howard street and watchin' that blackboard?*"
"*Why sure, George, I remember that...but...what'd we do then? I remember some girls come by and you says...you say...*"
"*The hell with what I says. You remember about us goin' into Murray and Ready's, and they give us work cards and bus tickets?*"
"*Oh, sure, George, I remember that now. George...I ain't got mine. I musta lost it.*"
"*You never had none, you crazy bastard. I got both of 'em here. Think 'd let you carry your own work card?*"

George's name use by Lenny distinguishes the speaker. Without this, George's simple dialogue and Lenny's swearing would expose the speaker. You can guess what type of characters we are dealing with here due to the diction and dialect being used by Steinbeck throughout.

"*I forgot,*" Lennie said. "*I tried not to forget. Honest to God I did, George.*"
"*O.K.—O.K. I'll tell ya again. I ain't got nothing to do. Might jus' as well spen' all my time tell'n you things and then you forget 'em, and I tell you again.*"
"*Tried and tried,*" said Lennie, "*but it didn't do no good. I remember about the rabbits, George.*"
"*The hell with the rabbits. That's all you ever can remember is them rabbits. O.K.! Now you listen and this time you got to remember so we*

don't get in no trouble. You remember settin' in that gutter on Howard street and watchin' that blackboard?"
"Why sure, George, I remember that...but...what'd we do then? I remember some girls come by and you says...you say..."
"The hell with what I says. You remember about us goin' into Murray and Ready's, and they give us work cards and bus tickets?"
"Oh, sure, George, I remember that now." He said, "George...I ain't got mine. I musta lost it."
"You never had none, you crazy bastard. I got both of 'em here. Think I'd let you carry your own work card?"

The speaker is clear, yet something is missing. We are only getting the words. Additional beats from the writer would complete the picture. Below is the final version of a masterful dialogue scene.

"I forgot," Lennie said softly. "I tried not to forget. Honest to God I did, George."
"O.K.—O.K. I'll tell ya again. I ain't got nothing to do. Might jus' as well spen' all my time tell'n you things and then you forget 'em, and I tell you again."
"Tried and tried," said Lennie, "but it didn't do no good. I remember about the rabbits, George."
"The hell with the rabbits. That's all you ever can remember is them rabbits. O.K.! Now you listen and this time you got to remember so we don't get in no trouble. You remember settin' in that gutter on Howard street and watchin' that blackboard?"
Lennie's face broke into a delighted smile. "Why sure, George, I remember that...but...what'd we do then? I remember some girls come by and you says...you say..."
"The hell with what I says. You remember about us goin' into Murray and Ready's, and they give us work cards and bus tickets?"
"Oh, sure, George, I remember that now." His hands went quickly into his side coat pockets. He said gently, "George...I ain't got mine. I musta lost it." He looked down at the ground in despair.
"You never had none, you crazy bastard. I got both of 'em here. Think I'd let you carry your own work card?"
Lennie grinned with relief.

One tool to help with your dialogue writing is a dialogue map. Create columns on a paper for each participant in the conversation. Put the dialogue in the column associated with the speaker and keep it lined up by row based on the sequence in the conversation (first line of dialogue in row one, etc.). This tool will help you identify if certain lines of dialogue are required, or additional lines needed. Do the participants answer or ask the questions you want addressed in the scene? It will also allow you to determine if every line of dialogue by a participant is consistent with their character. If a character's dialogue has slang in one line but is formal in another, you must fix one of the lines. A version of this tool exists in the Vibrant Prose Toolbox.

In your writing process, you should have your words read aloud. This includes the dialogue. There are several ways you can do this. Read it aloud to yourself. Perhaps buy dinner for someone and ask them to read with you, like actors practicing lines. Another option is to have your computer read the words aloud. Microsoft Word has a read aloud feature in the latest upgrade. Other software applications perform the same task. Either way, have the words read back to you. Something you write appears fine on the page, but stilted or clunky dialogue will become apparent if read aloud.

To improve your dialogue skills, try writing in another form. For example, focus on your dialogue by writing a one-act play. Informing the audience of a play's happenings is best done through dialogue. It worked out pretty well for Shakespeare.

At this point, you should have a better understanding of dialogue, monologue, non-verbal communication, and their purposes: telling characters apart, identifying tension between characters, providing information, and achieving plot objectives.

EXERCISES

1. Write a scene without dialogue tags.
2. Use a Dialogue Chart to plot out a conversation.
3. Write an edited scene with dialogue tags and beats.
4. Record a family conversation (with permission). Transcribe the conversation and then edit it into a functional conversation for a story.

REFERANCE MATERIALS

Crafting Dynamic Dialogue: The Complete Guide to Speaking, Conversing, Arguing, and Thinking in Fiction by Writer's Digest Books

Due to the large amount of dialogue in fiction, this is a common subject in writing guides. Numerous individual tomes are dedicated to this topic, and every guide has a chapter about it. Writer's Digest's tome covers the topic extensively, exploring dialogue's diverse roles in storytelling, such as internal dialogue and subtext.

19 – DESCRIPTIVE LANGUAGE

Description is perhaps the most difficult of the narrative modes to master. You may be a natural with dialogue or action. Exposition you could figure out. Emotions and thoughts might be your jam. Description takes work, time, and talent to understand. You must master your use of language and know when you have gone too far.

Writers and readers dislike how description slows down stories. They want the action and dialogue to quicken the pace. The fast-paced style of fiction that dominates the market today requires brief description, at least compared to the classics of yesteryear. Description sometimes has to be slipped in like the way your mom hid vegetables in your food as a child.

Description grounds the reader in the setting and events of the story. It assists in understanding the story's context, characters, and elements. Description helps foreshadow events and enhance theme through imagery and symbolism. Description characterizes players within the story through emotional tugs and creates tension and conflict at the same time. Description enriches a reader's experience and immerses them in the story's world.

SETTING DESCRIPTIONS

Our goal is to enthrall readers with the world we create in every story. We want them to experience it fully. Often, we struggle with what we want to include in that setting. Our focus is on a few items, which we believe suffices as writers. More is involved in creating a descriptive setting.

Think about anywhere you go. What do you see? You probably overlook wandering strangers, or the squirrels and other small animals roaming the space looking for food, or the cars and other things passing by that create sounds, smells, and other sensory experiences we take for granted. We should include those items without boring or overwhelming the reader. But attempt to be evasive to the point you can hide something that becomes important later, a version of Chekov's gun, perhaps.

For example, when we examine characters, we fixate on the nuances that make them unique, less bland, and more appealing. The settings of our stories demand the same level of treatment. Everything within the setting that you provide to the reader should have a reason for inclusion. Every mentioned piece should add color to the imagery, depth to the setting's character, and reveal a portion of the story to the reader.

It helps if you drill into what makes your setting unique. Every place is unique, nothing is identical. The pathways may be cobblestone or the trees could be limited to a certain type. Dive into that element and bring it out to the reader. Expand your exploration to understand the impact of that item on the world. And this needs to matter to the character conveying the imagery, otherwise it won't matter to the reader. Our goal is to describe the setting and evoke the desired reader experience.

Inhabitants are reflected by the setting. If your character is an art critic, you would expect them to have beautiful art hanging around their home. But this can also be a perfect point to subvert the expected. Perhaps the art critic is so immersed in the artistic world that they choose to avoid that world in their home and leave their walls barren. They could avoid art to prevent biasing their opinions. Or perhaps you go with the complete opposite and the character only wants pictures of clowns on their walls. These idiosyncrasies present the lead in for all kinds of potential stories. But we must connect these setting elements to the POV character for the reader. If the character doesn't care, the reader won't.

Our wish is for the reader to enjoy their presence in our setting. Make it inviting, make one element wonderful in a way that it captures the reader's imagination. Regardless of the awful setting, offer readers a motive to revisit.

"Dawn came glassy orange, stained from below by a gelatinous band of pale green. The sooty bulk of the mountain paled slowly until it was the same color as the smoke from Ennis's breakfast fire. The cold air sweetened, banded pebbles and crumbs of soil cast sudden pencil-long shadows and the rearing lodgepole pines below them massed in slabs of somber malachite." – Annie Proulx, *Brokeback Mountain*

CHARACTER DESCRIPTIONS

Character descriptions were not thoroughly examined in the previous chapters of this book but learning to describe characters is essential for writers. Your main character may not be described at any point in the novel, but they will describe the other characters. This will display the judgements and prejudices the POV character may have to the reader. This provides information used within the story. Focusing on specific elements will bring these characters to life.

For non-viewpoint characters, the description process is much simpler. Focus on one prominent feature of the character, whether it's their lips, eyes, or a scar. And make that focal point either appealing or appalling to the viewpoint character. Lack of interest equates to boredom. The POV character won't note the characteristic unless it impresses on them. And if it doesn't impress upon the character, it won't on the reader either.

You should also use the character's appearance to hint at their internal character, either through the clothes they wear, how they do their hair, or the way they walk. This is a great opportunity to use subversion. Perhaps they dress elaborately because of their job, but they hate that about themselves and are purposefully informal outside of the workplace. The outward appearance needs to speak to their internal character in some way.

As for our viewpoint character, that is more difficult. Unless they are narcissistic, they will not go around looking in mirrors. So, we need to avoid that cliché and get them in situations where we highlight their appearance. The easiest thing is to have another character comment on their appearance. This includes something that might point to their age. If they take care of themselves, they will look younger. If they don't, they will look older. The other option is having the viewpoint character compare themselves to other characters. In the following excerpt, the main character of *Argent's Menagerie* looks at themselves in a mirror and describes his own appearance.

"Argent closed the cabinet and peered at his reflection in the mirror. The image revealed how ruffled his silver feathers were and his lean nature testified to his recent diet. Thoughts drifted to a possible trip to Aviara, his home world, to enjoy home-cooked meals and regain a semblance of good health."

CONCRETE VS. ABSTRACT

One of the most valuable pieces of advice for any writer is in handpicking their words. Much of this goes back to our chapter on showing and telling. You want to have active prose with concrete nouns and active verbs. This works especially well with description where you are portraying a specific scene to the reader. We wish to avoid abstraction as much as possible.

How do we determine the right words to avoid vagueness and abstraction? Jane Cleland espouses the principle of FURY in *Mastering Plot Twists*. Color is a perfect tool to demonstrate the use of the FURY technique. Let's say you are trying to describe the color of a purplish house. F stands for familiar, and purple is distinctive and familiar to everyone, a good starting point. U stands for unique and heather would be a more unique color of the purple family. R stands for rich. A color like tyrian fits the bill of sounding richer. Y represents your own voice, aligning more closely with you. Something like lilac may fit a specific place in the author's mind because lilacs make them sneeze. The specific word choices can influence the writer's tone, mood, or theme.

Word choice ties to the feeling of the world you are attempting to evoke in your writing. We influence the displayed world mood. The reader's perception depends on our description, whether it's melancholic or jovial. If we wish for the reader to feel more suspense, we might have a thunderstorm raging outside of a house at night with tornado warning sirens blaring in the surrounding neighborhood. The character has heard these warnings a hundred times, so they don't seek shelter. Then they hear the sound of a train coming toward their house. That sets a specific mood that the reader will be able to grasp.

Tone is much more about attitude. Perhaps the words you choose are edgier than other writers because you are coming at the story with a mindset of sarcasm or cynicism. It seems like you're highlighting the significance of a row of neighborhood pubs as women go bar hopping on a Saturday night. Perhaps that isn't your scene, and you don't think it should be anyone's, but you write it in your book because it sets up the storyline. Your beliefs will come through with the word choices you make. But a skilled writer will see that.

Thematic imagery also drives home a certain point from the story. Perhaps you have a story with religious ramifications in a small town and you keep running across bushes set ablaze, crosses, or men walking alongside the road. These all allude to famous religious stories and carry a specific heft based on the reader's personal experience.

Imagery is best used to pull forward the emotions of the character based on the tone of the story or scene. The tone created impacts the reaction. How many people have seen a building during a sunlit day and then it appears the opposite on rainy days? These fluctuations provide variations in the emotional journey of the character. Also, if you have multiple viewpoint characters, they may have different reactions to imagery in the story. This is based on their own emotional baggage and backstory. In some instances, the imagery provides something akin to the personification of objects. Fog crawls, tree roots clutch, and bushes grab in the scariest of scenes. You can characterize the surrounding setting and use it to evoke tone, mood, and drive suspense.

Like dialogue and other narrative modes, descriptive language is flexible in conveying story elements to readers. It goes beyond simple descriptions of appearance and setting. Descriptive language evokes the greatest emotions and also opens up new worlds for the reader.

COMPARISON & CONTRAST

Comparison and contrast are another facet of the broad category of description that uses figurative language to better resonate with the reader. There are several types of figurative language devices (figures of speech) that perform this function for a writer. The most popular tools are bulleted below.

- Similes involve comparing in a specific pattern of words using "like," "as," "than," or "resembles." Examples would be "cute as a button" or "sweet like sugar" in everyday vernacular.
- Hyperbole is an exaggerated simile or metaphor that overstates the comparison and is often used for comedic effect.
- Allusions compare objects to known references. Phrases like "wide as the Grand Canyon" or "cold as the North Pole" convey specific comparisons.
- Analogies use a formula, like A is to B as C is to D, to compare relationships. For instance, a tornado to a household and a lion to a mouse.
- Symbolism uses aspects of items to convey messages that resonate with the deepest of our emotions. Corporate logos and religious emblems are the most prominent of these symbols in our everyday

life. Utilizing such elements produces a profound effect on a story, especially when addressing themes.

The king of the comparative tools is the metaphor. Metaphors are more difficult to construct than the other tools mentioned. They also have a richer language and provide greater depth to the reader. Let's be honest for a moment. Metaphors are difficult to master and, many times, require an advanced writer. It might be one of the more difficult skills for any writer.

At its core, a metaphor is the transference of the image from one item onto another. You compare two dissimilar items. The compared object adopts qualities from the other component. For example, Coors Beer uses the metaphor of cool mountain streams to connotate their beer has a more refreshing taste than other beers. In *Argent's Menagerie*, a dagger serves as the inspiration for the shape of a particular spaceship. The image of the dagger allows the reader to visualize the spaceship without seeing it.

The metaphor has two components: tenor and vehicle. The subject, represented by the spaceship, can be anything. The vehicle is a concrete image, in this case the dagger, that delivers the intended message. The ship's shape imitated a dagger meant for enemy destruction. Perhaps it was a poor choice, but it delivers the image desired by the author. In your metaphor, the words need to be precise. Precision allows the reader to visualize the image clearly and connect the metaphor in their mind. If done correctly, those precise words take two familiar images and create a new fresh image.

There are times you will write implied metaphors. Implied metaphors transfer the image, but there is no tenor. For examples, "…the ship, slicing through and leaving gashes and mechanical wounds, destroyed its enemy." We still have the spaceship, our tenor, but we don't expressly mention the dagger, our vehicle.

You may wonder how to work on metaphors. Start by examining your own writing. Search your writing for clues to images in your mind to produce metaphors. Perhaps you write a lot of imagery around birds and fill your prose with references to birds. Key in on that and use free word association to mine for richer descriptions to create. This provides the imagery to use as the vehicle in your metaphor. Another option is to refer to technical guidance in areas where your metaphors are leaning. This will expose you to more precise words and could evoke more imagery.

What should you avoid? Foremost, don't call attention to the metaphors at the expense of the writing. This leads to purple prose, hyperbole, or melodrama when not intended. Also, avoid contrived or cliché metaphors. Not every splendid work uses extended metaphors. Avoid chasing metaphors just to have them. Bad metaphors are worse than not using them at all. When using these tools, it's important to maintain a proportional scale for comparison. Don't compare elephants to cockroaches.

"The sun in the west was a drop of burning gold that slid near and nearer the sill of the world." – William Golding, *Lord of the Flies.*

DESCRIPTION DOING ITS JOB

Each character has their own voice and perspective on how they see the world, as we mentioned. Your viewpoint character communicates the world in a manner that seems natural to that character. If your character is a blacksmith, they notice metal elements and displayed weapons. OCD individuals obsess over perceived irregularities and disorder that induce anxiety. They enter the room, but each will perceive it differently. Their personal mood could also trigger different responses. Calm characters also perceive the world differently than nervous ones, while acting and reacting differently to the world around them.

We should depict those actions and reactions with physicality. There should be little standing still. It reminds us that characters should not remain static in the story. We wish to avoid that as much as possible. In short, we want the actions to be quick and sharp.

Though description comes through the perspective of our viewpoint character, we need to also realize it has a role in doing more than providing characterization and information. Descriptive prose increases tension and progresses the plot.

Scene description affects story pacing. Most people associate descriptive prose with flowery language that puts a roadblock on story progression. It actually controls the pace by speeding up the story or slowing it down. This is based on the words we use and the diction. It also depends on the sentence structures we use and the punctuation within those sentences. If we wish to establish a fine rhythm, write a longer sentence with fewer pauses. If you want to provide the illusion of higher pace, write a bunch of short choppy sentences that have commas and periods to slow the reader.

USE OF THE SENSES

The best advice is to communicate what your character takes in, but don't describe everything in detail. Focus on one or two details, but give a complete picture to the reader. To make the picture unique, allow your character to spin the image oddly based on their life experience. But don't paint a still frame. Give additional depth by having things move. The wind will flip leaves around, tiny animals will scour for nuts, people's hair will be flowing in the breeze.

Sight is the most common sense used to describe things. It is the first sense we use when encountering new people or places. Sight also provides us with the greatest level of detail. No visual description should be vague. The issue is an overemphasis on sight in stories, neglecting other senses. You must allow your characters to use all their senses and depict that information to the reader.

Sound is the second most used sensory experience. The problem with sound is difficulty in conveying it. We use onomatopoeias to get the actual sound across, but sound resonates in other ways. Certain sounds provide a tone, a creaking door. Some bring back memories and evoke emotion, the sound of a branch breaking because your father was cutting a switch. And certain words evoke sounds in our mind, like ooze. Make the sounds in your world benefit your writing.

Taste is perhaps the sense used the least in writing. If your character is eating something, describe it. Don't just say they ate it. Go into depth on the luxuries of pepperoni pizza. Allow the character to experience unique tastes in their mouth: blood after they get hit, the salt from ocean air after taking a deep breath, the bitterness of something they believe to be poison, or whatever that is in your mouth after you vomit. You get the point.

One of the most overlooked aspects of any story is food culture. Every character consumes food. Use this to dive into their character by revealing their likes and dislikes. Use food as a bridge to the surrounding culture and provide context for a society. Allow a sensory tool to open up your world-building.

Smell is often noted as one of the most emotionally charged senses because it brings back memories and reactions. When detailing smells, always introduce the smell as the character enters the scene. For example, a gas leak creates tension at the start of the scene. Other smells could raise suspense or mystery. To make a powerful impact with smell descriptions, compare them as good or bad. Some writers will choose a smell to use throughout their work, either the character's favorite, or one that holds a special place in their heart, or one that unlocks their memories.

The complexity of touch surpasses all other senses. It conveys many aspects pertaining to the surrounding world. The character experiences changes in temperature or humidity. Texture of materials or clothing evokes certain thoughts and emotions. Pressure and pain can be used for intimacy, threats, or humor. Touch is the most versatile sense and enhances your world. This can even be expanded to create a sense of space. A character might fear enclosed spaces or feel anxious in large groups.

The last sense to touch upon is the "sixth sense," intuition. The character's intuition often relies on their experience. Don't forget to account for this in your writing. We all understand the feeling that something ominous is about to occur. We have all experienced the sensation before. The book *Outliers* by Malcolm Gladwell touches on how experts in their field can often anticipate what will happen with no evidence other than seeing the situation arise. Experience prepares them for such moments, eliminating the need for data reliance.

Regarding sensory description, there are other options for describing tastes, sounds, scents, and sights. Synesthesia is an actual condition that occurs when you experience one sense through another, such as seeing colors when you hear music. Who hasn't experienced the taste of their favorite food when someone else mentions it? This can be a powerful tool for recalling emotional events in a character's past. In *Argent's Menagerie,* one character suffered a traumatic attack, they awoke from their slumber and underwent a transformation due to that trauma. Their senses were misaligned. The author used this situation for some comedic relief, but also demonstrated the trauma the character endured and caused them to transform and rewire their mind.

Descriptions may involve all five senses, whether it's in a scene, experiencing something, or meeting a new person. Amateur writers often only stick with sight and sound in trying to convey setting and description. Good writers will work in descriptions that impact smell, taste, texture, temperature, pain, and other levels of sensory interpretation.

Avoid using all five senses to describe every aspect of the story. First, it may not be possible. Second, it will become tiresome. As you go through the story, alternate between senses, and use only one or two at smaller sensory incidents. Save the use of all the senses for major scenes. When creating a scene, avoid listing the senses without interrupting the action. Make these descriptions blend into the narrative for an enchanting effect. Make use of your skill to "show" these items to the reader.

"I heard the rain still beating continuously on the staircase window, and the wind howling in the grove behind the hall; I grew by degrees cold as a stone, and then my courage sank." – Charlotte Bronte, *Jane Eyre*.

OTHER TECHNIQUES

Before concluding this chapter, let's examine some additional techniques and tools that enhance description. Using word sounds is the first technique. Alliteration is the use of the same letter or sounds in multiple words within a sentence or paragraph. Many excellent examples of prose and poetry include alliteration. The following is a brief excerpt from Robert Louis Stevenson's *The Strange Case of Dr. Jekyll and Mr. Hyde*.

"...his appearance: something displeasing, something down-right detestable. I never saw a man I disliked and yet I scarce know why. He must be deformed..."

Assonance is the repetition of vowel sounds in phrases. Consonance is an approach focused on a specific consonant sound. Onomatopoeia is the attempt to use facsimiles of sounds as words. Other techniques include the use of cadence or rhythm with the words to provide a clearer description of an item. Repetition is another effective tool. Don't repeat information, but using repetitive descriptions enhances thematic imagery and motifs.

The circling technique is another technique for conveying description. Picture a scenario where a character enters a room, taking note of various details, but captivated by the last image. The character's focus could center on a woman, a gun on the wall, or the bouncer in the bar's corner. It would be whatever is natural for that character to focus on. All people focus on one thing when they interact with others. Your characters should be no different. Also, the character will notice things in a certain order based on their biases. Think that through before finalizing your descriptive elements.

VIBRANT PROSE

We have two concerns when we discuss description in our stories. First, descriptive and figurative language must multi-task and do more than one thing. Second, we want to keep our prose from becoming "purple" or overworked. Our description should support the story and scene objective without overshadowing them. Use these techniques and tools to demonstrate how the setting influences the plot, characters, and other story elements.

EXERCISES

1. Evaluate the room you occupy and describe its many details.
2. Develop a simile and metaphor about something within that room.
3. Recreate an experience you had at a restaurant by calling out at least one sensory aspect for each of the five senses.

REFERENCE MATERIALS

Word Painting: The Fine Art of Writing Descriptively by Rebecca McClanahan

Similar to dialogue references, there are many description references available. McClanahan's writing style is straightforward to read and draws you into the tale she is trying to tell about descriptive language. A well-written book and one every writer should have on their shelf.

20 – THE ACTION/REACTION CYCLE

In a previous chapter, we discussed the structure of scenes and sequels and how those progress the plot. This chapter explores the Action/Reaction Cycle. This cycle relates to the notion of causality through the storyline; each event builds upon those that occurred before. Using this cause-effect relationship creates a plot that progresses toward an eventual and believable ending. Along the way, we experience the emotions, thoughts and actions of the characters while making them more rounded and easier to relate with for the reader.

Having said that, we will begin by diving into the cycle and looking at the various reactions: instinctual, emotional, logical, and non-sensical. We'll showcase applying these techniques in your writing with examples from fiction.

ACTION/REACTION CYCLE

Have you even heard of this cycle? Maybe not. It is key to progressing the plot and ensuring the reader understands how the character moves through the story and maintains their agency through the novel.

The cycle begins when an action impacts the character. Once this act is committed onto a character, it prompts a reaction from that same character. In many scenes, this initial act may not be displayed. Especially, in scenes where the writer begins them *in media res*. In those scenes, that initial act needs communicated to the reader, so they understand what prompted the entire sequence.

Emotions initiate the reaction, causing the character to respond to stimuli. In the case of a fight, the character may react in kind. Or they may flee. These reactions are all driven by emotion and reflexes. A character's background and experience shape these reactions, often without thinking. Thus, underscoring the need to understand the character's backstory.

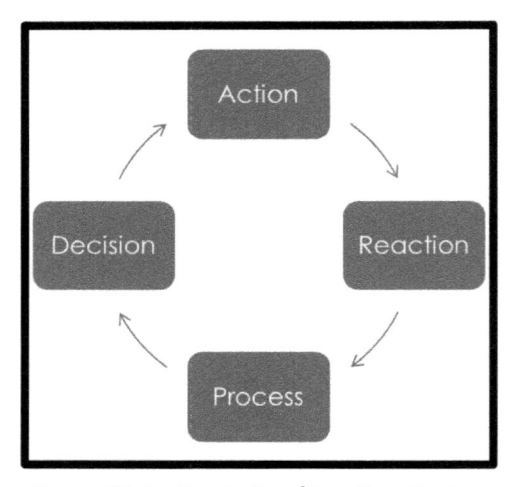

Figure 20-1 - The Action/Reaction Cycle

Next, the brain kicks in and the character begins the decision-making process. The character pieces together information in their brain and decides what to do next, or draws a conclusion that will dictate their next decision. Some writers often summarize this piece or skip the process. The problem with taking this approach is that experiencing a character's emotions and thoughts connects the reader and this process reveal the character's true makeup.

In many stories, countless heroes react without considering consequences and make nonsensical choices. This can be exploited as a flaw in the character, but people don't operate in this manner, and this creates a credibility gap. In Brandon Sanderson's recent novel, *Tress of the Emerald Sea*, the narrator of the tale points this out and commends the main character, Tress, for thinking through her decisions. We want our characters to be believable.

The character must follow through on their decision, or state why they disregard the decision. This action, in turn, leads to the character saying and doing stuff and moves the plot forward. The consequence of this action initiates the next reaction, continuing the cycle. In theory, the first act of the story creates a logical loop of yes/no decisions that create causality, continuity, and cohesion throughout the entire work.

REACTION TYPES

When something dramatic happens, our body responds with our initial reaction. This reaction is typically physical. They can be extreme and visceral, like passing out or vomiting. They can be subtle where our eyes dilate or the hair on our neck rises. That initial reaction is our body putting up its defense systems and depends on the person and what they are reacting to. Your characters should be no different.

The divergence lies in what happens next for each character. The mind activates and elicits a specific physical reaction often termed fright-flight-fight-freeze. Based on your character's makeup and the challenge in front of them, they will take on one of these postures. To use Jim Holden from *The Expanse* series as an example, he has UN Navy training, has a quick temper, a deep streak of hatred for injustice, and is not afraid to hurt someone. He usually defends himself and others, using blunt force or a sidearm. However, not all characters receive such training. You can't expect Miss Muffet to turn into a ninja and tear apart a crew of rustlers taking her sheep. We need to demonstrate that embedded training exists before allowing it to show itself in a response situation.

Next, we will look at the emotional reaction. This is where the character is overwhelmed and turns to fright, flight, or freeze. All are possible reactions for anyone in any situation. We don't like being confronted. Our characters shouldn't either, especially if they are unprepared. The emotional reaction can often lead to surprising results. In *Cibola Burn*, the fourth book in *The Expanse* series, a character is in an argument and appears to be under complete control and he shoots someone who threatens him. There was no cycle progression and no attempt to deescalate. The character jumped to the violent response. In doing this, the writer is telling us this character has a problem. We realize he is psychotic, and the rules of the reaction cycle don't apply to him. But we as writers need to tread this line carefully.

A single character's one-time action could be an isolated incident. Once the number of responses surpasses that threshold, the response becomes part of a trend. This trend, if multiple characters follow suit, isn't believable. That means the reader won't stay with the story. Desperate individuals resort to extreme actions. However, even in such cases, you will witness their journey through conflict and tension, as well as delve into their thoughts and emotions that drive them to that outcome. An immediate jump is non-sensical in almost all circumstances. Readers won't stand for that.

Next is the logical reaction type. This is where we show the character dealing with their emotions, struggling with their personal thoughts, making an informed decision, and stepping forward to take action. Or they decide to do nothing. That potential result of the process often gets lost in the possibilities. All options are available to your characters, but we must justify the reaction and explain the choices the character makes to the reader.

EMOTIONS IN WRITING

The internal narration of the character always breaks down into either emotions or thoughts. A character may remember something, triggering emotions and leading to a response and further actions or thoughts. Sensory experiences evoke sensations, emotions, thoughts, and actions in characters. Every instance prompts emotions and thoughts, resulting in action or inaction.

When we deal with emotions in writing, we are driving to the core of the character. Thoughts can be controlled, but our emotions on the inside of us reveal our base selves. The following paragraphs will not review every emotion and how to write them. You can acquire a copy of the excellent book by Angela Ackerman and Becca Puglisi, *The Emotion Thesaurus: A Writer's Guide to Character Expression* to view that type of detail. The goal is to provide you with a standard process on how to represent your character's emotional responses in writing. Then include the specifics of the desired emotion based on what you are trying to achieve in your writing.

First, let your reader identify with your character. We need to set up scenes early that expose who they are inside. This means fleshing out the character and exposing their wounds and warts. Hoping to make the reader empathize or sympathize with them. The reader wants to make this connection, or they wouldn't be reading your story.

To convey emotions, we must illustrate the trigger. Is it a building from their childhood, a smell of their favorite food, or something else? Present this to the reader. The other element is showing why this creates the emotional response and the revelation. Does the stimulus induce a flashback or evoke a memory? Conveying the reason behind the reaction to the reader is essential. Knowing a character's motivation for their actions is essential.

Then the reaction must be demonstrated. What type of reaction does the stimuli generate? The reader must know that. Show the response to them and don't say the girl blushed. Add something to the description. "The girl's cheeks turned a color I had only seen in a red velvet cake." Draw a comparison to make the reaction more concrete to the reader.

As the story progresses, we need to increase the intensity of our characters' reactions. They will be under increased tension and stress throughout the story. We need to build them up to their breaking point at the Crisis plot point. The more we punish them, the stronger their reaction. If they break down, what happens next?

People desire to witness genuine reactions. When portraying these emotions and the resulting reactions, we want to use varied descriptions and strong concrete word choices. We want the reader to experience these emotions as well and believe the character can overcome their struggle.

Dramatic points (the Big Event, the Midpoint, and the Crisis) elicit these visceral reactions from the characters. Visceral reactions are the strongest we can produce: fainting, vomiting, complete breakdowns, the ugly cries. For example, if your character has diabetes, this condition explains nausea in intense situations and a tendency for low blood sugar and potential vomiting. The character shouldn't experience this consistently. This presents a fragile psyche and a melodramatic character.

Also, your character will reveal their feelings through their body language. Use this to add to your dialogue beats or to give an image of a character attempting to remain composed but giving signals of the complete opposite. With involuntary actions, the character shouldn't realize they are wringing their hands or fidgeting their leg. If they thought about their action, they would hide it better.

Emotions of characters can be shown through their interactions with the world. If they are feeling paranoid, they will not act normally around people, especially those they are comfortable with. They may avoid certain settings when they have a particular emotion dominating their thought process. Add people to the character's life who elicit varying emotions, perhaps someone who brings them joy despite any challenges. Or someone they cannot stand. Our goal is to create authentic characters, like real people.

We also want to make sure these reactions feel real. We can't have someone that gets annoyed by a bug hovering near their head and reacts by shooting at someone. It's a nonsensical leap. Make sure the emotional reactions match the stimulus.

Remember, the emotions of your character are the doorway to their reactions to the conflict and tension they face in the story. The emotions get brought to the surface and lead to thoughts, with resulting actions. We must ensure the reader follows the character's reactions in a clear and sequential manner. This allows us to show changes within the character as their emotions and thoughts mature though the character arc and lead to the decisions that impact resolving the story.

THOUGHTS AND DECISIONS

Thoughts in your character bridge the gap from emotion to action. Showing this connection will open your story up to the reader and keep them invested. Presenting the character's internal thoughts can be done if a particular character is the viewpoint character, or if there is an omniscient narrator. It gives the reader inside knowledge of what that character is thinking. It develops trust with the reader and builds a connection. It can also clue you into there being an unreliable narrator, as covered in the viewpoint chapter.

Our primary goal is to steer clear of introspective thinking. We want to avoid scenes where the character waxes poetic and halts the story by becoming self-aware. Employ character thoughts as a principal source for the story but avoid excessive self-focus to keep readers engaged. Basically, don't let the characters impede the story.

Thoughts are informative because they allow us, the reader, to observe the process a character makes toward a decision. Think of any mystery novel. Part of the enjoyment is seeing the detective solve the puzzle. Poirot, sharing his thoughts with you, the audience, pulls you into the story and creates a specific challenge. Who can figure out the puzzle first?

These thoughts lead to a decision. The decision by the character creates a pivotal point in the story each time. The character has weighed the costs of their action and come to terms with the decision/moral dilemma. They have decided the consequences, or stakes, are worthy enough to warrant whatever their action is. We have given the character agency over their life, and they are ready to act, or not, regardless of the stakes, consequences, or costs.

Now, our protagonist gazes into the enemy's eye and moves forward or flees, hides, and evades conflict. We discuss conflict avoidance in more detail in the conflict chapter. For specific details, refer to that chapter, but the character must eventually accept this challenge to advance the story.

ACTION SCENES

You know what you almost never hear about a book? "I wish the book plodded along because I enjoy slow reads where nothing happens." People don't want that. They want action. Now, the kind of action is debatable. It might not be car chases, explosions, or fight scenes. The action might take the form of simple incidental acts or non-violent action. We need our story's characters to do something and perform actions that push the story forward.

What is action and why do we want this element in our fiction? Action involves the characters doing something that suggests they have agency over their fate. This action aims toward an objective. That objective could be to provide characterization, add tension, resolve conflict, progress the plot, or all the above. All action should be moving the story forward. If there's no objective, the action is pointless and should be excluded from the story.

Before delving into grand action scenes, two additional action types take place in the story. The first one is always prominent, known as body beats. You can't avoid these beats, they happen and using them to augment your story will show off your skill. Dialogue is often accompanied by slight body movements. She shrugged, he smiled, and they nodded. All of these are beats. It's crucial that beats mirror the character's emotions and stay in tune with presenting their characterization. If the beat doesn't match up to the emotional state of the character, there is a problem. This small action beat must be demonstrated to reflect the character's emotions. Otherwise, the character appears to be disingenuous. A great resource to use to check if your beat matches the emotions you wish to draw from your characters is *The Emotion Thesaurus*.

The second of these types of action is something we have referred to a couple times in this book, the THAD (talking heads avoidance device). This excellent tool presents action as a secondary device in a scene to distract from the fact that an intense conversation about details important to the story is occurring. In her book titled *Mastering the Process*, Elizabeth George explains the THAD through an example. The scene's forefront conversation revolves around the farm owners' relationship. In the background, the characters help an animal deliver babies while having difficulties with that task. The scene enables distraction, subtext, and the passage of time. You will have instances where using such a device is the perfect answer to present subtext heavy scenes in the story.

There are three general categories of action scenes we will discuss. The initial element is the fight, involving shootouts and battles. The fight becomes more intense with the addition of weapons and people. There are several craft books detailing how to write a fight scene. These scenes are typically shown through a first person or third person limited narrative. It helps the writer and reader focus on events from a character's perspective. In a battle, head-hopping among characters can cause confusion and reader fatigue.

The second action scene is the chase. These can occur by walking, running, or using a vehicle. The objective of the chase depends on the point-of-view character. If they are doing the chasing, the objective is to capture. In the opposite situation, the goal is likely to escape. Only two outcomes exist: getting caught or escaping. One of the benefits of a chase scene is the action immerses your characters and readers into the story world. The setting has a large impact on the chase.

The third action scene is referred to as non-violent and happens throughout the story. Simple acts in a story include walking to a neighbor's house or phoning a friend. The intensity of these acts can fluctuate. Perhaps a bank robber tries to crack a safe, or someone scales a wall with a rope, or someone walks their dog. It's crucial to assess their impact on the story and plot progression. As stated before, if they don't meet an objective, regardless of how cool they may seem, they need cut.

Action scenes cause subsequent reactions in various characters. This reaction caps the scene and allows the reader to understand the impact, while also controlling the pace of the story. This function as a break, regardless of how short, and allows us to move to the next scene where we witness the ramifications of the prior action. This also helps the reader as their journey should match the characters. The character can't physically continue, and the reader needs a break from time to time, primarily in longer stories.

Once we move beyond the action, there must also be consequences. Whether the result is property damage following a car chase, physical damage after a fight, or mental anguish. Action scenes have consequences and require a reaction to the consequence after they finish. Superhero movies often neglect the aftermath of urban conflicts. The amount of property damage in New York City during *The Avengers* would have crippled the city, but we see none of that.

Within the scene's structure, the action can be lumped into three levels. The stunt is a single action or a flurry of related actions. In writing, these are brief and are perhaps one sentence or two. They serve as excellent tools for introducing characters or conflicts.

A series of stunts is known as an engagement. This may be an entire scene. Engagements can be useful for transitioning into another set of stunts (chase into a fist fight), as character development (two brothers duke it out), or as a resolution moment (catch the bad guys).

Engagements combine to form sequences across multiple scenes. We would hope to have several sequences within a novel of any significant length. In *The Avengers*, the storyline is dominated by a continuous action sequence, from the fight in New York City to Iron Man's heroic act with the bomb. It's a single sequence, albeit with multiple small engagements.

TIPS AND TRICKS

Once you have selected what type of action scenes to include in your story, map them out. A hole in the main action sequence ruins the reader's immersion. Action sequences, like a good story, have a cause-effect pattern. Everything in the scene builds off what happened before. To plan a fight scene, consider sketching a basic room map and diagramming the fight's flow. Or, for a chase, map out the route. This will help you frame the action in the setting and allow you to pull in details to add realism. You'll be aware when the combatants crash into a lamp, roll over a chair, or bust through a closet door. A mini-plotting exercise of the stunt sequence will make the writing easier and allow the reader to follow the scene.

Next, we get to the actual writing of the scene. A major factor of the scene is the vocabulary you use. Everyone likes a good punch, but using the same word fifteen times in one sequence might be over the top. Create a comprehensive list of synonyms for the repetitive actions in the sequence. Also, make the verbs powerful and the nouns concrete. Use the active voice. Our goal is to engage the reader, not bore them with passive voice. Lastly, with action, we want to show more and tell less. Don't give a detailed play-by-play analysis of the scene. Stick to the essentials and hasten to the next element of the scene. The following is a gun fight from *Red Sky in Morning* by Paul Lynch.

> "The rasp of a door opening slow on its hinges and board squeak from the men stealing in. Faller stood and turned and collared the little girl beside him with his left hand and lifted her out of the grasp of her mother clean into the air. He hoisted her in front of his body, and he turned towards the door and little girl screamed and her mother scrambled the air with her hands towards her. Faller kicked her back down and then the men from outside were coming in, their rifles pointed in the door and the first man paused as he came through to take in the sight of the girl hanging in the air in front of him and in the moment of his hesitation Faller shot him dead.
>
> The man's legs collapsed from under him and Faller dropped the child into a swing and launched her into the air at the other man taking aim with his gun and the man recoiled in horror as the child flew towards him, dropped the weapon to catch the child as she crashed into him and Faller was already on top of him as they fell to the ground and he smiled into the man's eyes and fired the other round into his head. He looked up towards the hall and took the man's rifle and swung smoothly upwards on the ball of his foot and then he was out the door."

One of the fundamental aspects of action scenes is the use of pacing. The aim is for the reader to perceive the story's swift advancement. First, we need to draw them in. The writing must become more immediate. Pull them in with a much closer point of view, either first person or third person deep. Change the tense to present tense for the sequence and create the illusion of real-time events. Next, if you want the scene to feel a little out of control, use longer sentences with shorter words. Longer, descriptive verbiage and punctuation slows down the pacing. Use short bursts of reactions in your writing. Then, as the sequence draws toward the end, focus the reader on the details that matter. Use shorter sentences. The pauses will force the reader to slow down. It will draw their attention to the aftermath and make an impact.

But what about tension or suspense? Action scenes are natural places to build out tension in the story by using cliffhangers, reversals, or plot twists. We also add to the suspense by focusing in on the details of the incidental or non-violent actions leading into the sequence. As we gather these small actions, suspense for the reader grows until the scene's payoff. Who doesn't anticipate a shoot-out when someone walks into a saloon and brandishes their six-shooter? One of the greatest scenes in *Tombstone* is where the bad guys interrupt a card game and start whirling around their guns. Doc Holliday mimics them by doing the same thing with a tin cup. He mocks the characters and adds tension, all while foreshadowing their future meeting.

As you write your action scenes, there are times you focus on certain details. Your hero may get injured, your bad guy may have a certain type of weapon, etc. Here is when you win over the reader with your world-building. It harkens back to the Iceberg Principle. If you get the details right on these items, the reader will assume you have done your research on everything else. This is where you earn their trust. Let's be honest, in fiction, we sometimes need the reader to go along for the ride.

How do you handle simultaneous events? In movies, you will watch the action shift from multiple viewpoints or parallel plotlines through quick cuts. In a visual format that is much easier to pull off. Don't try this in your writing unless you have practiced the technique. Refrain from doing this for an extended portion of text. One method involves writing a prolonged action sequence, syncing up with the other section at the climactic moment. In *The Lord of the Rings*, Tolkien balanced Aragorn's storyline with Frodo's this way.

Alternate between the two to give the impression of simultaneous closure. As you approach the climax of the sequence, make the swaths of text for each plot line shorter and shorter until you hit the end. A great example from movies is the end of *The Dark Knight* where the explosions occur at almost identical times and Batman saves Harvey Dent, but he hears the explosion that kills Rachel through the radio. Alternating viewpoints intensifies the story's emotional impact.

WRITING ACTION

Action in writing takes many forms. Subtle actions such as biting nails and twirling your hair convey emotional conflict in the form of beats. Larger actions scenes, such as fights, or car chases, provide physical conflict and exhilaration to the writing. Action involves psychological exchanges and physical encounters.

- Action should be active in voice. Putting action sequences through the passive voice almost negates the impact. It needs to keep the narrative alive and moving.
- Include pertinent details. This is your chance to show some world-building skills by including details around injuries or the fighting skills of your characters.

- Action must drive the story forward and work toward achieving the goal. The character may fail in his attempt, but he is working toward the objective. Pointless action is unnecessary and should be avoided.
- Post scene reflection should reveal character development as well. Slow down for reflection, your characters must show change.
- Keep the scenes short and the pacing high. Shorter sentences with crisp words that convey clear visuals are best. This makes the story move faster. If your action scene slows down the story, you need to revisit the scene.
- Make sure there is an aftermath. Actions follow the laws of physics. There must be consequences from the cause. Use these to foreshadow something that comes to the forefront later in the story. Perfect for building Yes-But-No-And scenarios and Try-Fail cycles.
- Consider reversing the stimulus-response order of events. But it still follows the cause-effect mantra, you show the result of the action first. *The chess pieces flew across the board. Across stood a man, anger on his face and revenge in his eyes.*
- Enter an action scene in the middle of the event, *in media res*. Avoid buildup and work that into the scene as needed for additional context.
- Ensure the action sequence concludes with the main character's status established. They can lose that battle, they can agree to a draw, or they can win. Whatever the outcome, make the result clear. Defeats are great for the lead because they learn and draw inspiration. Acceptable draws happen when characters mutually decide not to settle their battle at that time. It keeps the tension for later. If the protagonist wins, you remove that antagonist from the story. The lead has overcome that challenge and that opponent no longer holds any tension. The lone exception is if the antagonist allows the hero to win to advance their plans.
- Always leave the scene with conflict on the horizon. The protagonist cannot have a break until they achieve their objective. They must have conflict and unyielding tension hanging over them. The lead cannot have an action sequence in each scene, but tension needs to linger and be palpable to the reader whether the conflict is internal, external, or interpersonal.
- Always impact the character. Emotional resonance is necessary for the lead. If they get their butt kicked, there must be a

development. Change is inevitable with their victory. If the character remains unchanged, the scene is pointless. Even fan-pleasing scenes, like the Avengers battle in *Captain America: Civil War*, create character development.

Along with all these bits of advice, there are certain pitfalls you must avoid in writing action sequences and scenes. The first problem in writing action is the issue of head-hopping. In large battle scenes, it might make sense to jump from character to character. But this creates issues within the scene. Do this carefully.

Try not to be elaborate and fall into the trap of purple prose. Stick to the action and make it fast-paced and direct. Flowery descriptions slow down the writing and the story, the exact opposite of what needs to happen in an action scene. Resolution scenes present one exception for when you dive into a specific point of the story for emphasis.

Using a reflection scene is almost always needed after a large action sequence. Have your character be frantic at various junctures in your story, but there must be a breaking point. Humans cannot go through high-octane action for extended periods unless they are superhuman. Your reader will appreciate the break as well.

Another warning regarding the use of quick cut scenes. Yes, sometimes these can be useful, but use them sparingly. Create imaginative shifts between your scenes to illuminate different settings and viewpoints that add impact to your story. If not possible, find alternative ways to convey the information without the cut scene.

A final warning: avoid unnecessary violence. This is not only gory, gross, or extensive violence, but unnecessary action. You may have your main character jumping through hoops and or doing unsavory things. Consider if their actions align with the plot's objectives. If a character's action disrupts the plot or repels readers, reconsider its inclusion and possibly remove it.

In writing reaction/action cycle elements, we aim to check off several things at once. We must be progressing the story and achieving an objective. We want the sequence to have a cause-effect relationship throughout and provide a conclusion with a reaction and consequences. Our goal is to control the pace and create a sense of immediacy for the reader. We want to use language that is active, strong, and concrete to reinforce the action. We want to use the setting to our advantage and show the action through the surrounding world, instead of providing a step-by-step summary. Our successful execution and avoidance of pitfalls will captivate the audience with gripping scenes. They will turn the page and read the next one. Which is what we want.

USING THE CYCLE

Let's discuss how writers can use this action/reaction cycle. We'll review two examples, discussing the positives and potential negatives of each. The first example will be Joe Abercrombie's *A Little Hatred*, the first book in the *Age of Madness* trilogy. Abercrombie is very much a character driven writer and pulls in various viewpoints throughout his stories. Abercrombie uses a third-person limited viewpoint and occasionally drifts into a third-person deep viewpoint to create dramatic effect. Abercrombie explores his characters through witty conversations and very intimate acts. No scene captures this better than one featuring Orso and Savine, two of the main characters of the book. Orso is a Prince, and Savine is his clandestine lover. She is also a wealthy investor in growing industries. Due to the length of the scene, a summarization follows.

The two begin the scene amid an amorous moment. During the moment, Orso makes a request upon Savine to help him by financing the development of a small army. While in this third-person limited viewpoint, we witness the subtle physical reactions of the characters and their playful dialogue. Orso's unforeseen behavior prompts Savine to deviate from her usual response and agree to the request. Orso leaves the scene and Abercrombie shifts his viewpoint into third-person deep and dives into the thoughts of Savine. She realizes her emotions took over and forced a reaction from her without going through the entire reaction process. Savine realizes why she did this. She loves Orso.

Abercrombie does something he's famous for. He closes the scene before we complete the cycle and see the resulting action. His characters convey their intentions in the scene, but rarely explicitly depict it in writing. The subtext carries the action until the character's next appearance. Because Abercrombie writes almost exclusively from a character-driven perspective, the action is secondary to him. If not a crucial scene, he emphasizes characters' emotions and thoughts. The drawback to the lack of action is the illusion of no story progression. It leaves some readers desiring something that signifies the plot is moving forward. Yes, the plot moves, but without seeing the progression on the page, the reader sometimes loses that impression.

Abercrombie succeeds in this technique thanks to his exceptional dialogue and character moments, but it's a tough task for most writers.

To contrast this, we will move to Pierce Brown's *Red Rising*. Brown writes in a first-person perspective and explores the entire cycle. His main character, Darrow, is among the lowest members of his society, the Reds, and works as a driller. He desires freedom from the chains that bind him and his people, yet feels responsible for his wife, Eo. Eo shares his desire, even willing to sacrifice her life as the spark for their revolution.

The scene we examine is one where Eo and Darrow are caught committing a crime. They are taken into custody and lashed in front of their community as punishment. Eo decides to sacrifice herself at that time. She sings a forbidden song and is hung in front of the community to send a message. This breaks Darrow and we witness his emotions and thoughts as he processes the loss of his wife. He is presented with the chance to pick up the torch and carry the cause forward, but he refuses.

We observe the entire process of Eo's sacrificial act through to Darrow's decision and lack of action. Brown does something at the end of that scene that makes Darrow's situation even worse, as is his style. Brown shows us the entire cycle, not leaving anything to the subtext. As a result, we see the resulting action, or inaction in this case, that pushes the plot forward.

One of the reasons for the varied approaches is the use of the first-person viewpoint versus third person limited. Brown's story follows Darrow, so we are going to witness everything he does, see his emotions, and experience his thoughts. Whereas Abercrombie is writing a multiple third person POV story involving a dozen or so characters. Abercrombie has a larger world to engage with many more perspectives. His luxury is he can present the story from multiple angles to give the entire view to the reader. Both writers decided how to best represent their story and present the characters' action/reaction cycle to readers.

Understanding the Action/Reaction Cycle is key to understanding the basics of novel writing. It teaches you the proper flow of emotions, thought, action, and reaction and helps to build a cohesive plot. These aspects of the cycle are the key to understanding and presenting the interiority of the character and intertwining multi-faceted characters with your story's plot.

EXERCISES

1. Design an action scene on a map of a room or city.
2. Write a scene without the reaction cycle being followed and then rewrite it following the cycle.
3. Provide a summary of the reaction cycle chain of events.

REFERENCE MATERIALS

The Emotion Thesaurus: A Writer's Guide to Character Expression by Becca Puglisi and Angela Ackerman

This book is within easy reach when I am writing for a quick reference when I need to write any type of emotional reaction or body movement. This is one of a complete reference library produced by Puglisi and Ackerman. The tome is easily organized by the emotion and creates a nearly perfect resource. This book is essential for writers.

21 – REVISION, THE NECESSARY EVIL

Now you have completed your first draft. Take a deep breath. You accomplished a lot. Make a second copy of the document and save the file somewhere offline. Relax, enjoy, and escape for a few days. Then, get ready to trash the thing. When reviewing the document, you may doubt your sobriety or abilities. Almost everyone views their initial draft in this manner. This is a common experience for writers when they write for the first time. Scan the quote below for verification of your self-doubt.

> *"The first draft of anything is shit."* - Ernest Hemingway

But don't lose heart. This chapter will walk through various editing and revision strategies. Just like writing, you must find your own path through revisions and experiment to determine what works best for you. The following paragraphs provide a detailed glimpse at one typical process and highlight a few other noteworthy ones. It may help to visualize the book as a work-in-process and assigning various stages with a certain percentage of completion, much like any project. Or you can imagine the process as a flowchart, as shown below.

1. Rough Draft completed – 33%
2. First Revision pass completed – 50%
3. Receive Manuscript Review – 60%
4. Make changes based on Manuscript Review – 66%
5. Second Revision pass completed – 90%
6. Beta Readers Reviews and changes made – 95%
7. Detailed Line Edit – 99%
8. Final Pass and Detailed Review – 100%

```
First Draft → Story & Development Editing → Second Draft → Critique Groups/Beta Readers → Line Edits → Finished Manuscript
```

You may think, "Wow, only five review passes?"

The experienced writer would reply, "Bless your heart. No, double that. And that's if the rough draft is fantastic." After the rough draft, at best, you're maybe a third of the way towards finishing a book. Many individuals begin anew once they finish their initial rough draft. Some see that approach as wasteful, but your response at this point relies on your developed process. Now, let's explore the revision steps of the process in detail.

Set the book aside for sometime before revising it. It is best to review the document with fresh eyes. Get the document in some format you will use for the review. Print out a copy, get an electronic version ready, or even an audio file to edit. Get any supplies you might need like sticky notes, notecards, or red ink pens.

With those items taken care of, you are now ready to start. In this first revision pass, you will focus on the big pieces: characters, plot, setting, theme, and conflict. Ask yourself several questions about the major aspects of the story as you go through the manuscript.

- Do the characters come across as you intend them to?
- Does the plot point in each chapter move toward completing the story?
- Does the setting make an impact on these scenes? If not, should you change it?
- Is the setting adequately described?
- Does the conflict contain all the components?
- Does the chapter end on a tension note?
- Are there consequences and costs to the conflict?

- Does the dialogue work? Is it overtaking the other parts of the chapter/scene?
- Does the action move the plot along?
- Is the pace where you want it for the scene?
- What do you need to cut or add to make the pace correct?
- Does your theme come through in the story?

You can approach this first pass in a multitude of ways. Once you complete a chapter, make the edits in your document and repeat that chapter by chapter. Before returning to edit, consider making notes throughout the entire document. There are other approaches as well, but the important thing is to make sure you go through the document. Many writers will use any editing software they prefer. A section discussing editing software will be at the end of this chapter. Also, many will use a read aloud feature in some software to hear another voice read each chapter. This often reveals things that read fine to the eye, but sound awkward when they hit your ear.

After completing that first pass through the entire first draft, you may wish to obtain someone's input on if the story works. Seek feedback on your manuscript from a trusted editor or fellow writer. If you have confidence in the story, search for alpha readers as well. Alpha readers are people you will review your story and provide feedback. Give them an overview of what you specifically desire feedback on and send a secure version of the document to them. Once you review this feedback, decide what to incorporate. Approach their comments with an open mind. But ultimately, this is your choice to adopt anything they recommend. Then implement the changes and prepare for the second major pass through the book.

This second pass focuses on the prose aspects of the manuscript. You may review all the dialogue in one review and then the narrative elements or go chapter by chapter. Whatever your approach, be consistent with the approach through the end of the document. Editing often requires a thorough analysis using software, which we cover in a later section. Another audio reading of the manuscript will also be helpful.

After you get the prose to where you like it, contact beta readers (a second round of people to review your document). Consider having a different editor review the book. It is difficult to find people to read your story. The important thing is for someone else to review your writing with a critical eye prior to submitting the document anywhere. This doesn't mean your mother, unless she is an editor by trade. Opening up your writing to other eyes is important, but also difficult. Perhaps find a writing group to review your writing and provide honest and meaningful feedback. Sometimes, having multiple opinions about your story may give you an idea on a new direction to take if problems exist.

Once you receive feedback from any readers or an editor, incorporate that. A complete rewrite suggests a previous round of awful edits. However, try not to be too negative toward yourself. All writers have experienced this frustration, and many persist. Don't get your head down.

The last piece of the puzzle is the detailed line edit, or copy edit. This is where you uncover the remaining errors in your manuscript. Misspellings, grammar, style choices, punctuation. Awful sentence structure and hidden typos will haunt your sleep during this process. Then, once you complete the review, do it all one more time. This last step is the most tedious and makes you question if the process is worth the effort. It is.

REVISION PYRAMID

The next approach is the Revision Pyramid, made popular by Gabriela Pereira. This approach takes a five-layer view of the manuscript. At a minimum, you will go through your story five more times, with each pass focusing on specific aspects of the manuscript. The following rundown highlights the layers and their focuses in this approach.

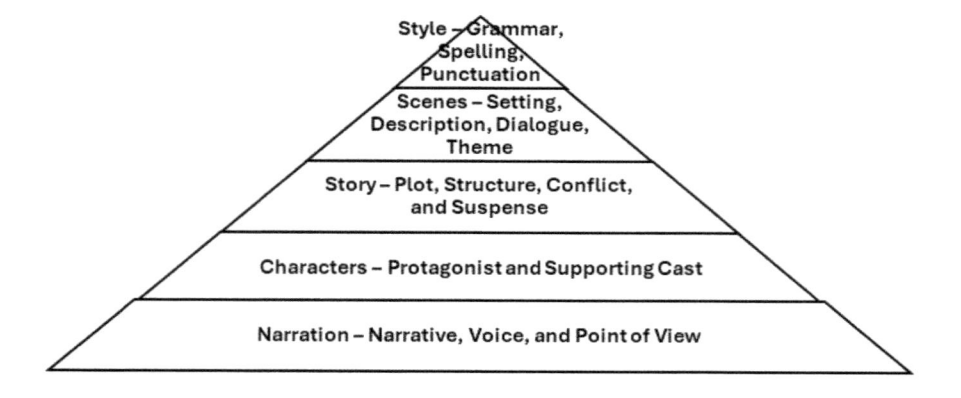

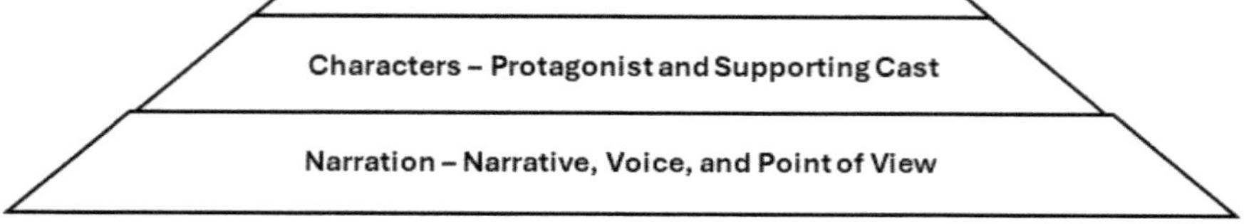
Style – Grammar, Spelling, Punctuation
Scenes – Setting, Description, Dialogue, Theme
Story – Plot, Structure, Conflict, and Suspense
Characters – Protagonist and Supporting Cast
Narration – Narrative, Voice, and Point of View

1. Narration – Focus on voice and POV and change narration and POV so that these are consistent throughout the work. Rewrite sections in a new POV as needed. Rework the narration to refocus the lens of how your reader sees the story.
2. Characters – Focus on making sure the protagonist does not come across as a flat character. Experiment by giving them different situations to achieve their objective. Also, make sure your supporting characters are not serving duplicate roles and support the main character(s) of the story.
3. Story/Plot – Review your story to make sure the following items work. You hit all the major plot points in your format. There are no plot holes. Your characters aren't driving a problem with the plot because they want to go another direction. Ensure there are no extraneous scenes that do nothing to move the plot forward.
4. Scenes – Once you finish revising the story and characters, focus on the scenes. Review each scene (with your scene tracker handy) to make sure every scene hits on all the key points. Verify the dialogue is sharp. You provide sufficient information and make sure the theme of your work comes across.
5. Cosmetics – This pass focuses on the style elements and looks much like a line edit. You will review every sentence for word choice, proper grammar, correct spelling and punctuation, sentence structure, and typographical errors. This will end the pyramid process and give you a polished product.

Once you have completed this, review the major components of the draft and the details to provide the best product possible. You will want at least one more review once you complete the pyramid process. The approach is lengthy but effective. One issue with the pyramid is the process neglects certain story aspects, such as setting, description, and tension. But that would involve adding additional layers of review.

THE MACRO-MICRO APPROACH

Another approach to discuss is a popular method among several writers and is the basis of the book *Intuitive Editing* by Tiffany Yates Martin. Martin, and those that use a similar approach, believe you should make multiple passes through the story to focus on various aspects. Not dissimilar to the Revision Pyramid, but different buckets. Simultaneously combine some review processes, but avoid mixing Macro-edits with Micro-edits.

- Macro-edits focus on the plot, conflict, and characters of the story. The bulk of your work lies here. Changes to these three elements are like major surgery to your story. Some writers include theme and setting issues in this bucket.
- Micro-edits focus on other aspects of the story that are fixable but require much work. These equate to outpatient procedures. This list includes tension, viewpoint, description, structure, pacing, and voice. You can do multiple passes to focus on this or combine them into one pass. However, covering this much ground in one pass sounds challenging.
- The third major component is the line edit. This is a review of every sentence for word choice, proper grammar, correct spelling, punctuation, structure, and typographical errors. Much like any other approaches mentioned.

OTHER METHODS

Another popular revision methodology is the checklist approach. In this methodology, the writer has a pre-defined checklist of items they review and mark off the items as they complete them. The checklist typically has a section of questions that pertain to the major components of your novel, like plot, characters, setting, viewpoint, etc. Despite exhaustive checklists, there's always an uncaptured issue on each project. Upon discovering these items in your work, include them in the list for future reference and acknowledge that the checklist has its limitations.

One fundamental aspect about the checklist is the easy customization for each project. If, for some reason, you are going to try writing an epistolary novel, you may have specific questions you wish to ask yourself along with those on the checklist. Adequate checklists exist across the internet and can be downloaded for free. Many writing resource books also include one for use by the writer. One is included in the Vibrant Prose Toolbox.

Some writers, especially full-time writers, use an approach of revision as they go. They will write a sizeable chunk of text one day, or in the morning session of their work. In the next session, edit and revise the work until it meets the requirements for the scene, chapter, or story section. For writers with inconsistent time blocks, this may not be the best approach. Effectively working this approach may be challenging without the right mindset and rhythm. This would only be suggested for writers with an established writing routine.

Funneling involves focusing on a specific aspect of the manuscript. Are you concerned about your dialogue or description? Focus on that aspect alone, then transition to the next writing aspect. Many writers do this with their dialogue scenes and then focus on narrative separately.

Reverse outlining is a technique to use if cohesion or cause-effect issues exist within your story. This technique builds an outline after you complete the story. Before addressing other concerns, utilize this process to identify and rectify any story gaps. An alternative approach is to utilize a story tracker, such as the one found in the Vibrant Prose Toolbox. Both tools help you identify missing story beats that fill the gaps and create a cohesive plot.

As mentioned earlier, a valuable resource in the process will be beta readers and critique groups. Soliciting the opinions of a specific target audience at this point could be key. At times, you may even need a contractual agreement with them, especially if there is some sort of payment for their services. Be explicit about your desires and expectations from them. When they give you feedback, listen and don't interrupt them. You asked for their feedback, so let them provide it. Sort out their comments to find what you want you to use after they are done. Let them know you appreciate the feedback and take their comments with a smile.

Another approach is sometimes referred to as the flyover method. The flyover method will require three read throughs of the manuscript with specific goals in each read through. This technique works best if you created notes while writing the story. Refer to those as you progress through this exercise. Jot down extra notes in the margins as you go through the manuscript to review later. Have your scene tracker and story bible at the ready to serve as reference materials.

1. The initial read is for identifying major plot, setting, and character issues. It will also address any major narrative issues. You will carve up your manuscript. Use multiple colors of pens to signify specific things (red=errors, blue=narrative adds, black=plot issues). You are looking for plot holes, flat characters, awful narrative, pedantic description, and dull settings. It may feel like you are rewriting the entire story, but you need to do this.
2. Once these rewrites are done, the second review is to detect any remaining problems. Spelling, punctuation, sentence structure, and the style details. The goal is to attain the most polished product possible after this pass. Once you finish this step, give yourself a week off from your project to create some distance.
3. A fresh set of eyes is needed for the third read through. Approach the story with no prior knowledge and highlight any inconsistencies you identify. Do the supporting characters work? Is the setting immersive enough? Does the lead feel three-dimensional? These are the questions you are trying to answer. Once you correct any remaining issues and nothing else needs changed, you are ready for someone else review the manuscript.

EDITING OPTIONS

To avoid doing all the revision and editing yourself, you can hire someone to assist you. Finding talented editors can be difficult. The key inquiry is always: how much should you compensate? These individuals earn their livelihoods as editors. Requesting free work from them is unacceptable. Imagine someone wanting you to do your day job without paying you. The amount you pay depends on what you want them to do and depends on your financial capability.

In your search for an editor, be aware that various services exist. Conduct thorough research and request references and work samples from potential hires before deciding on a course of action. Examples of services and their impact on your story appear below.

- Book Doctor – Freelance editor who edits your complete novel.
- Manuscript Evaluation – Editor gives you feedback on strengths, weaknesses, and general suggestions for change.
- Developmental Edit – Edit notes problems with structure, pacing, and style. May make revisions or provide you with guidance on how to fix issues.
- Copyedit – Editor corrects grammar, spelling, punctuation, and usage. Catches inconsistencies and continuity problems.
- Line Edit – Editor focuses on sentences and words. Fixes same things as a copyeditor.

Below are items to consider for developmental edits:

- Ensure the structure you are using helps to tell the story. Don't be afraid to move scenes or cut them to get to the best story.
- Ensure your character's motivations and goals are evident in the story. This ensures that the reader understands the stakes that exist.
- Ensure that the main plot line is in the fore front through the novel.
- Pay attention to the sub-plots and supporting characters, but remember they come after the main character. Make sure they end to help the story.
- Evaluate your pacing to make sure it keeps the tension of the story at a level that keeps the reader interested.
- Ensure that your setting impacts the story in some way through the manuscript. If not, why does it matter?
- Ensure you are writing the scenes and characters required for your genre and you are suing or subverting them appropriately.
- Make sure the theme comes across but is not preachy or pounded into the reader's head.
- Make your scenes are solid structurally.

Below are tips for line edits:

- Eliminate Passive Voice in all narrative sentences. Passive Voice in dialogue can be fine in certain situations.

- Eliminate vague words, adverbs, and adjectives that provide unclear imagery to the reader.
- Eliminate as many filler words as possible.
- Reduce the number of repetitive words, phrases, and starts to sentences unless it serves a purpose.
- Vary sentence lengths to break up repetitive rhythms unless there is a specific style choice being made.
- Look for show opportunities that improve the text and eliminate tells.
- Ensure you are using all senses to describe action, setting, and emotions in the story.
- Look for paragraphs and sentences that are too slow or complex.

WRITING SOFTWARE

In the day and age of Hemingway, he never envisioned the technological age we inhabit today. Let alone the existence of an editing tool bearing his name. Though many of us wish to avoid technology in our writing habits, writing software might be an option for you. Yes, some of you swear by writing everything out by hand or using dictation to write your book. But eventually, technology will be involved. Can you find the tool you need?

If you wish to hand write your books, there are transcription software tools on the market that help get your work into an electronic format. Rev, Dragon, and Descript are a few of the foremost tools on the market. Investigate which best meets your needs from a use and price perspective.

Writers almost always need word processing software. Many computer applications are available. Microsoft Word is the most used. Another option is Google Docs, which is free and has nice collaboration applications but has speed issues once you exceed a certain word count. There are several other word processors out there but pick one that best suits your needs as a writer.

Writers often use editing software, even if they only choose the editing tool included in their word processor. Tools have improved, but some prefer a tool that focuses on functionality. Popular tools include Grammarly, Hemingway, and ProWritingAid. There are free versions of these tools, but they only allow limited use or exist only for online content. Beyond the free versions, these tools require a subscription license for continued usage.

Another popular software package is Scrivener. This tool, and its copycats, help with organizational issues. They support effortless movement of scenes within the story and also incorporate some of the editing tools mentioned above. However, tool costs and the learning curve can be daunting. If writing is your primary source of income, you might sing a different tune. Don't get sucked in by the pretty on-line marketing. Do your research before buying one of these applications and play with any free trial versions you find. Each one of these tools also feature specific capabilities that they highlight. Confirm the tool meets your requirements, because some of these options can be expensive.

Publishing software is a specialized tool. If you are serious about publishing your own work and starting your own imprint, the benefit of Vellum, Atticus, or another publishing software tool could be worth the expenditure. You would reclaim your investment with a few sales. Each of these tools also offer different features that make them usable on various platforms. Again, research and make the best decision for your needs.

Does the absence of a tool pose a genuine issue? Do you need these tools or are you making excuses? We are familiar with the guy that buys the fancy golf equipment or the high-end Craftsman tools and never uses them. Once your neighbor realizes the hard work still exists, does he remain committed? These tools might help you with certain portions of the job, but we know the truth. Writing is a difficult yet liberating endeavor, and nothing can diminish the satisfaction of typing or composing words. You must still do the writing, which is the actual work.

People often overlook the importance of revision in writing, but having a pre-defined approach makes the process less intimidating. In theory, revisions should be exciting because all you are doing at this point is improving your story. And we all want one thing, the best story we can produce.

EXERCISES

1. Change the POV in your story for a chapter and see how it works?
2. Re-write a scene and change the structure of it to see if the same major points come through.
3. Re-write a scene by changing the punctuation to impact pacing.
4. Edit (developmental, copy, and line) the restaurant history of one of your writing partners.

REFERENCE MATERIALS

Intuitive Editing: A Creative and Practical Guide to Revising Your Writing by Tiffany Yates Martin
Getting the Words Right by Theodore A. Rees Cheney
Self-Editing for Fiction Writers: How to Edit Yourself Into Print by Renni Browne & Dave King

Martin's take on the editing and revision journey is an enjoyable read. Despite its dry nature, the pacing and style make the topic entertaining. Unlike other books that often say they discuss editing and drift into writing style, Martin sticks to the topic and provides meaningful advice on how to go through the arduous process to improve your story. Cheney's book contains the technical merit of Strunk & White, along with the stylistic requirements for most fiction writing. Browne and King's effort is often considered one of the must haves of any writer and focuses very much on the prose aspects of writing.

AFTERWORD

After reading this book, we still may be faced with the question of what makes *Vibrant Prose* different from every other writing craft book on the market. *Vibrant Prose* is a textbook style attempt to catalogue as many good ideas on how to develop a concept, understand the basic components of the story, and how to write effective prose as possible. The goal is to create a truly unique book, offering abundant ideas, techniques, and tools for writing like no other. Examine the bibliography to gauge the extent of research for this book. We seek a text that combines the best of other books in a concise, vibrant style. It is a firm belief that this is the best writing book out there. But it won't speak to every reader or writer. That's fine. The goal was to provide a resource for those who want to learn how to write or teach a group on the topic. There is more to this package than the book

We strongly believe that resources should not just talk about helping you, but also provide the necessary tools for putting the advice into action. This toolbox includes a workbook with over twenty individual tools that you can use to help write or revise your work-in-progress. Along with that is a customizable story tracker file that provides updatable graphs and charts to help diagnose any issues within writing. This tool also comes with a series of guides to help you identify certain key components of the most popular genres of fiction. For those who are plotters, also included are a set of beat sheets to help you plan your story or review your story with any of the many popular approaches to plotting a book, including one that allows you to create your own method. Another addition is a complete revision checklist to help you to verify you have not forgotten anything in your story. All of these are tools free for your use in developing your story and aiding your craft.

We just ask that you kindly limit your downloads of the tools to one per person, as they are provided to you at no cost. *Vibrant Prose* benefits from every book purchase. Consider each book a license that gives you unlimited access to the other tools you will receive. Thank you for your support.

CHRISTOPHER CLOUSER

GLOSSARY

Accountability – The responsibility to deal with the consequences of a decision made by the character.

Action – A form of narrative that depicts physical movement and progression through the story.

Adhesiveness – The quality of two characters stuck together through the story, usually hero and villain.

Agency - The ability of a character to act, control their responses, and make choices.

Allegory – A story that can be interpreted to reveal a hidden meaning.

Alliteration - The occurrence of the same letter or sound at the beginning of adjacent or closely connected words.

Allusion – An expression designed to call something to mind without mentioning it explicitly; an indirect or passing reference.

Analogy - A comparison between two things, typically for the purpose of explanation or clarification.

Anchoring – The act of providing details so the reader feels they are included in the scene and action taking place.

Antagonist – The character that provides the obstacles that get in the way of your protagonist and prevent them from achieving their objective.

Apotheosis – A part of the Hero's Journey where the character gains a higher understanding due to an experience in the alternative world.

Apparent Depth – level of development to potentially create a story from a given idea.

Archetype - A very typical example of a certain person or thing. A recurrent symbol or motif.

Assonance - The repetition of the sound of a vowel or diphthong in nonrhyming stressed syllables near enough to each other for the echo to be discernible.

Backstory – The background information around a character that informs the character and the conflict in the story.

Beats – Narrative components of the story that reflect physical movements tied to dialogue.

Brainstorming – A problem-solving technique that involves the spontaneous contribution and creation of ideas.

Cauldron – The location of a key scene within the climax of the story.

Causality – The premise that each event in a story is based on those prior and directly impacts those that follow.

Character Arc - The emotional and developmental journey a character undergoes within the story.

Chekhov's gun - A dramatic principle that states that every element in a story must be necessary, and irrelevant elements should be removed.

Cliché - A phrase, character, or technique that is overused and betrays a lack of original thought.

Cliffhanger - A tool that abruptly ends a scene that leaves the conclusion in doubt

Climax – The point where the final conflict occurs in the story from which the resolution will be derived.

Concept – A brief summary of the story within in two or three sentences.

Conflict – The struggle to overcome an obstacle between the protagonist of the story and their ultimate goal.

Consequences – The resulting impact of a character's choices.

Consonance - The recurrence of similar sounds, especially consonants, in close proximity.

Continuity – The premise that the story should flow as one narrative stream and not have any interruptions that disrupt the reader's processing of the story.

Counterpremise – The premise of the story should the antagonist become the lead character of the narrative.

Denouement – A point in the story after the resolution that shows or suggests the final impact on the lives of the characters.

Description – The act of providing details to convey the image of a scene to the reader.

Deus Ex Machina – A proverbial all-powerful item that resolves all plot problems at the end without proper leadup or explanation.

Deuteragonist – The secondary lead in a story, behind the protagonist.

Dialogue – Spoken communication between characters in a story.

Discovery Writing – Writing without the use of plotting tools, also referred to as organic writing and "pantsing."

Dramatic structure - The flow of drama throughout a work of fiction and provides the framework for the entire story

Dystopian – A style of book that presents a future version of society that has been drastically changed by negative influences such as government or war.

Epilogue – A conclusion that occurs post-story that imparts additional information about the characters.

Epiphany – A moment of clarification or understanding to a character that reveals the path to their resolution.

Epistolary – A literary work in the form of letters or official communications.

Exposition - A narrative insertion of background information within a story.

Fable – A short story, typically with animals, conveying a moral.

False protagonist – When the writer pushes forward a character as the protagonist to then reveal later that another character was the true protagonist.

Flashback – The act of taking the story to a prior period to present necessary information important to the main story.

Flashforward - The act of taking the story to a future period to present potential information important to the main story.

Foreshadowing – A narrative tool used to suggest a potential event that may happen later in the story.

Freewriting – A form of spontaneous writing, possibly in a classroom setting, to develop something through stream of consciousness.

Genre – A categorization of stories with similar material, ideas, and structures.

High Concept – An artistic work that can be easily pitched with a succinctly stated premise.

Iceberg Principle – The idea of representing only what the character needs to know in the story, while maintaining the appearance that there is more information below the surface.

Idea Mapping – A visual presentation of the thought process in creating ideas.

Imagery - Visually descriptive or figurative language, especially in a literary work.

Imposter Syndrome – The thoughts that center around the inadequacy of ones work.

Interiority – The act of reflecting the interior thoughts and emotions of a character.

Intention – The decision by the character to undertake the task of fulfilling their main desire in the story.

Irony – The use of language to suggest something the opposite of the typical meaning for humorous effect.

Kishotenketsu – Eastern story format that features a twist at the end of the story.

MacGuffin - An object or device in a movie or a book that serves merely as a trigger for the plot.

Master of Fine Arts – An advanced degree that focuses on creative writing and storytelling.

Melodrama - The act of creating an overdramatic piece with exaggerated characters and events that overly appeals to the emotions of the reader.

Metaphor - A figure of speech in which a word or phrase is applied to an object or action to which it is not literally applicable.

Mindmap – An artistic representation of a multi-faceted idea.

Monologue – Internal dialogue with the mind of the character that is only communicated to the reader.

Mooding – A form of creative mediation where you reflect on ideas and the emotional resonance.

Motif – A significant element within writing that reflects a mood or emotion throughout the work.

Motivation – An underlying desire the character wishes to fulfill and is often prevented from achieving due to an obstacle.

Obstacle – The item, person, or other item that stands between the protagonist and their main motivation in the story.

Ockham's razor - The idea that, in trying to understand something, getting unnecessary information out of the way is the fastest way to the truth or to the best explanation.

Onomatopoeia - The formation of a word from a sound associated with what is named.

Plot – The organization and sequencing of events to tell the story in the best possible manner.

Premise – The truth ascertained by the character after their conflict in the story.

Prologue – A part of the narrative that is set aside and presented prior to the main story.

Protagonist – The main character of the story that in most instances drives the action of the story. Very often considered the hero of the work.

Purple Prose – Language in a story that is so flowery and pronounced that it detracts and draws the reader away from the story.

Repetition – The continued use of like or similar symbols, motifs, or other items to achieve an effect in the story.

Resolution – The point where the conflict in the story is settled and the story ends.

Reversal - An event in the story that create additional obstacles for the character.

Scene – One portion of a story, usually contained within one location with the same characters until an objective is achieved.

Setting – Anything the conveys the location through the place, time, or atmosphere within the story.

Simile - A figure of speech involving the comparison of one thing with another thing of a different kind.

Stereotype – A widely held but fixed and oversimplified image or idea of a particular type of character or thing.

Stock Character – A character that is used for a specific function within a story.

Story – A tale told that includes all of the necessary literary elements.

Story Prompt – A word, phrase, or idea that is used to prompt a free writing exercise.

Storyview – A view of the story world from the perspective of a specific character.

Structure - The resulting form of the story once the plot has been implemented.

Style - The way a writer writes through the technique and usage of words and grammar in his writing.

Subplot – A secondary plot line that deals with an issue in the larger story.

Subtext – Not revealing everything to the reader through narrative but provide enough information through context to fill in the blank.

Subversion – The method of contradicting a stereotype or trope within writing.

Symbolism – The use of visual cues to exemplify the theme of the work.

Synthesizing - Method of taking one idea and melding it with another.

Tension - The element of your writing that keeps the reader glued to the page. Conflict is an example of tension.

Tritagonist – The third lead in a story, behind the protagonist and deuteragonist.

Theme – The central concern the reader derives from the overall story.

Trope – A recurring theme or motif in literature that establishes a predictable stereotype.

Twist – A change in the plot that is unexpected by the reader.

Viewpoint – The perspective used to tell the story to the reader.

Vocabulary - The body of words used by a particular author.

Voice – The narrative expression or author's emotions, attitude, tone and point of view through artful, well thought out use of word choice and diction.

Worldview – The comprehensive view of the story world.

World-Building – The process of creative a setting for a story that encompasses creating a focal point of the story, as opposed to a place and time that are referenced in the story.

Writer's Block – An issue that prevents the writer from moving forward in their storytelling.

CHRISTOPHER CLOUSER

BIBLIOGRAPHY

Ackerman, Angela and Becca Puglisi. *The Emotion Thesaurus: A Writer's Guide to Character Expression.* JADD Publishing. 2019

Alberts, Laurie. *Showing & Telling: Learn How to Show & When to Tell for Powerful & Balanced Writing.* Cincinnati, Ohio: Writer's Digest Books. 2010.

Alderson, Martha. *Writing Blockbuster Plots: A Step-by-step Guide to Mastering Plot, Structure, & Scene.* Cincinnati, Ohio: Writer's Digest Books. 2016.

Baig, Barbara. *Spellbinding Sentences: A Writer's Guide to Achieving Excellence & Captivating Readers.* Cincinnati, Ohio: Writer's Digest Books. 2015.

Bates, Joseph. *Writing Your Novel From Start to Finish: A Guidebook for the Journey.* Cincinnati, Ohio: Writer's Digest Books. 2015.

Bell, James Scott. *Plot & Structure: Techniques and Exercises for Crafting a Plot that Grips Readers from Start to Finish.* Cincinnati, Ohio: Writer's Digest Books. 2004.

Bickham, Jack. *Scene & Structure.* Cincinnati, Ohio: Writer's Digest Books. 1999.

Bickham, Jack. *Setting.* Cincinnati, Ohio: Writer's Digest Books. 1999.

Bird, Matt. *The Secrets of Story: Innovative Tools for Perfecting Your Fiction and Captivating Readers.* Cincinnati, Ohio: Writer's Digest Books. 2016.

Black, Sacha. *The Better Writer Series.* Atlas Black Publishing. 2017

Booker, Christopher. *The Seven Basic Plots: Why We Tell Stories.* Continuum. 2005

Bork, Erik. *The Idea: The Seven Elements of a Viable Story for Screen, Stage, and Fiction*. Thousand Oaks, California: Overlook Press. 2018.

Brody, Jessica. *Save the Cat! Writes a Novel: The Last Book on Novel Writing You'll Ever Need*. New York: Ten Speed Press. 2018.

Brooks, Larry. *Story Engineering: Mastering the 6 Core Competencies of Successful Writing*. Cincinnati, Ohio: Writer's Digest Books. 2011.

Browne, Renni & Dave King. *Self-Editing for Fiction Writers Second Edition: How to Edit Yourself Into Print*. New York, New York. Harper Collins. 2004.

Buckham, Mary. *A Writer's Guide to Active Setting: How to Enhance Your Fiction with More Descriptive, Dynamic Settings*. Cincinnati, Ohio: Writer's Digest Books. 2014.

Burroway, Janet. *Writing Fiction: A Guide to Narrative Craft*. Chicago, Illinois: The University of Chicago Press. 2019.

Card, Orson Scott. *Characters & Viewpoint*. Cincinnati, Ohio: Writer's Digest Books. 2010.

Card, Orson Scott, Philip Athens, Jay Lake, and the Editors of Writer's Digest. *Writing Fantasy & Science Fiction: How to Create Out-of-this-world Novels and Short Stories*. Cincinnati, Ohio: Writer's Digest Books. 2013.

Cheney, Theodore A. Rees. *Getting the Words Right: 39 Ways to Improve Your Writing, Second Edition*. Cincinnati, Ohio: Writer's Digest Books. 2005.

Chiarella, Tom. *Writing Dialogue*. Cincinnati, Ohio: Story Press. 1998.

Cleland, Jane. *Mastering Plot Twists*. Cincinnati, Ohio: Writers Digest Books. 2018.

Cron, Lisa. *Story Genius*. Berkeley, California: Ten Speed Press. 2016.

Cron, Lisa. *Wired for Story*. New York: Ten Speed Press. 2012.

Coyne, Shawn. *The Story Grid: What Good Editors Know*. New York: Black Irish Entertainment, LLC. 2015.

Dibell, Ansen. *Plot*. Cincinnati, Ohio: Writer's Digest Books. 1999.

Dixon, Debra. *GMC: Goal, Motivation, and Conflict: The Building Blocks of Good Fiction*. Memphis, Tennessee: Gryphon Books. 1996.

Edelstein, Linda. *Writer's Guide to Character Traits: Second Edition*. Cincinnati, Ohio: Writer's Digest Books. 2006.

Editors of Writer's Digest. *Creating Novels & Short Stories: The Complete Guide to Writing Great Fiction*. Cincinnati, Ohio: Writer's Digest Books. 2011.

Editors of Writer's Digest. *Creating Characters: The Complete Guide to Populating Your Fiction*. Cincinnati, Ohio: Writer's Digest Books. 2014.

Editors of Writer's Digest. *The Complete Handbook of Novel Writing Third Edition: Everything You Need to Know to Create & Sell Your Work*. Blue Ash, Ohio: Writer's Digest Books. 2016.

Editors of Writer's Digest. *Crafting Dynamic Dialogue: The Complete Guide to Speaking, Conversing, Arguing, and Thinking in Fiction*. Cincinnati, Ohio: Writer's Digest Books. 2016.

Editors of Writer's Digest. *Writing Voice: The Complete Guide to Creating a Presence on the Page & Engaging Readers*. Cincinnati, Ohio: Writer's Digest Books. 2017.

Edson, Eric. *The Story Solution: 23 Actions All Great Heroes Must Take*. Studio City, California: Michael Wiese Productions. 2011.

Ephron, Hallie. *Writing & Selling Your Mystery Novel Revised & Expanded: The Complete Guide to Mystery, Suspense, & Crime*. Cincinnati, Ohio: Writer's Digest Books. 2016.

Friedman, Jane. *Publishing 101: A First-Time Author's Guide to Getting Published, Marketing and Promoting Your Book, and Building a Successful Career*. MBA for Writers. 2014.

Gerke, Jeff. *Hack Your Reader's Brain: Bring the Power of Brain Chemistry to Bear on Your Fiction*. Self-Published. 2017.

Gerke, Jeff. *Plot Versus Character: A Balanced Approach to Writing Great Fiction*. Cincinnati, Ohio: Writer's Digest Books. 2017.

Hanika, Tanja. *Writer's Workbook: A Personal Planner with Tips, Checklists and Guidelines*. Tanja Hanika. Germany. 2019.

Hardy, Janice. *Understanding Conflict: And What It Really Means*. Fiction University Press. 2016.

Hardy, Janice. *Understanding Show, Don't Tell: And Really Getting It*. Fiction University Press. 2016.

Harrington, H. C. *World-building for Writers: The Complete Handbook*. Self-Published. 2021.

Healy, Ian Thomas. *Action!: Writing Better Action Using Cinematic Techniques*. Local Hero Press. 2012

Heffron, Jack. *The Writer's Idea Book 10th Anniversary Edition: How to Develop Great Ideas for Fiction, Nonfiction, Poetry, & Screenplays*. Cincinnati, Ohio: Writer's Digest Books. 2011.

Hilt, Jennifer. *The Trope Thesaurus : An Author Resource Guide*. Self-Published. 2022.

Hood, Ann. *Creating Character Emotion*. Cincinnati, Ohio. Story Press. 1998.

James, Steven. *Story Trumps Structure: How to Write Unforgettable Fiction by Breaking the Rules*. Cincinnati, Ohio: Writer's Digest Books. 2014.

Klaassen, Mike. *Fiction-Writing Modes: Eleven Essential Tools for Bringing Your Story to Life*. Pennsauken, New Jersey. Bookbaby. 2015.

Kennedy, Marcy. *Deep Point of View*. Toronto, Ontario. Marcy Kennedy. 2015.

Kennedy, Marcy. *Description*. Toronto, Ontario. Marcy Kennedy. 2013.

Kennedy, Marcy and Chris Saylor. *Grammar For Fiction Writers*. Toronto, Ontario. Marcy Kennedy. 2013.

King, Stephen. *On Writing: A Memoir of the Craft*. New York, New York. Scribner. 2000.

Kress, Nancy. *Beginnings, Middles & Ends*. Cincinnati, Ohio: Writer's Digest Books. 1999.

Kress, Nancy. *Dynamic Characters*. Cincinnati, Ohio: Writer's Digest Books. 1998.

Lamott, Anne. *Bird by Bird 25th Anniversary Edition: Some Instructions on Writing and Life*. New York, New York. Anchor Books. 1994.

Maass, Donald. *The Emotional Craft of Fiction: How to Write the Story Beneath the Surface*. Cincinnati, Ohio: Writer's Digest Books. 2016.

Martin, Tiffany Yates. *Intuitive Editing: A Creative & Practical Guide to Revising Your Writing*. FoxPrint Ink. 2020.

McClanahan, Rebecca. *Word Painting: The Fine Art of Writing Descriptively*. Cincinnati, Ohio: Writer's Digest Books. 2014.

McKee, Robert. *Story: Substance, Structure, Style and the Principles of Screenwriting*. New York: Harper Collins. 1997.

Morrell, Jessica Page. *Between the Lines: Master the Subtle Elements of Fiction Writing*. Cincinnati, Ohio: Writer's Digest Books. 2006.

Munier, Paula: *Plot Perfect: How to Build Unforgettable Stories Scene by Scene*. Cincinnati, Ohio: Writer's Digest Books. 2014.

Noble, William. *Conflict, Action & Suspense*. Cincinnati, Ohio: Writer's Digest Books. 1999.

Ortman, Mark. *A Simple Guide to Marketing Your Book: What an Author & Publisher Can Do to Sell More Books*. Bellingham, Washington. Wise Owl Books. 2003.

Orwell, George. *Politics and the English Language*. India: Grapevine Press. 2022.

Osborne, Jon R. *World Building for Novices*. Coinjock, North Carolina: Quillcraft Press. 2023.

Payne, Johnny. *Voice & Style*. Cincinnati, Ohio: Writer's Digest Books. 1999.

Presley, M. D. *Forging Fantasy Realms: Worldbuilding for Fantasy Fans and Authors*. M. D. Presley. 2020.

Roof, Judith. *Tone: Writing and the Sound of Feeling*. New York: Bloomsbury Academic. 2020.

Rosenfeld, Jordan. *How to Write a Page Turner: Craft a Story Your Readers Can't Put Down*. Cincinnati, Ohio: Writer's Digest Books. 2019.

Rosenfeld, Jordan. *Make a Scene: Writing a Powerful Story One Scene at a Time.* Cincinnati, Ohio: Writer's Digest Books. 2007.

Schmidt, Victoria Lynn. *45 Master Characters: Mythic Models for Creating Original Characters*. Cincinnati, Ohio: Writer's Digest Books. 2001.

Strunk, Jr., William & E. B. White. *The Elements of Style Fourth Edition: With Revisions, an Introduction, and a Chapter on Writing*. Needham Heights, Massachusetts: Allyn & Bacon. 2000.

Swain, Dwight V. *Techniques of the Selling Writer*. Norman, Oklahoma: University Oklahoma Press. 1965.

Tobais, Ronald. *20 Master Plots: And How to Build Them*. Cincinnati, OH: Writer's Digest. 2012

Truby, John. *The Anatomy of Story: 22 Steps to Becoming a Master Storyteller*. New York. Picador. 2007

Truby, John. *The Anatomy of Genres: How Story Forms Explain the Way the World Works*. New York. Picador 2022

Turco, Lewis. *Dialogue*. Cincinnati, Ohio: Writer's Digest Books. 1999.

VanderMeer, Jeff. *Wonderbook: The Illustrative Guide to Creating Imaginative Fiction*. New York: Abrams Books. 2013.

Weiland, K. M. *Creating Character Arcs: The Masterful Author's Guide to Uniting Story Structure, Plot, and Character Development*. PenForASword Publishing. 2016.

Weiland, K. M. *Structuring Your Novel: Essential keys for Writing an Outstanding Story*. PenForASword Publishing. 2024.

Weiland, K. M. *Writing Your Story's Theme: The Writer's Guide to Plotting Stories That Matterwww*. PenForASword Publishing. 2020.

Wood, Monica. *Description*. Cincinnati, Ohio: Writer's Digest Books. 1999.

Zeidner, Lisa. *Whos Says?: Mastering Point of View in Fiction*. New York: W. W. Norton & Company. 2021.

Internet Resources:

Callahan, Diane. 2016. *Diane Callahan – Quotidian Writer*. From https://www.youtube.com/c/QuotidianWriter/featured

Gilbo, Savannah. 2024. *Fiction Writing Made Easy*. From https://savannahgilbo.com/podcast

Glass, Ira. 2009. *Ira Glass on Storytelling*. Retrieved From https://www.youtube.com/watch?v=5pFI9UuC_fc

Hardy, Janice. 2020. *Fiction University*. Retrieved from https://www. blog.janicehardy.com

Moreci, Jenna. 2013. *Writing with Jenna Moreci*. Retrieved from https://www.youtube.com/c/JennaMoreci/featured

Sanderson, Brandon, Mary Robinette Kowal, Howard Taylor, and Dan Wells. 2015. *Writing Excuses*. Retrieved from https://www.writingexcuses.com.

Sanderson, Brandon. *2020 Creative Writing Lectures at BYU*. 2020. Retrieved from https://www.youtube.com/user/BrandSanderson/featured.

Weiland, K. M. *Helping Writers Become Authors*. 2024. Retrieved from https://www.helpingwritersbecomeauthors.com.

CHRISTOPHER CLOUSER

INDEX

45 Master Characters, 75, 78
7 Basic Plots, 38-39
13 Steps to Evil, 70, 78

A Christmas Carol, 39
A Farewell to Arms, 118
A Horse and His Boy, 221
A is For Alibi, 28
A Little Hatred, 288-289
A Natural History of Dragons, 151-152
A Tale of Two Cities, 247
A Writer's Guide to Active Setting, 166, 172
Abercrombie, Joe, 214, 288-289
Ackerman, Angela, 241, 248, 290
Action/Reaction Cycle, 275-290
    Action, 281-287
    Reactions, 277-278
    Thoughts, 280-281
Adams, Ellery, 60
Adventures of Huckleberry Finn, The, 121
Alderson, Martha, 154-155
All of Us, 229-230
Anatomy of Genres, The, 36, 42
Anatomy of Story, The, 42, 140, 155
Animal Farm, 39, 99
Antagonist, 69-71
Archetypes, 74-76
Argent's Menagerie, 18, 24-25, 37, 48-49, 84, 98, 100-103, 116, 146, 153, 166-167, 178, 184, 265, 271
Aristotle, 128
Arrival, 127, 129, 144
As the City Burns, 54, 80, 82, 83, 87, 175-176, 180, 210, 239
Austen, Jane, 54, 89, 218, 235
Author's Intent, 220-221

Avatar, 35
Avengers, The, 115, 159, 207, 283

Babel, 50, 106
Bastards of the Revolution, 205
Bates, Joseph, 119-120
Batman, 69, 77, 187
Beginnings, Middles and Ends, 125
Bell, James Scott, 22, 29, 125
Bird by Bird, 5, 15
Bickham, Jack, 145, 150, 155
Bishop, K. J., 231
Black, Sacha, 70, 78
Blackgoose, Moniquill, 106
Blood Over Bright Haven, 174
Bone Shard War, The, 237
Booker, Christopher, 38-39
Boone, Jo, 57
Bork, Erik, 23-24. 29
Brennan, Marie, 151-152
Brody, Jennifer, 133, 140
Brokeback Mountain 264
Bronte, Charlotte, 272
Brooks, Larry, 125, 131
Brown, Dan, 49
Brown, Pierce, 289
Browne, Renni, 302
Buckham, Mary, 166, 172
Buffy the Vampire Slayer, 31
Burroughs, Edgar Rice, 174
Burroway, Janet, 1, 86, 94
Butler, Octavia, 12

Campbell, Joseph, 75, 134-136
Captain America: Civil War, 287
Card, Orson Scott, 20-21, 29, 66, 78, 94
Cardinal in the Kremlin, The, 204
Cartographers, The, 4

Carver, Raymond, 229-230
Castaway, 72
Catcher in the Rye, The. 199, 203
Cauldron, 159
Cervantes, Miguel de, 235
Chandler, Raymond, 221
Characters & Viewpoint, 29, 66, 78, 94
Character Web, 101
Chekhov, Anton, 235
Cheney, Theodore, 302
Christie, Agatha, 21, 39, 65, 80, 211
Cinderella, 38
Clancy, Tom, 85, 204
Clash of the Titans, 38
Cleland, Jane, 197, 210, 215, 266
Cliffhangers, 210
Cline, Ernest, 199
Cogman, Genevieve, 28, 246
Collins, Suzanne, 120
Conflict, 185-198
    Objectives, 188-189
    Obstacles, 191-194
    Outcomes, 194-197
    Sources, 186-187
CORE, 64-65
Coyne, Shawn, 107-108, 145
Cron, Lisa, 51
Cujo, 27
Curator of the Gods, 4, 27

Dante, 160
Dark Knight, The, 285
Dark Lord, The, 71
Daughter of the Moon Goddess, 145
David Copperfield, 27, 54, 56
DaVinci Code, The, 49
Deep Point of View, 94
Description, 263-273
    Character, 265
    Comparison, 267-269
    Sensory, 270-272
    Setting, 262-264
Dialogue, 249-261
    Subtext, 252-254

Dick, Philip K., 177
Dickens, Charles, 28, 39, 54, 89, 136-137, 235, 247
Dixon, Debra, 100, 107-108
Doctorow, Cory, 5
Doctor Who, 139
Don Quixote, 27
Dossier Method, 65
Doyle, Arthur Conan, 33, 174
Dr. Faustus, 39
Dracula, 31, 87, 123, 129
Dragnet, 247
Dresden Files, The, 139
Dressel, Caleb, 8
DuMaurier, Daphne, 209, 230
Dune, 26, 166, 177-178
Dynamic Characters, 66, 78

Edelstein, Diane, 56, 66
Edson, Eric, 134, 140
Editors, 298-300
Elantris, 84, 127
Elements of Style, The, 225-226, 234
Ember in the Ashes, 60-61
Emotion Thesaurus, The, 241, 248, 278, 281, 290
Emotions, 278-280
Expanse, The, 277
Exposition, 245-248

Faulkner, William, 92, 229, 231-232
Fellowship of the Ring, The, 193
Fiction University, 46, 51
Fiction Writing Made Easy, 94, 155
Fiction Writing Modes, 1, 228
Fifth Season, The, 81
Flight of Nevada Lee, The, 18
Flynn, Gillian, 92-93
Footloose, 162
Forsaken Protector, The, 27, 122, 144, 207
Foreshadowing, 207
Freytag's Pyramid, 128-129
Friedman, Jane, 15
Friends, 74
FURY, 266

Genre, 31-42
George, Melissa, 207, 281-282
Gerke, Jeff, 51, 56, 66
Getting the Words Right, 302
Gilbo, Savannah, 94, 155
Girl With the Dragon Tattoo, The, 204
Gladiator, 167
Gladwell, Malcolm, 271
Glamourist Histories, 177
Glass, Ira, 28-29
GMC, 100, 102, 107-108
Goblet of Fire, The, 114, 147, 171, 252
Golding, William, 97, 104, 267
Gone Girl, 92-93
Gone With the Wind, 253
Grafton, Sue, 28
Grapes of Wrath, The, 47
Gravity's Rainbow, 92
Great Expectations, 136-137, 168
Great Gatsby, The, 104, 167
Green, John, 4
Green Lantern, 167
Greenbone Saga, The, 162

Hack Your Reader's Brain, 51
Half-Blood Prince, The, 114
Hamlet, 39
Hammett, Dashiell, 221
Happy Feet, 19
Hardy, Janice, 46, 51, 197, 241, 248
Harmon, Dan, 136
Harrington, H. C., 179, 184
Helping Writers Become Authors, 172
Hemingway, Ernest, 118, 178, 218-219, 229
Herbert, Frank, 26
Hitchcock, Alfred, 237
Hero, 123, 129
Hobbit, The, 38, 85, 111
Hunger Games, The, 120, 122, 177

I am Not a Serial Killer, 117
Iceberg Principle, 178
Idea, The, 23, 29
Ideal Reader, 43-45
Imposter Syndrome, 8
Inception, 129
Inferno, The, 160-161
Interiority, 89-93
Intuitive Editing, 296-302
Invisible Library, The, 28, 246
Invisible Life of Addie LaRue, The. 90, 144
Irony, 205-206

Jackson, Peter, 206
James, Steven, 197-200
Jane Eyre, 272
Jaws, 170-171
Jemisin, N. K., 81
Jewell, Lisa, 27
Jordan, Robert, 85
Journey to the Center of the Earth, 20
Journalistic Technique, 24-25
Journey to the Center of the Earth, The, 14
Joyce, James, 92, 231
Jung, *Carl*, 74
Jurassic Park, 97, 105, 187

Kennedy, Marcy, 94
King, Dave, 302
King, Stephen, 13, 15, 27, 177
Kishotenketsu, 129
Klaassen, Mike, 1, 228
Kuang, R. F., 50, 106
Kole, Mary, 64-65
Kowal, Mary Robinette, 177, 218
Kress, Nancy, 66, 78, 125
Kuang, R. F., 50, 106, 188

Lamott, Anne, 6, 13, 15, 235
Land that Time Forgot, The, 174
Lee, Fonda, 162
Legends in Addington, 28, 96, 175
LeGuin, Ursula K., 230-232

Lewis, C. S., 221
Li, Jet, 123
LOCK System, 22
Lord of the Flies, 97, 104, 118, 120-121, 267
Lord of the Rings, The, 38, 74-75, 129, 139, 145, 194, 206, 285
Lost World, The, 174
Luceno, James, 71
Lynch, Paul, 284

Maass, Donald, 96, 235
MacBeth, 233
Magnetar, The, 57
Make a Scene, 155
Man in the High Castle, The, 177
Man of a Thousand Faces, 75
Man of Steel, 76, 187
Mandalorian, The, 34
Martian, The, 87, 123
Martin, George R.R., 8
Martin, Tiffany Yates, 296, 302
Mastering Plot Twists, 197, 210, 215, 266
Mastering the Process, 281-282
Maxson, Press, 205
McClanahan, Rebecca, 273
McKee, Robert, 100-101, 133, 140
Melville, Herman, 96-104
Men in Black, 211
Merchant of Venice, The, 233
MICE Quotient, 20-21
Midnight's Children, 231
Mindmap, 18
Moby Dick, 96, 104, 248

Monologue, 255-256
Monologue Method, 65
Mood, 223-224
Morelli, Michael, 223
Morrison, Toni, 232
Murder of Roger Ackroyd, The, 80, 211

Name of the Wind, The, 87
Narrative Modes, 227-228
Nineteen Eighty-Four, 177

Oates, Joyce Carol, 230
Oathbringer, 152
Odyssey, The, 134
Of Mice and Men, 258-259
O'Keefe, Kat, 134
Old Man and the Sea, The, 218-219
On Writing, 15
Orwell, George, 39, 99, 231-232, 234
Osborne, Jon R., 184
Outliers, 271
Outlining, 138-139

Pacing, 212-214
Paper Towns, 4
Perfect Storm, The, 166
Pereira, Gabriela, 294
Plot, 109-125
    Character Arcs, 116-119
    Problems, 123-124
    Subplots 119-122
Plot & Structure, 29, 125
Plot vs. Character, 56, 66
Poetics, 128
Politics and the English Language, 234
Pomodoros, 12
Poppy War, The, 187-193
Presley, M. D., 184
Pride & Prejudice, 54
Princess Bride, The, 87
PROBLEM, 23-24
PROMS, 64
Prose, 226-234
Protagonist, 66-69
Proulx, Annie, 264
Publishing 101, 15
Puglisi, Becca, 241, 248, 290
Pynchon, Thomas, 92

Raiders of the Lost Ark, 146
Raybourn, Deanna, 147
Ready Player One, 199
Rebecca, 209
Red Rising, 289
Red Sky in Morning, 284
Red Team Blues, 5

Reveals, 210
Revelation, 137
Reversals, 209
Revisions, 291-302
    Checklist, 296-297
    Flyover Method, 297-298
    Macro-Micro, 296
    Pyramid, 294-295
Rick & Morty Show, 136
Roadhouse, 162
Romeo & Juliet, 31, 206, 233
Roof, Judith, 222. 234
Rosenfeld, Jordan, 155
Rowling, J. K., 54
Rushdie, Salmon, 231

Salinger, J. D., 199
Sanderson, Brandon, 4, 6, 64, 84, 125, 138, 145, 152, 231-232, 236-238, 240, 276
Save the Cat!, 62, 133, 140
Scene & Structure, 145, 155
Scenes, 141-155
    5 Commandments, 145-149
    Flashbacks, 143-144
    Flashforwards, 143-144
    MRUs, 150
    Scene/Sequel, 145-149
Schmidt, Victoria, 75, 78
Schwab, V. E., 71, 90, 144, 153
Scott, Michael, 69
Secret, Book & Scone Society, The, 60
Secrets of Nicholas Flamel, The, 69
Self-Editing for Fiction Writers, 302
Setting, 159-172
    Evolution, 170-171
    Setting Spectrum, 174-178
    World-building, 173-184
    Worldview, 164-165
Shakespeare, William, 39, 65, 89, 107, 233

Shawshank Redemption, The, 202
Shepherd, Peng, 4
Show, not Tell, 235-245
Slaughterhouse Five, 230
Snyder, Blake, 133
Software, 300-301
Sound and the Fury, The, 231
Stand, The, 177
Star Wars, 7, 33, 62, 75, 113-114, 116, 131-132, 134-136, 170-171, 245
Steinbeck, John, 258-259
Stevenson, Robert Louis, 272
Stewart, Andrew, 237
Stoker, Bram, 31, 123
Story, 140
Story Engineering, 125, 131
Story Grid, The, 107-108
Story Solution, The, 134, 140
Story Trumps Structure, 197-200
Strange Case of Dr. Jekyll and Mr. Hyde, The, 272
Structure, 127-139
    27 Chapter, 134
    Chiastic, 137
    Monomyth, 135-136
    Plot Circle, 136-137
    Three-Act, 130-131
    Seven Point, 131-133
Structuring Your Novel, 133, 140
Style, 224-226, 227-232
Supporting Characters, 72-74
Swain, Dwight, 2, 125, 155
Symbolism, 104-105

Tahir, Sabaa, 60-61
Taming of the Shrew, The, 233
Tan, Sue Lynn, 145
Taylor, Howard, 148
Techniques of a Selling Writer, 2, 125, 155
Tension, 199-215
    Informational, 203-205
    Tension Fiction, 199-203

THAD, 148, 207 281-282
Then She Was Gone, 27
Theme, 95-108
Theme Square, 101
Thor, 207
Thrawn: Alliances, 72
To Kill a Mockingbird, 21-24, 96-97, 121, 162
To Shape a Dragon's Breath, 106
Tolkien, J.R.R., 111, 179, 194, 218, 285
Tombstone, 284
Tone, 222-223
Tone, 222, 234
Tress of the Emerald Sea, 237, 276
Trottier, Dan, 131
Truby, John, 36, 42, 100-101, 131, 133, 140, 155
Truth Chart, 103
Twain, Mark, 7, 28, 121
Twists, 208-211

Understanding Conflict, 197
Understanding Show, not Tell, 241, 248
Unspoken Truths of Casemiro, The, 7, 10

VanderMeer, Jeff, 172
Verne, Jules, 20, 174
Vicious, 71, 153
Viewpoint, 79-89
    Choosing, 86-89
    First, 79-80
    Second, 81
    Tense, 85-86
    Third, 81-84
Voice, 217-226

Voices, 230-231
Vonnegut, Kurt, 230

Wang, M. L., 174
Weiland, K. M., 100, 103, 107-108, 133, 140, 172
Weir, Andy, 123
Wells, Dan, 65, 117, 131, 138
Wired for Story, 51
Wheel of Time, The, 85
Who Says?, 94
Wizard of Oz, The, 115-117, 131-132
Wonderbook, 172
Word Painting, 273
Worldbuiding for Fantasy Fans and Authors, 184
Worldbuilding for Novices, 184
World-building for Writers, 184
Writer's Block, 9
Writer's Guide to Character Traits, 56, 66
Writing Blockbuster Plots, 154-155
Writing Excuses, 6, 17, 148
Writing Fiction, 1, 86, 94
Writing Voice, 234
Writing Your Novel From Start to Finish, 119-120
Writing Your Story's Theme, 107-108

Young & the Wicked, The, 181

Zahn, Timothy, 72
Zeidner, 94

ACKNOWLEDGEMENTS

First, I want to thank Carol Hall for reading this book ahead of the release. Your comments were especially helpful.

I want to tip my cap to what has almost become my personal hype squad of Paulette Brooks, Nichole Mathews, and Joanne Flood. Paulette just released her first book and the other two are working on their first fiction books currently. Thank you for the kind words about *Craft the Draft* over the years.

Next, I need to call out all those people that have been involved and led many of the writing groups I have participated in over the years. Groups led by Kirsten Edwards (another published writer), Jan Bridges, the folks at CIWA led by Carol Michael and Karen Zimmerman, Jeff Couch, the folks from Porter Bread & Books, and anyone involved with those groups over the years. Our time together has been an influence on what is in this book.

I also should mention the author community in the Indianapolis area. Many of you have impacted me and my writing in some way.

And I can't finish this without mentioning my wife, Danielle, and how much she has supported this effort over the years. She is really my daily inspiration.

CHRISTOPHER CLOUSER

ABOUT THE AUTHOR

Christopher Clouser, by day a finance and accounting professional, lives in the Indianapolis, Indiana area and pursues writing speculative fiction in his free time. His family consists of his wife, two children, and multiple grandchildren. He has written seventeen books, novels, and novellas and one play in the fantasy, science-fiction, mystery, and sports history genres while contributing to several compilations, along with multiple articles in national publications. He also has spoken to many local and national organizations on fixed asset accounting, creative writing, and the career of Perry Maxwell, a noted American golf course architect.

https://clouserwritesbooks.wordpress.com
www.facebook.com/christopherclouser.authorpage
instagram.com/christopherclouserauthor